Wellcome Mead

Books by Laura Angotti:

Historical Brewing Sourcebook I: Cider and Perry in Britain to 1700

Historical Brewing Sourcebook II: Wellcome Mead

Wellcome Mead

105 Mead Recipes from 17th and 18th Century English Receipt Manuscripts at the Wellcome Library

Historical Brewing Sourcebook II

Laura Angotti

ISBN: 1-7324646-1-8

ISBN-13: 978-1-7324646-1-2

Library of Congress Control Number: 2019915475

Published by Mt. Gilboa Miscellany; Arlington, MA, USA

www.mysteryofmead.com

Table of Contents

Illustration Credits

Like the recipes, all illustrations, other than those created for this book and credited or copyright Laura Angotti, are taken from the Wellcome's extensive image collection (which includes some from the Science Museum, London). The Wellcome images are used under CC-BY license allowing use with credit.

Cover: Wellcome Collection MS 1407 Buckworth, 1725. Credit: Laura Angotti.

p.2: 14th c. silver drinking horn. Engraving by J. & H. S. Storer, 1821.

p.5: *A further discovery of bees* (Rusden, 1679).

p.8: Woodcut of drinking and vomiting.

p.9: Photograph: the Wellcome building: Euston Road, 1930s Studio Corot.

p.11: Wellcome Library MS 7976 (Palmer, 1700-1739, p.75).

p.16: *A further discovery of bees* (Rusden, 1679).

p.21: Title page *Grete herball*, 1529.

p.23: The elements and humors. © Laura Angotti.

p.26: Hydrometer, France, 1810–1820. Credit: Science Museum, London.

p.29: Der butner (the cooper) (Amman & Sachs, 1568/1884).

p.32: Innkeeper composed of wine bottles and grapes. Engraving, c. 1660.

p.34: Der bierbreuwer (the beer brewer) (Amman & Sachs, 1568/1884).

p.43: A witch at her cauldron surrounded by beasts. J. van de Velde II, 1626.

p.46: Title page of *Grete herball*, 1526 (Rohde, 1922).

p.49: Bee keeping at Chelsea Physic Garden, London. Credit: Sue Snell.

p.53: Leeuwenhoek's first microscope. Photograph.

p.55: Yeast cells. *Saccharomyces cerevisiae* (Coplin).

p.58: *A new orchard and garden* (Lawson, 1623/1858, p.19).

p.64: Sloe or blackthorn. C.H. Hemerich c.1759.

p.72: Pomander c.1610.

p.74: Nutmeg (Acosta, 1578, p.35).

p.75: Pepper plant (*Piper nigrum*). Line engraving after C. de Bruin, 1706.

p.76: Spanish herb cutter 18th c. Credit: Science Museum, London.

p.81: Betony.

p.82: Buck's horn plantain (*Plantago coronopus* L.). Etching by M. Bouchard, 1774.

p.87: A carnation and hollyhock. Etching by N. Robert, c. 1660.

p.88: Illustration and description of Colts-Foot (Gerard, 1636, p.811).

p.90: Cowslip, herba paralysis, (Brunfels, 1532a, p.96).

p.94: Common fennel (Gerard, 1633, p.1032).

p.97: *Juniperus communis*. Juniper. David Blair.

Preface

For the majority of my 25+ years of mead making I have had a strong interest in finding and making meads from historical recipes. I am specifically drawn to recipes from the time before science became an integral part of brewing. Beyond the intrinsic appeal of re-creating recipes that are hundreds or even thousands of years old, my interest is driven by the desire to understand how people who did not know the scientific underpinnings of fermentation, chemistry, and sanitation applied their intelligence and resourcefulness to make fine drink. I have to date collected and cataloged several thousand mead recipes dating up to 1750 CE, and made well over one hundred of them.

Most readers are probably aware of the long history of mead, but available information on that history is largely anecdotal. In bringing mead history forward to the modern day, writers often apply pieces of information to times and places far afield, or exaggerate and extrapolate from minimal or uncertain data. Others take the viewpoint that history has nothing to teach because it predates the modern science that is embedded in many modern mead making procedures. All of these, to my mind, both misrepresent and undervalue mead's amazing history.

My overall goal is to create a concrete understanding of how mead was made in different times and places, primarily by focusing on mead recipes. For this book, that is England across a roughly 125-year period in the 17th and 18th centuries. In this geography and time period, the ingredients and methods used produce meads of astonishing variety and flavors. For modern mead makers, these recipes can be employed as is, modified as desired, or used as a source for creative inspiration.

Understanding the recipes sufficiently to make educated interpretations of their contents, methods, and results requires a general knowledge of an amazingly large number of subjects: agriculture, apiculture, beer/ale brewing, botany, culinary arts, economics, geography, horticulture, language, medicine, politics, and the daily lives of people as they changed over hundreds and even thousands of years of history. All of these subjects, and more, are relevant to how mead was made and how the product would have tasted. Each topic therefore also plays a role in recipe interpretation and modernization.

While my focus is on the recipes themselves, I try to present them within the complexities of history. The outlook is generally scholarly, but not in every detail. It is my hope that the scholar will not be offended by the occasional lack of rigor, and the reader looking for a more dynamic presentation does not find tedious the attention to historical detail. I am optimistic that the reader will accept the compromises that come with this hybrid approach, and take the opportunity to follow up by themselves on some of the numerous topics that are perforce only touched upon.

This volume owes its existence to the Wellcome Library in London, England, with which I have no affiliation other than as a delighted user. The library's on-line resources are impressive. I have also gratefully used their resources in-person. The library's generous dedication of works to the public domain, most notably digitized manuscripts and illustrations, has enabled this volume. Thank you.

Personally, I will always thank Mike, Lissy, Peter, and the rest of my family for their support and commentary (often couched in extreme sarcasm). Thank you, Dr. Todd Huhn, for allowing yourself to be convinced to provide your broad expertise in reviewing; your help was invaluable. Thanks also to Robyn, Darcy, and Bob for your precise eyes and thinking.

Therefore, I present this book. I hope you find reading it as interesting and informative as I found the process of creating it.

Laura Angotti
November, 2019
www.mysteryofmead.com

Introduction

The mystery of fermentation. For the mead maker, this means turning honey, itself a mysterious product of bees' labor, into a drink that has become synonymous with luxury, feasting, warfare, and love. Most of the mead makers I have encountered feel these associations deeply as they carry out their art. They also, almost universally, have a love for experimentation. What better way to feed that love than detailed recipes from the fabled history of mead, bringing old ingredients and methods forward in time to produce results which are new again.

The core of mead: honey, water, and yeast, is unchanging. Yet the details of mead making vary greatly. And the context in which mead exists is always one of time and place. The end goal, however, appears to have remained constant for millennia – to produce a drink whose flavors and effects are much desired. This remains true no matter the ingredients, equipment, and methods or whether the mead is used for every day drinking, feasting, or competition.

As mankind began to write about their lives, experiences, and opinions, they wrote about fermented drinks, including mead. Many of these writings are general in nature and establish simply that mead was known and appreciated. Yet the number and variety of actual mead recipes in the historical record is much greater and more varied than most would suppose. The earliest of these is the 4000-year old Hymn to Ninkasi, famed as a recipe for beer, but which also includes honey, making the product arguably a braggot – a mead. The earliest recipes for drinks more clearly identified as meads can currently be reliably dated to the first century Common Era, but evidence suggests they have earlier origins.

1

Introduction

These earliest mead recipes were transmitted only by word-of-mouth or in individual manuscript copies. Manuscripts passed from hand to hand, were copied in whole or part, and were relatively rare, reflecting the effort involved in creating them.

Starting with the advent of the printing press in Europe, mead recipes were included in printed texts. The early printed books frequently copied, collected, and annotated Classical authors and the texts of Arab physicians. These included a base group of mead recipes. Printed books soon expanded to include additional subjects, and contemporary mead recipes, although many were still located in texts not directly focused on food and drink.

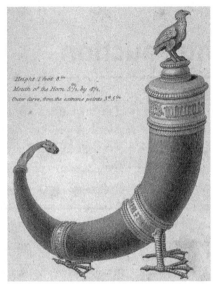

14th century silver drinking horn

In the 17th and 18th centuries, household "receipt books", containing family records for cooking and medical recipes, became common, moving mead recipes back into the sphere of manuscripts, although they remained frequent in printed texts.

On the whole, the source documents for early mead recipes are scattered in location, date, language, topic, current repository, and other factors. The recipes themselves demonstrate the continuing presence of mead in diverse times and places. They show an extraordinarily varied universe of mead ingredients and styles.

This volume looks at a small but rich microcosm of historical mead recipes, representing a small slice of mead history. Dating from about 1629 to 1750 CE (roughly 390 to 270 years ago), the recipes are all drawn from English-language receipt books held in the Wellcome Library in London, England. The intent is to make this diverse group of historical mead recipes accessible to the modern mead maker. Despite its limited geographic and temporal scope, this group of recipes presents many insights into mead, the making of mead, and history.

At its core, this is a recipe book. The majority of the text focuses on presenting the recipes themselves, the information required to understand the original texts, and detailing the derivation and final instructions for the modern recipes developed from each of the historical recipes. The history of yeast, identification and nomenclature of herbs, the place of mead and other drinks in society, purpose and history of receipt books, and a host of other topics could each be (and in many cases have been) subject to book-length analysis. The discussions of these topics herein are often superficial, presenting only essential context, to retain focus on the mead recipes themselves.

This book also serves as a reflection on the position and significance of mead within the complex agricultural, economic, cultural, and political atmosphere of the 17th and early 18th century time period in England.

Making Mead from Historical Recipes

Turning a historical recipe into a useful modern one requires multiple skill sets and the ability to think creatively about potential meanings. When working with a recipe, I keep three rules constantly in mind:

1. Work to develop a wide range of possible interpretations for recipe elements. Consider possibilities of error in the original. Acknowledge points of uncertainty.

2. Be aware of the difference between choices that are clearly indicated by the historical record, choices where a selection is made from varied possibilities, choices that are educated guesses based on specific evidence, and choices that are guesses. I try to ensure each choice has some justification for why it was "best", even if that means "unlikely but interesting" or "most convenient given the circumstances." I also try to acknowledge the strengths and weaknesses of each choice.

3. Do not allow uncertainty to get in the way of progress. Voltaire is credited with saying "Le mieux est l'ennemi du bien" or, "The best is the enemy of the good." Perfection is rarely essential.

Introduction

The modernized recipes in this book are presented in a format that assumes the mead maker is familiar with mead making processes, comfortable calculating amounts for their own recipes, and has sufficient knowledge and experience to modify recipes and procedures to achieve their desired ends. I have relied on my experience from making well over 100 such recipes to develop modern interpretations of the original recipes that are both accurate and expected to produce good results. The actual testing of recipes, however, is ceded to the end user, who hopefully finds that process as engaging and as worthy a pursuit as I do. In cases where I have made a test batch using a specific or similar recipe, my experience and notes are provided. Choices made by individual mead makers, including difference in materials and methods, will almost always give results that differ from my own.

Some mead makers will want to make mead from the Wellcome recipes in a way that adheres as closely as possible to how it would have been done hundreds of years ago. Others will use the full range of modern technological knowledge, equipment, and materials to manage the mead making process. Most will fall somewhere in between.

The mead maker using a historical recipe must always have foremost in their mind their ultimate purpose and goals with respect to historical accuracy and the purpose of the drink they are making. A historical re-enactor will approach mead making differently from the person focused on creating an award-winning entry for a national mead competition. The person with time and energy to experiment will choose a different process than someone who desires the greatest chance for immediate success. And the same person may very well be all of these at different times. The purpose and goals will affect choices of ingredients, equipment, and methods, resulting in profoundly different products.

In presenting recipes and options, I try to remain agnostic to the choices of the individual mead maker, specifically with respect to utilization of modern equipment and techniques.

Each of the recipe interpretations herein is truly a starting point, with the heavy lifting of interpretation, identification, and calculation already done, leaving the joy of making to the reader. I fully expect that individuals may disagree with some of the interpretations I have made, or may prefer an alternate choice where there are multiple options – in which case they are invited to substitute their own interpretations, and place their own imprint upon the recipe.

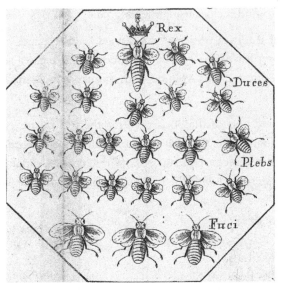

A further discovery of bees (Rusden, 1679)

Using this Book

The first part of this book presents general information on historical mead making in four chapters as follows:

Recipes in Context presents an overview of the Wellcome Library and its manuscript collection, the topic of receipt books in general, the process of reviewing the manuscripts and the recipes within them, and the transcription and selection of recipes for this volume.

Old Recipes into Modern Mead Making briefly discusses some of the challenges faced in translating recipes from times with very different technologies, language, and understanding of the world into instructions and processes that make sense in the modern world. These topics are globally applicable to the recipes, and represent insights and procedures which are not repeated at the level of the individual recipes.

Ingredients provides a summary description for each ingredient used in one or more recipes. This typically includes modern identification, historical background, and a summary of the use of the ingredient in the recipes in this volume and in historical mead recipes in general. The index can be used to find recipes using each ingredient.

Selected Recipes presents an overview of the recipes as a group. It also provides a list of the source manuscripts and recipes selected from each manuscript for this volume with summary information on each recipe.

The second part of the book presents the recipes sorted roughly by the types of ingredients that will primarily determine the end character of the mead. Where a recipe contains options that create a variant recipe these are typically presented with the original recipe to avoid repetition. These chapters are:

- Plain Meads
- Meads with added Sugars
- Citrus Meads
- Flower Forward Meads
- Spice Focused Meads
- Non-Spice (Herb) Focused Meads
- Meads with Multiple Flavors
- Complex Meads
- Braggots
- Miscellaneous Meads

General considerations for ingredients, equipment, and process discussed in the initial chapters are not repeated with individual recipes.

The reader interested in skimming recipes can do so in three ways. First, the recipes are grouped into chapters by ingredients/flavors with the earlier chapters generally presenting simpler meads than later. Second, the index lists all meads containing a given ingredient under the name of that ingredient. Finally, the list of recipes given by manuscript source summarizes the original gravity (OG) and ingredients for each mead.

Introduction

Each recipe or group of recipes is presented in the same manner.

- The recipe(s) are introduced with relevant context.
- A transcription of the recipe from the source manuscript is provided.
- Notes clarify issues with the recipe and possible interpretations of elements of the recipe.
- An abbreviated recipe is presented for a selected interpretation and a one-gallon (US) test batch.
- Modifications for not boiling honey are given in [square brackets].
- Options for variations are presented in {curly brackets}.

The individual mead maker will need to adapt the instructions to accommodate their preferred fermentation protocols (understanding that that will affect flavors and the fermentation end point), aging methods (including racking and clarification), and bottling choices (with particular attention to potential dangers of bottling with incomplete fermentation). It is assumed that mead makers wishing to use nutrient addition, degassing, and other such techniques are familiar enough with those processes to insert them appropriately into recipes.

Numbers and statistics in this text are approached in a general manner, and terms such as "seem to", "may", and "indicate" are frequently used. This is entirely intentional. The Wellcome recipes in this volume are all from England in a roughly 125-year time span, but the corpus of cataloged historical recipes to which they are compared covers most of Europe (with occasional forays into other geographies), and a time period more than 10 times longer. In addition, the catalog of recipes is continually expanding. Statistics are also complicated by challenges of how to count duplicate and variant recipes. Therefore, trends and statistics contain inherent uncertainty.

Safety

Vomiting

A note of caution.

This book speaks of historical brewing practices and how they can be re-created in the modern day. Despite the claims sometimes made in the texts, historical recipes do not provide any objective or scientific promise of medicinal or other safety.

Recognize that some of the ingredients, materials, and methods called for in the original recipes are risky or dangerous. Certain ingredients in particular may be poisonous or otherwise dangerous under certain circumstances. Brewing and fermentation can also produce dangerous conditions or results such as exploding bottles when incompletely fermented liquids are sealed.

I have called out specific risks where I am aware of them. The individual mead maker is expected to carry out all required research to understand the safety concerns surrounding ingredients, equipment, and methods to assure themselves that they are not placing themselves or others at risk.

No claim or assurance is made of the safety of any of the materials, methods, or processes presented in the historical texts herein.

Recipes in Context

Other than to provide a catchy title, why focus on the Wellcome Library manuscripts to produce this book?

The Wellcome Trust states they exist "to improve health by helping great ideas to thrive." The museum and library of the Wellcome Collection aim, "to challenge how we all think and feel about health." The Library more specifically, "seeks to explore the connections between medicine, life and art in the past, present and future." Pursuing these goals, the library has collected numerous manuscripts, dating from the 13th century to the modern day.

The Wellcome Building Euston 1930's

Several hundred of the Wellcome's manuscripts are English receipt books. These types of manuscripts became notable in the 17th and 18th centuries, and are typically collections of instructions and recipes on varied household subjects such as cooking, medicine, cleaning, and even veterinary medicine. Recipes were sourced from relatives, friends, acquaintances, books, and professionals. Most were written by the people who used them; professional scribes were involved in creation of others.

These manuscripts were often added to and used across multiple generations, reflecting changes in the world around them. They provide an enormous amount of information about daily life. They exhibit an unprecedented level of involvement from women. Contents were transmitted through complex social networks. They mirrored the transition of published books from a focus on repeating old knowledge to developing new knowledge, often informed by the Scientific Revolution.

These manuscripts routinely contain mead recipes.

The Wellcome Trust and Library

Sir Henry Solomon Wellcome (1853–1936) was born in Wisconsin in the USA. In 1878 he moved to England with his business partner Silas Burroughs, and started the pharmaceutical firm Burroughs Wellcome. Over 140 years and numerous mergers later, this original company has become part of GlaxoSmithKline, one of the ten largest pharmaceutical companies in the world.

In 1895, on the death of his partner, Wellcome became sole owner of Burroughs Wellcome. About the same time, he began to collect books and artifacts, focusing on medicine and medical history. His goal was to create both a library and a museum, to educate the public, and to advance the practice of medicine. When Wellcome died in 1936, the majority of his estate funded the Wellcome Trust, a charity for "the advancement of medical and scientific research to improve mankind's wellbeing."

The first public exhibition of Wellcome's collection was in 1913. The initial museum opened after the first World War. In 1949 the Wellcome Historical Medical Library was opened to the public. The Wellcome Collection, including both the library and museum, was founded in 2007.

The Wellcome Collection occupies quarters close to the British Museum and British Library in London. The use of the library is open to all, albeit with restrictions on physical access to rare and delicate material.

Recipes in Context

In 2010, the Wellcome Library started a digitization program for their holdings, including books, manuscripts, paintings/prints/drawings, photographs, ephemera, video, and audio and began placing the digital files on-line. These digitized documents have been dedicated to the public domain (as long as source credit is supplied).

This extraordinary work to make these materials freely available has led to this book. All of the recipes, and almost all of the illustrations have been drawn from the Wellcome Library collections.

Selecting Recipes

The Wellcome Library holds approximately 500 receipt books; almost all are currently online. These documents date from the 15th century to the early 20th century. The shortest are a few dozen pages and the longest over 400. They are written in a variety of languages including English, French, German, Greek, Latin, and Welsh.

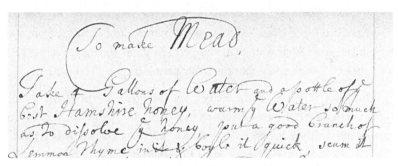

MS 7976 (Palmer, 1700–1739, p.75)

After beginning review of these manuscripts in search of mead recipes, and recipes for other fermented and distilled drinks, it quickly became clear that they include a substantial number of recipes. I became interested in collecting the mead recipes for publication.

In an effort to define a cohesive group of mead recipes I initially selected manuscripts using date and geography. I first noted English language manuscripts (about 350), indicating an origin in the United Kingdom. Next, I culled the list to about 200 manuscripts dating before 1750. I have reviewed all but a handful of these manuscripts (either on-

11

line or in-person) for mead recipes. In most cases this was a page by page review. Indexes are common, but later additions to many manuscripts make those unreliable. Despite indices in some manuscripts, review was typically page-by-page, looking at recipe titles, with more in-depth reading of recipes that appeared likely to be for fermented drinks.

About half of the manuscripts contain at least one recipe for mead. About 40% of those contain a single recipe, and about 65% contain one or two. One manuscript includes 14 recipe entries for mead, and 27 total mead recipes when significant variants are counted.

As I identified mead recipes in a manuscript, I transcribed and cataloged them with the source, materials used, methods employed, and ingredients included. I enter duplicate recipes once for each appearance, because these typically differ from version to version. Many recipes include variants, using terms such as "if you", "many", "if you please", "others", or "if you have it." Variations I judge to have a significant effect on the final drink are cataloged separately — a somewhat subjective process.

I have cataloged over 300 mead recipes, including variants, from these English language Wellcome manuscripts. The dates for these recipes range from about 1590 to a few that probably post-date the 1750 cut-off.

This was still too many recipes for adequate coverage in a single volume. Therefore, I have selected a representative group of recipes with varying styles, ingredients, dates, trends, and processes. As is typical of such a process, some recipes of great interest have been omitted.

Managing the Manuscripts

Manuscripts are as individual as their writers, and a single manuscript will often have multiple "hands", each indicating a different person who wrote down recipes or notes over a period of time. Sometimes manuscripts were in use for generations. With such complex histories, dating and transcription of manuscripts can be difficult, page number are duplicated or absent, and deciphering the individual words may be a challenge. Each topic is touched upon below.

Manuscript Dating

Manuscript dating is a complex task with many uncertainties. The range of factors relevant to dating include the paper (possibly with watermarks) used in the manuscript, binding, the individual hands and writing styles of each of the persons writing in the manuscript, dates mentioned in the contents and the context of those dates, identification and dating of named persons, identification of sources for material included in the manuscript, and correlation with other dated sources.

The drafting of these manuscripts over a period of years, often including a number of contributors, makes it difficult to assign precise dates to individual recipes. Any given recipe may be associated with the earliest or latest date of the manuscript as a whole, or may even lie outside the cataloged manuscript dates.

Even if a specific date is associated with a manuscript, a recipe may be significantly earlier in ultimate origin. As an example, I have traced one mead recipe through its ingredients and process from an initial (so far) appearance in a 1570 herbal through multiple countries, languages, and texts to a final (so far) appearance 272 years later in an 1842 book. The majority of these appearances give no indication of the history of the recipe. Recipes written down at the end of my period of study (1750 CE) contain instructions which echo those given in Dioscorides' c. 70 CE *De Materia Medica,* almost 1700 years earlier.

Each of the manuscripts has been given a date or date range by the library catalogers. Their experience typically provides reliable date estimates. I have used these dates here.

Pagination

Many manuscripts have no pagination, pagination is unclear, or multiple pagination schemes are present, some of which may have been added long after the manuscript was written. Where possible, original manuscript page numbers are used for reference. Page numbers added by later scribes are the fall back choice. If there are no page numbers at all, the scan number within a PDF of the complete document is used.

A peculiarity of these household manuscripts is that medical recipes are sometimes written from one end and culinary recipes from the other end, with the book physically turned and flipped. In these cases, the pages are typically numbered from both ends.

The term f. for folio or leaf is for a physical page with a front (r – recto) and a back (v – verso).

Transcription

Transcription turns handwritten manuscript text into a machine mediated text form like this book. Like other activities, it is done with varied purposes. The rules and conventions vary based on the purpose. At one end of the spectrum is diplomatic transcription, which aims to present every detail of the original in machine-readable form. The other end of the spectrum is normalized transcription which uses modern spelling and letter forms, expands abbreviations, and sometimes even rewrites content; this approach is intended to maximize readability and searchability. Semi-diplomatic transcription is in the middle. Among other factors it typically preserves spelling and letter forms and expands, but marks, abbreviations.

Because the focus here is the information content of the text, I use a modified semi-diplomatic transcription scheme, moving towards normalized. Specifically:

- Word choice and spelling of the original is maintained.
- Old letter forms such as the long s, use of v for u, and of i for j are normalized to modern usage. Ligatures are presented as separate letters without being specifically marked.
- Abbreviations are usually expanded without specific indication; ampersands are maintained.
- Symbols are generally written out without specific indication.
- Capitalization is normalized to modern conventions, except where it appears to denote a point of emphasis or identification.
- Line divisions are not maintained.
- Deletions are shown as strikethroughs.
- Insertions are placed in line with other text.
- Punctuation is maintained.
- Marginal comments and missing letters filled in with informed guesses are inserted using square brackets [ ].

The end goal is a text that maximizes the readability for those who are not accustomed to reading old texts, while making effort to maintain the character and important ambiguities of the original. Scans of almost all of the original texts are readily available, and the curious reader is referred to those for better understanding of the original presentations.

The 17th and 18th Centuries

The 17th and early 18th centuries were a time of great political, economic, social, religious, and technological change. These changes are reflected in many of the more specific names given part or all of the roughly 1500–1800 CE Early Modern Era: Age of Discovery, Age of Exploration, Scientific Revolution, Age of Enlightenment, Age of Reason, and Industrious Revolution.

This story of global change can be seen writ small in mead recipes themselves. The period starting about 1600 marks the beginning of a number of significant changes in the general character of mead recipes. The existence of the receipt books from which the Wellcome recipes are drawn is part of the overall changes taking place. Broad trends in mead recipes of this time period include:

- Citrus, not seen as a mead ingredient previous to 1600, surges to appear in about one-third of all recipes by the end of the century.
- Refined sugar appears as a replacement for honey in making fruit wines, greatly reducing the number of recipes for fruited meads.
- Refined sugar also appears as an ingredient in mead recipes as a replacement for some of the fermentable sugars in the must.
- Proportionally more recipes contain herbs and spices.
- Bottling becomes the prevalent storage method.

Many aspects of mead making did not change:

- The amount of honey in musts remains highly variable, from a low of a bit over one lb/gal to well over four lb/gal.
- The number of different ingredients added to recipes in this time period is consistent with the variety in earlier periods.

In other words, while the general character of meads saw significant shifts, the overall variety of recipes did not increase or decrease.

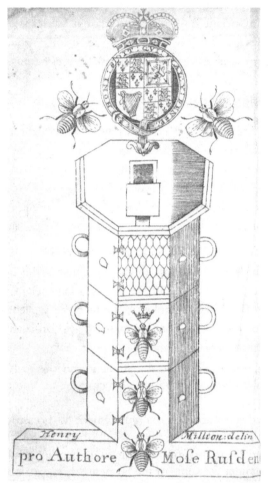

A further discovery of bees (Rusden, 1679)

Old Recipes into Modern Mead Making

The historical mead maker's list of priorities almost certainly matched those of the modern mead maker. They wanted to produce a product that tasted good, was free of contamination or undesired elements, and was ready to drink when it was wanted. They developed, through hundreds of years of experience, methods that ensured these goals, within the limits of their knowledge and resources. Evidence indicates they consistently succeeded in producing meads that were tasty and greatly appreciated.

The instructions written in historical recipes are not as readily interpreted for execution in the modern world.

This chapter discusses the general issues associated with turning historical written instructions for mead making into a set of modern instructions, which requires three critical steps.

First is **understanding what the recipe is saying**. This somewhat academic process involves transcription, translation, and investigation of word and phrase meanings to derive a text.

Next, **placing the instructions into historical and modern context**. This involves identifying ingredients, materials, and methods as they would have been originally used, and understanding them in both historical and modern context. This typically requires multiple areas of expertise and looking at all possible interpretations of individual recipe elements.

Finally, **translating the original into a modern version**. This process takes into account the mead maker's ultimate goals (historical research, modern competition), resources (equipment, time, money), and, most importantly, their preferences and choices within those goals (to choose specific possible interpretations of the original recipe).

The resulting recipe can range in outlook from completely historical to almost completely modern. Any approach is equally valid, but it is important to stress that while there is no intrinsic reason why one approach is "better" or "worse" than another, it is certainly true that individual choices may be more or less historically "accurate."

When the one-gallon modern instructions are presented for each of the recipes in this volume, they represent a single interpretation within a range of possibilities. While I have applied my experience and knowledge in developing each of the recipes, I will stress that there are almost always alternative interpretations.

The elements of the processes discussed below to understand and interpret recipes are each relevant to most or all of the recipes in this book. Because they are universal concerns, they are not generally reiterated for each recipe.

A few notes on general mead making techniques and a table of gravity/brix/honey versus potential alcohol are given at the end of the chapter for reference and for the relatively new mead maker.

The Texts

The technical aspects of manuscript dating and transcription are addressed in the previous chapter. Translation is not an issue for these manuscripts, as all are in English. Interpreting the texts is best done with additional background, as discussed below.

Names for Mead

The word "mead" in this book is used as a general term, referring to any member of the group of fermented beverages made from honey as a majority fermentable sugar, or to that group of drinks as a whole.

The names given the individual recipes in this book are those given in the source manuscripts, regardless of their historical or modern meaning.

Historical mead naming conventions were not normalized or consistent during the time of the Wellcome recipes. One Wellcome manuscript contains a recipe for plain mead titled "metheglin", which historically and today usually indicates a mead with herbs and/or spices added. A number of recipes are called "quick" or "small" which would not match modern ideas of a low alcohol session mead, while others are called "strong" or "sack" without being particularly high in sugar or alcohol.

Modern mead makers may find this even more confusing, because current naming conventions have adopted a number of historical mead designations and assigned them meanings that differ from historical usage.

For example, hydromel ("water honey") historically could refer to any mead, but in modern parlance it is specifically a low alcohol mead. "Bochet" is an old French word that means "mead", yet as a modern term bochet is universally identified as mead made with caramelized honey.

Finally, spelling in manuscripts of the 17th and 18th centuries was variable. Therefore, we have metheglin, methiglin, metheglan, methegling, matheglin, and many other spellings for the same core word.

To manage confusion, I recommend, in the immortal words of Charlie Papazian, author of the iconic *The new complete joy of homebrewing*, "Relax. Don't worry. And have a homebrew."

Intentional Change and Scribal Error

It is not uncommon to read a historical recipe and identify differences from another appearance of the recipe, or a word or phrase that does not make sense in context. These changes may be intentional or unintentional. Intentional changes usually make sense in context, and we can compare versions across different manuscripts and see shifts in the ingredients, proportions, and instructions that affect the final character of the recipe. Unintentional changes may make sense in context or not. Sometimes it is impossible to tell whether a change was intentional or unintentional.

As a mead maker focused on re-creation, I view all changes, whether error or intentional, as valid recipes, because the mead maker looking at the recipe in isolation has no way of knowing that an error or change has been made. In many cases the new recipes are not intrinsically better or worse. When aspects of a recipe are suspected to be due to error or are likely to lead to undesirable results, I identify them as such.

Measurements

The Wellcome meads use many measures unfamiliar in the modern day. Most are relatively easy to understand. We have a solid basis of documentation for the meaning of various weights and measures for 17th and 18th century England. Measures of ounces, drams, and pints are clear and easily interpreted. A pennyweight of spice would be a weight of the spice equivalent to the weight of a penny (which is known). Finally, other measurements such as handfuls or "one lemon" are clear, but open to interpretation as to actual objective size or how the size changed over time.

There are three different gallon measurements in play in the period of the Wellcome recipes. The old English wine gallon of 231 cubic inches was standardized in 1707 and is equal to the modern US gallon. The British Imperial gallon is 269 cubic inches, or 1.17 US liquid gallons, and the Elizabethan-era beer and ale gallon holds 282 cubic inches (1.22 modern US gallons). For the most part, measurements as a volume ratio make this irrelevant, but in some cases, it is not.

Kirkby (1735, p.14) wrote "In *Wine Measure* the *Gallon* equals 231 *Cubic Inches*, by which are measured all *Wines, Brandies, Spirits, Mead, Perry, Cyder, Vinegar, Oyl, Honey, &c.*" While there is no guarantee historical mead makers universally adhered to this standard, I have used the English wine, equal to the modern US gallon, as the basis for my recipe interpretations.

Some measures are much more difficult to understand, but are specific enough in time and place that an interpretation can be made without an attempt to rigorously define. For example, a pennyworth of spice is the amount which could be bought with a penny, and that amount would vary based on date, locale, and recent trading results.

Plant Identification and Portions Used

When we refer to *Homo sapiens*, we give the Genus – *Homo*, and Species – *sapiens* (when writing them out, the names are placed in italics with the genus capitalized). Similarly, *Laurus nobilis* is the bay tree which produces both the bay berry and the aromatic bay leaf of the laurel crown used to mark heroes, poets, and wise men since classical times.

These two-word Latin, or Latinized, identifiers are the best way to clearly identify a plant, and we see many plant names in our recipes and reference herbals using such names. But caution is required. Typical 17th and early 18th century plant names were based on tradition, copying of previous texts, and identification using woodcuts. These woodcuts could be of dubious accuracy or even printed next to the wrong description.

Title page *Grete herball*, 1529

The core of our modern plant identification system was not published until 1753 in Linnaeus' *Species Plantarum*, which is just after the end of my period of interest for mead recipes. Many names changed as this system was implemented and classifications were made more scientific.

Based on these factors, names of plants used in historical recipes can differ from the modern, be uncertain, or misleading, or even wrong. Irregular spelling and variable handwriting complicate identification.

There is also no guarantee that the makers of any given recipe named individual ingredients accurately, or in practice actually used the ingredient that is named.

Many ingredients have multiple types. Both cardamom and cinnamon have different forms, which are often confused or substituted. Common herbs such as sage and thyme have multiple cultivars with differing characteristics and flavors.

Another issue, with some recipes is deciding what portion of the plant is intended to be used. A good example is fennel, where the root, seed, and herb are all possible mead ingredients. In some recipes, the form is called out specifically. In others, it is clear from context, e.g. when fennel is listed as part of a group of roots or seeds. But in some cases, the portion is not specified and the mead maker needs to decide which is most likely, or alternatively, which suits their needs best.

Misidentification, naming errors, and changes of form are all possible problems in ingredient identification. Typically, I do not assume any of these unless other indicators suggest it is a possibility. Instead I use the available knowledge to identify a most likely case, and use that.

Fresh, Dried – New, Old

The form of herbs and spices used in historical recipes, whether fresh or dried, is not typically specified. In some cases, such as for most spices, a common form can be assumed. In other cases, it is unclear whether fresh or dried is called for. Particularly for herbs, the question of fresh versus dried can significantly affect the flavor and strength. Some herbs can be collected throughout a relatively long growing season, others have only brief periods for harvesting. Directions to use handfuls of herbs may seem to imply fresh herbs, but dried herbs can also be measured in this way.

Comments in several recipes suggest that powdered herbs and spices were not considered desirable. MS 1510 Carpenter (1715) wrote, "an ounce of ginger half an ounce of cinnamon and ounce of cloves & an ounce of Mace grosly beaten if it be finely beaten it will foul the Metheglin."

The modern mead maker will probably use fresh herbs where available and dried where not. It is important to keep in mind that relative volume and potency will vary with the form used and the herb's age.

Assumed Medicinal / Humor Properties

Medicine, particularly the assumed medicinal properties of ingredients, is a major undercurrent for historical meads and other historical food and drink. This connection is confirmed by the many mead recipes co-located with medical recipes in texts and by medicinal effects attributed to others.

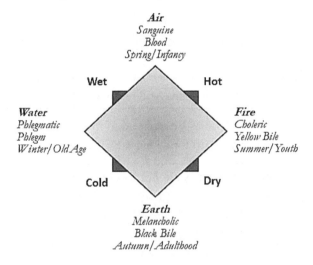

The elements and humors

Greek and Roman physicians first promulgated the idea that people, foods, and drinks all embodied, in varying degrees, the qualities shown in the above diagram. This view continued as a central tenet of medicine and diet through the time of the Wellcome meads. In this medical model, it was critical to balance humors; medicines and food and drink were used to counteract or increase specific humors as desired. Specific foods were typically characterized as hot or cold and wet or dry in the first, second or third (strongest) degree.

This theory extended to honey, mead, and metheglin. Those interested in mead purely as a culinary beverage may find this unimportant, but to understand how herbs and spices were historically added to meads, or the context of the many medicinal mead recipes, knowledge of this theory of health is critical.

In 1541, in his *Castel of helth,* Thomas Elyot said of mead and metheglin (pp.35–36):

Of this excellent matter, moste wonderfully wrought and gathered by the lyttell bee, as wel of the pure dewe of heven, as of the most subtyll humor of swete & vertuous herbes & floures, be made lykors commodious to mankynd, as mead, metheglyn, and oximell. ...

Alsoo meade perfectly made, clenseth the breast and lunges, causeth a man to spytte easyly, and to pisse abundantly, and purgeth the bely moderately. Metheglyn, whiche is moste used in wales, by reason of hotte herbes boyled wih hony, is hotter than meade, and more comforteth a colde stomake, if it be perfectly made, and not new or very stale.

Additionally, in 1638, Tobias Venner said of metheglin in his *Via recta ad vitum longam* (The correct path for a long life, pp.53–4):

But it is not good for such as are hot by constitution, nor in the hot seasons of the yeere, because it overmuch heateth the body, and is very quickly turned into red choler, and therefore let such as are cholerick, beware how they use it. If in their old age, cold fleame shall somwhat abound in their stomacks and lungs, then sometimes mornings fasting, a small draught thereof may be profitable for them. It must not be drunk while it is new, for then, because it is not fined from the dregs, nor the crudities thereof digested, it is very windy and troublesome to the belly. But after that it hath well purged it selfe, and setled in the vessell three or four moneths, and made as afore described, there is not for very cold, old and phlegmatick bodies, especially in the cold seasons of the yeere, a better drink

Historical mead makers would formulate their recipes with the perceived medicinal properties of the ingredients in mind. Sometimes the intent would be to balance these properties to create a more neutral effect, but for the most part, the intent would be to align the properties of ingredients to promote a single focused effect.

Freedom to Experiment

Just as modern mead makers are prone to vary aspects of written recipes to suit their preferences, we have ample evidence that this was a common practice for historical mead makers. These changes might come from the desire to make a drink more suited to personal tastes, or from a simple desire to experiment with different results.

Over 10% of the historical recipes calling for addition of herbs and/or spices instruct the mead maker to choose ingredients, often from a group with given characteristics. This instruction is repeated in many recipes for the honey:water ratio used in the must. Proof that personal choice has always been an element of mead recipes is further provided by the variations observed in recipes that appear in multiple manuscripts or written sources. These recipes often change from appearance to appearance, and while some changes do appear to be a result of scribal error, many more are almost certainly intentional.

For the mead maker interested in historical accuracy this permission to change recipes must be approached with caution. Many potential choices are limited by other concerns of the world our historical mead makers inhabited. A thorough understanding of that world is needed to make informed choices.

The modern mead maker less focused on strict historical accuracy can take any recipe as a starting point from which a vast universe of experimentation is possible.

Equipment

Every recipe interpretation needs to consider the effect of the mead-making equipment on the final product. Here, I focus on two aspects which have the most significant effect on the final product. The first is the use of eggs to measure liquid density, serving as a functional hydrometer. The second is the broad topic of the types and construction materials of containers used for brewing, fermentation, aging, and storage, and their wide-ranging effects on the final mead product.

The Egg as Hydrometer

A notable minority of 17th and 18th century mead recipes use an egg to assay the sugar content of mead must. The earliest such use of an egg in brewing may be in a French recipe for mead from 1576 (Estienne, p.143b), which instructed "they take the knowledge that it is cooked by an egg that they throw in; which if it swims over it is a sign that it is cooked, if it goes to the bottom, it is not cooked." This method is used in half a dozen of the Wellcome meads, which ask the must to bear an egg. This is often specified to be a fresh laid egg, because eggs get less dense as they age.

The Avian Egg (Paganelli, 1974) uses data from over 20 bird species to derive an equation for egg density, which gives an initial density for hen eggs of 1.063. If an egg in a honey/water mead must is neutrally buoyant, the mixture is also 1.063 gravity. This is equivalent to 1.35 lb/gal sugar or 1.7 lb/gal honey, with an alcohol potential of about 8%.

French hydrometer c. 1810–1820

Most recipes ask that the egg float, often to a width of shell showing that corresponds to the size of a common coin, implying positive buoyancy. The databases at the Portable Antiquities Scheme provide the following average diameters for the English post-medieval coinage mentioned in the Wellcome recipes: penny – 14.5 mm, two pence – 18 mm, three pence / four pence – 19.5 / 18.6 mm, and groat – 24.5 mm.

Experimentation with eggs, sugar syrup, and a modern hydrometer reveals that floating a fresh egg the breadth of a penny requires a gravity of about 1.088–1.098, with a three or four pence circle exposed about 1.095–1.11, and with a groat exposed about 1.105–1.122. The variation is due to differing egg shapes.

If buoyancy is measured in a hot liquid, there is an additional complicating factor. The above numbers assume room temperature. Boiling water has a density of 0.958. Assuming adding honey causes a proportional increase in density, a gravity of 1.063 at boiling temperature (where the egg is neutrally buoyant), increases to 1.11 at room temp. This intuitively would not be measured at a full boil, where an egg would bounce about and any assessment of floating would be near impossible, but a simmer, where its buoyancy could actually be observed.

The egg is an imperfect measure; variations in egg shape or a small error in judging the amount exposed will lead to significant differences in actual gravity. This conveniently leaves the historical mead maker a fair degree of flexibility in defining desired starting gravity for the must, based on how they want their mead to turn out.

Kettles, Pots, Barrels, Tuns, and Vessels

Enumeration of the types of containers historically used for cooking, fermentation, and storage, their construction materials, the effects on character and flavor of a drink made in them, and how those effects could change over the lifetime of the container is an enormous topic which will be covered here only in extremely abbreviated form.

The Wellcome recipes typically use multiple containers during preparation of the must, fermentation, and aging. Bottling is discussed following this section. Many of these containers are relatively inert, but others are not. Three basic types of materials were historically used for these bulk containers:

- Metal was used most commonly in cooking
- Earthenware could be used for cooking, fermentation, or storage
- Wood was typically used for fermentation and storage.

Metal containers were most likely to have been used short-term for cooking, where their ability to be placed directly over a fire was an advantage. Evidence does not suggest their use longer-term for fermentation or storage. Typical metals used in cooking pots included copper (reactive, especially with acid), tin (non-reactive), brass (reactive to salt and acid), bronze (less reactive), and iron (can add iron to food). Where mead recipes specify a material for the boiling container it is almost always copper or tin-lined copper, with brass sometimes mentioned as a second choice. Copper helps remove sulfur compounds and will donate trace copper to the must as a nutrient. Perhaps more importantly, it is easy to work into large vessels and conducts heat very well for boiling.

Earthenware vessels (both glazed and unglazed) made and fired in specific ways are useable to cook liquids over a fire as long as the majority of the heat is indirectly applied. The use of earthenware for storage, as in fermentation and aging is an ancient practice. Earthenware containers are relatively inert, but are somewhat porous, leading to small amounts of materials being carried over from previous contents.

The simplest assumption for the modern mead maker relative to use of metal and earthenware is that they are generally neutral, and the common stainless steel and glass used today are reasonable analogs. Suitable containers made of the specific materials used historically can be found, and experiments would demonstrate the effect on mead from using them. As with other decisions, the goals of the individual mead maker and the resources available to them, will determine their approach.

Wood is the far more interesting material in terms of the brewing process. The use and re-use of previously used alcoholic beverage barrels, enthusiastically re-discovered by the modern brewing world, is merely the past made present. Wood was used extensively in cooling, fermentation, and storage of historical meads. Often more than one wooden vessel would be used in the production of a batch of mead. Each container used would influence the flavor and character of the resulting mead. Wood potentially affects a mead that is kept in it in a number of ways:

- Flavor from the wood itself, diminishing over time
- Flavor from former contents that have soaked into the wood
- Effects on the drink from varied older contents including yeast
- Flavor from barrel treatment (cleaning, toasting, pitching)
- Evaporation and oxidation through the barrel (or barrel openings) during storage
- Ability of container to hold carbonation
- Off flavors from former contents or decay and contamination

Each of these factors is expected to vary in importance based on the history of the specific vessel and its use in the brewing process.

With such a variety of possibilities, this may seem impossibly complicated, but once again, the options should be viewed as liberating rather than confining.

Der butner (the cooper) (Amman & Sachs, 1568/1884)

The round wooden barrel appears to have been invented by the Celts well over 2000 years ago. It was a mainstay for storage and transportation of wet and dry goods until displaced by more modern materials in the past hundred or so years.

Wooden barrels, casks, tubs, and pails, both open and closed, were extensively used in historical mead making. In keeping with the value of these hand-made containers, they were used, re-used, and repaired. Barrels can have a useful lifetime of several hundred years; the use of old barrels to support the sides of wells testifies to their final practical use once they were no longer suitable for storage.

Maintenance and cleanliness of these containers was important. Bailey, (1742, Entry: CASKS) instructed on cleaning and sweetening casks:

If the cask be a butt, then first rinse out the lees clean with cold water; and having boiling water ready, put it in, and scrub the bottom with a long handled birch broom very well; and with a shorter broom cleanse the sides very well, either with water, sand or ashes; likewise cleanse it well about the bung hole, lest the yeast as it works over carries some of its filth with it.

But if it be a barrel, kilderkin, firkin or pin, the custom is in large brew-houses to put them over the copper-hole for a night together, that the steam of the boiling water or wort may penetrate into the wood.

But this method is so violent a searcher, that unless the cask has been new hoop'd just before, it will be apt to fall to pieces.

Another Way.

Put two quarts or more of lime stones into the cask, pour some water upon it, stop it up directly and shake it well about.

Another Way.

Dip a long linnen rag, in melted brimstone, light it at the end, and hang it in the cask, the upper part of the rag being fastened to a wooden bung. This way is both quick and sure, and at the same time will not only sweeten the cask, but help to fine the drink.

The Vintner's Way.

Take a quarter of an ounce of stone brimstone, one ounce of burnt alum, and two ounces of Brandy; melt all these together in an earthen pan over the fire, then dip into the mixture a slip of canvas, sprinkle upon it nutmegs, cloves, corriander and anniseeds powdered, set it on fire, and hang it in the cask, fastened at the end with the wooden bung, stopping it so close that no smoke can come out.

The mead maker choosing to use or model wooden containers should consider each of the flavoring factors mentioned above.

- The specific wood used to build the container and its age will determine the strength and specific essence of the wood character that can be donated. Even if oak is used, oak from different areas provides different tastes, and American oak was not in play in 17th and 18th century England.
- Flavor contribution from previous contents will vary between wine, ale, beer, or cider. Distilled spirit barrels are not mentioned in recipes, but would probably have been available.
- The methods for cleaning barrels as detailed above would potentially provide residual flavor.
- Toasting or pitching wood for maintenance or cleaning would also provide flavor.
- If a barrel was re-used immediately, it may not be cleaned, leading to carry-over of yeast and residue.

My preference when first trying a recipe is to model the wooden brewing, fermentation, and storage containers as well-used, clean and sound, thus protective against contamination and adding no notable flavor or character to the final product. Where a used sack cask is called for (for example Sack Mead MS 1127), I use oak cubes soaked in wine ("sack" of the time was not fortified) for at least a month, changing the wine several times to remove the initial extracted tannin and flavor (assuming the wine would have been in the barrel for at least several months).

Bottles

About 40% of the recipes in the Wellcome manuscripts call for bottling. These bottles could be either glass bottles or earthenware / "stone" (stoneware) bottles. The Wellcome recipes do not typically specify.

The use of small, medium, and large clay vessels to contain liquids is an ancient practice, as established by examples found at Egyptian, Chinese, and other archaeological sites. One of the best known is the amphora, invented by the Egyptians and used as a standard shipping container through the Roman period. These types of containers would have been available throughout the time period of the Wellcome manuscripts.

Glass bottles also have a long history, but their availability in sizes useful for storage of liquids like wine and mead is much shorter. It was in the 17th century that the glass wine bottle using a cork stopper was developed. Jones (1986) calculates the filling capacities of a number of styles of these early wine bottles. These capacities range from 759 ml to 1130 ml; a modern US quart is 946 ml.

Interestingly, the invention of the modern wine bottle has an unexpected connection to mead. Sir Kenhelm Digby's 1669 *The closet of the eminently learned Sir Kenelme Digbie Kt. Opened* may be the largest single collection of mead recipes ever published (this collection comes close, but does not surpass it). Sir Kenhelm, via a glassworks he owned in the 1630's, is credited with invention and commercialization of a practical wine bottle using a novel manufacturing process that made a thicker bottle, enabling storage and transport of liquids without unacceptable risk of breakage. It is entirely possible that the use of glass bottles in recipes had an element of demonstrating wealth and access to new technology, as well as serving the practical function of holding the drink for aging and storage.

Innkeeper composed of wine bottles and grapes c. 1660

Much like the modern mead maker, the historical mead maker was concerned about conditions that would make bottles explode or corks "fly." MS 7892 Birch Mead instructed, "care most be taken to set the bottles in a very coole place, to preserve them from flying & the wine is rather for present drinking then of long duration, unless the refrigeratory be extraordinary cold."

This concern is of particular importance relative to the Wellcome recipes, as many call for bottling a mead that can be expected to have residual or potential fermentation activity that will cause modern bottles with tight modern closures to explode.

Process

Modern mead makers use instruments to measure density, pH, temperature and other characteristics of their mead. They use procedures that ensure the yeast works well, and that other microorganisms are less able to compete. Historical mead makers had similar customary processes, which served many of the same purposes, and are of notable interest when understanding recipes.

Sanitization

Mead making intentionally creates an environment where yeast grows happily, to obtain one of the by-products of that process, ethyl alcohol. But the environment in which alcohol-producing yeast thrives is the same in which many other micro (and some macro) organisms also thrive. For the most part, the products and by-products of those other organisms are much less desirable, and in some cases they are actively unhealthy for human consumption. Sanitation is the primary technique used to ensure the only micro-organisms in fermentation are the desired ones.

Other than a recurring insistence for clean ingredients and brewing conditions, and typically boiling of must, there are few direct indications of intentional sanitization in historical recipes. As a result, contamination was likely more common in historical brewing than it is today.

In my opinion, using modern sanitization techniques mirrors the circumstances under which a historical brew did not get contaminated. In this respect, it does not fundamentally alter the character of the drink produced, but merely increases the overall success rate.

Mead and the Art of Beer/Ale Making

In 17th and 18th century England mead was not a rare drink, although beer, cider, and distilled alcohol were all produced in far greater quantities (A state of the revenue).

Der bierbreuwer (beer brewer) (Amman & Sachs, 1568/1884)

Beer brewing took place on a regular basis in many households, and they were furnished with the equipment to make beer/ale. Not only could this equipment be used in the production of larger batches of mead, but the detailed instructions in some texts on beer brewing give us insight into brewing and fermentation in general. As well, a number of mead recipes specifically refer to ale/beer brewing for the provision of yeast cultures and in reference to managing must during preparation and fermentation.

The complete family-piece (1736, pp.197–198) in the chapter on brewing for private families, started with a list of brewing equipment:

> The Copper we have agreed to hold 36 Gallons, then your Mesh Tun must be (at least) big enough to contain 6 Bushels of Malt (*Winchester* Measure) and the Copper of Liquor, and room for meshing (stirring) it; your other Vessels, (*viz.*) Underback, Coolers, and working Tuns, may be rather fitted to the Conveniency of the Room, than to a particular Size

This text noted that multiple vessels could be used for processes downstream of the initial mashing and gave instructions for sanitization, "scald all your Vessels well; a little Malt Dust or Bran thrown into each, will contribute towards sweetening and stopping them if leaky."

A number of the Wellcome recipes call for using "coolers" from the beer making process, broad shallow pans intended to allow rapid cooling – particularly important when large volumes were involved. Their use is notable due to the opportunity for capture of wild yeast (or other contaminants) as the must is cooling.

It is very common for mead recipes to call for ale barm or ale yeast. Barm from an actively brewing ale would be a very active yeast culture, and would often carry with it some ale wort. Beer yeast or barm is much less commonly specified. The distinction between beer and ale arose in the early 16th century, when beer with hops was first popularized in England from the mainland. It became common to distinguish the new hopped drink from the old, unhopped one by calling the hopped beer and the unhopped ale. This distinction is not absolute; Cornell (2011) demonstrated that in the 17th century, the term ale gradually came to signify a drink containing some hops, but still significantly fewer than beer.

Data suggests mead was typically made in much smaller batches than ale/beer. These smaller batches were more likely made using kitchen equipment than with specialized, often large-scale, ale/beer brewing equipment. This is supported by the inclusion of many mead recipes with cookery recipes in the manuscripts, whereas ale/beer recipes, except for the smaller volume medicinal "diet drinks" based on beer wort, are rarely seen in the manuscripts.

Measuring Honey

Honey is measured in historical recipes by both weight and volume. Whatever the measurement method, every mead maker is aware of the difficulty of introducing a precise amount of this viscous and sticky substance into the must. Given these challenges it is reasonable to assume that honey:water proportions in historical recipes contain a certain amount of inherent variability. My recipe interpretations treat stated proportions as relatively precise, but practically it was certainly less so.

Boiling the Must

The majority of historical mead recipes call for boiling the must, honey included. In order to preserve flavor and aroma, most modern mead makers do not boil honey.

Almost without exception, recipes can be readily modified to avoid boiling the honey, so long as attention is paid to two specific areas. The first is accounting for loss of liquid in the boiling process to maintain a starting gravity in keeping with the original recipe. The second area is to maintain the boiling steps (without honey) where other ingredients are added, to preserve the effect of boiling on added flavors.

Liquid loss due to boiling is affected by a number of factors including the amount of heat transmitted to the liquid and the type and configuration of the pot, specifically the surface area for evaporation. Other factors affecting evaporation include air temperature, wind, humidity, and atmospheric pressure (altitude). I have chosen to use a constant boiling liquid loss rate of 15% per hour, based on information in the recipes, my experience, and reported liquid loss rates for beer brewing.

The recipes confirm this rate choice. MS 3008 Jackson (1743) stated that 30 quarts of water with eight pounds of honey added will boil to 20 quarts in three hours a loss of 15% per hour. MS 2330 allowed two quarts liquid loss from five and a half gallons must in one-half hour "very fast" boil – a loss of 18% in one hour. These rates are confirmed by modern rules of thumb for liquid loss in boiling.

The effect of liquid loss from boiling on must gravity can be seen in the following table for a must starting with a moderate honey content.

Boiling Time	% of total liquid Lost	Honey lb/gal	Expected Gravity
0	0	2.0	1.075
30 minutes	8%	2.17	1.08
1 hour	15%	2.35	1.085
1 ½ hour	22%	2.56	1.095
2 hours	28%	2.78	1.10
2 ½ hours	34%	3.03	1.11
3 hours	40%	3.33	1.12

Many recipes do not specify a time for boiling but rather an event: "as long as any scum will rise", "boil it very well", or "when it is boiled anoufe." I typically assign a one hour boiling time to these, although either shorter or longer is plausible. Several recipes state a period as short as 15 minutes until "no scum rises." A shorter boiling time will lead to lower must honey concentration and lower original gravity (OG). A longer boiling time will lead to higher OG. Varying boiling time will also affect flavor extraction from any ingredients in the boil.

Varying the assumed evaporation rate, or the boiling time within limits allowed by a recipe, is another route for the mead maker to influence the final character of their mead.

Because boiling rates are unpredictable, and liquid loss continues during the cooling after boiling, the mead maker using these recipes may find themselves adding some water back into the fermenter to make the desired batch size of one gallon for each of the modernized recipes in this book. Alternatively, they may decide that variable liquid loss is part of the original uncertainty in the recipes and accept a slightly higher or lower OG for their mead.

Boiling also serves to removes impurities from the honey and must through removal of the scum that rises to the top. This removal of scum is a step in the majority of the Wellcome recipes. While it is true that the majority of modern honey has far fewer impurities than historical honey, this scum contains more than gross impurities and its removal also changes the character of the honey beyond loss of aromatics.

The belief that historical brewers boiled must to remedy contaminated water, or only drank beer because water was unsafe to drink, may have been true in some areas, particularly larger towns and cities, but current evidence does not suggest this was a common consideration.

When Flavors are Added and Removed

The Wellcome recipes tell us to add flavorings to mead at a number of points in the production process including during boiling, immediately after boiling during cooling, in fermentation, and sometimes after fermentation during aging or bottling. Sometimes ingredients are carried from one stage to another.

Instructions for removal of these same flavorings are sporadic. Final removal of ingredients placed into fermentation is almost never directly instructed. Removal of ingredients added during boiling is often not specified. Because those recipes that do direct removal of boiled ingredients almost always strain it out before fermentation, that is the general assumption in my versions of the recipes. Other interpretations are viable, and would affect flavor.

Typical treatment of flavorings differs by type. Herbs are most often added during boiling, and generally removed before cooling and fermentation. Roots are often boiled for a longer period. Spices are more often added during boiling, but are also commonly added during fermentation. Unlike herbs, spices are sometime carried from boiling to fermentation. Spices and certain aromatic elements are occasionally added to bottles. Citrus is used across the process from boiling to bottling.

If flavorings are added to a recipe in a fashion that varies from the original recipe, the flavor will change. The amount of flavor and the specific flavor compounds which are extracted from an ingredient are significantly affected by how that extraction occurs. Boiling is an effective way to extract flavor, but volatiles are often lost and flavors changed by the heat. Alcohol developed during fermentation extracts flavors which are not as soluble in water alone. There are also cases where an ingredient is macerated in wine or brandy and the tincture added to the mead. The timing for each step also affects how flavors are extracted and changed.

I typically follow flavoring addition and timing instructions in recipes as closely as possible to ensure flavors match to the original.

Managing Multiple Ingredients

Many historical recipes call for a number of flavoring additions, sometimes of widely differing characters. Effective management of multiple flavors is an important aspect of making good mead. An understanding of the flavor elements allows the mead maker to work from knowledge, and better correct any imbalance in the resulting mead. Where new flavors are being used, or they are being used in a new way, the mead maker should use test batches, maceration, or make a "tea" of individual ingredients to understand them individually and in concert.

Nutrient Substitutes: Bread, Flour, Lees

Modern mead makers work hard ensuring proper nutrition for their yeasts. Like all living things, the micro-organisms we depend upon to produce the alcohol we desire work better when they are properly fed and cared for. Yeast, when a full slate of nutrients is accessible, produce alcohol more quickly, ferment to completion more readily, and produce fewer side products. Stressed or starving yeast use metabolic pathways other than converting sugar to energy and alcohol, and produce side products with unpredictable and sometimes undesirable flavors.

The people writing the Wellcome recipes knew nothing about nitrogen, much less its critical role in yeast growth, and the words "alternate metabolic pathways" would have meant nothing to them. But, as with many other aspects of brewing, their lack of modern knowledge does not imply practical ignorance. Multiple methods and ingredients in the Wellcome recipes provide potential analogs to the scientifically designed yeast nutrients in modern use.

A common technique for adding yeast in the Wellcome recipes was to toast a piece of bread and coat it with yeast before placing it on top of the must to start fermentation. Roughly one-quarter of the recipes use this technique. Other recipes add wheat flour or a portion of ale/beer wort along with the yeast/barm. All of these methods add components that can be used by the yeast as nutrients. It seems probable that these practices were observed by experience to improve fermentation and therefore became a part of the mead making process.

A part of the rationale for using yeast nutrients is to avoid stuck fermentations. The recipes do not reflect stuck fermentation as a historical issue. It is possible that stuck fermentations were not recognized or acknowledged. It is also possible that modern yeasts have adapted to rely more heavily on nutrient addition than their historical counterparts.

Where the mead maker chooses to use a modern nutrient regime, they need to be aware that it may change the flavor and character of the mead by altering the pathways and efficiency of fermentation.

Timing

Timing of fermentation, aging, and storage presented in the historical recipes is often far out of line from what a modern mead maker would expect. Additionally, a great many of the recipes from the Wellcome manuscripts call for bottling the mead under conditions where fermentation is almost certainly still active, creating potential for "bottle bombs." As with other re-creation issues, the individual mead maker can choose to resolve this potential danger in a number of ways. They may neutralize the yeast and bottle as instructed without concern of further fermentation. They may decide to allow fermentation to continue in bulk until risk of bottling is acceptable. Or they may derive some other solution which matches their goal for the mead.

A recipe that instructs serving after a week can be easily brewed one weekend and served the next. If it is expected that a mead will be drunk over a two-month period but is said to last only one, a slight increase in honey may make it more durable.

Basic Mead Making

A vast quantity of information on making mead can be easily found on the Internet, although much is of questionable validity. Well established sites such as gotmead.com and larger home brewing sites can be a good place to start. Social media sites often have forums dedicated to mead making, most of which have resource libraries as well as readily available advice from experienced members. Many areas have local home brewing clubs with experienced mead makers as members. The new mead maker should always read available reference materials before asking questions.

There are two books in particular which are generally regarded as foundational references for modern mead making. Neither is expensive.

Piatz, Steve. (2014). *The Complete Guide to Making Mead: The Ingredients, Equipment, Processes, and Recipes for Crafting Honey Wine.* Voyageur Press. ISBN 13: 978-0760345641

Schramm, Ken. (2003). *The Compleat Meadmaker: Home Production of Honey Wine From Your First Batch to Award-winning Fruit and Herb Variations.* Brewers Publications. ISBN 13: 978-0937381809

The mead maker interested in historical mead making is well served by understanding modern mead making and brewing science, and then adjusting to use equipment, materials, and procedures appropriate to the time. Practices should be adjusted to fit goals and as needed to address safety or other relevant concerns.

Sugar, Gravity, Alcohol Potential

I created the following table for my own reference. It addresses sugar concentration, with associated gravity and potential alcohol, measurements for volume to volume and weight to volume additions of honey, and calculations for fruit sugar contributions.

The table is developed from my own calculations, based on NIST Circular 440, Polarimetry, Saccharimetry and the Sugars, (Table 114), Brix, apparent density, apparent specific gravity, and grams of sucrose per 100 ml of sugar solutions, 1942. Potential alcohol is calculated and shown as a range based on 5 different calculation methods. My lb/gal of honey assumes honey is 80% sugar and 20% water.

Percent sucrose by weight (Brix, weight per total weight) and sugar gram/Liter (g/L) (weight per total volume) diverge because the higher density of sugar makes the weight of the g/L solution increases from 1000 gram per liter volume as the amount of sugar increases. In the same way, specific gravity increases as the amount of heavier ingredients, like sugar, increases in a defined volume.

Specific Gravity	Brix (wt. % Sucrose)	Sugar (g/L)	Sugar (lb/gal)	Honey (lb/gal)	% Potential Alcohol (v/v)
1.00	0	0	0	0	0.0
1.005	1.3	13	0.11	0.13	0.0–1.6
1.01	2.6	26	0.22	0.27	0.5–2.2
1.015	3.8	39	0.32	0.40	1.1–2.9
1.02	5.1	52	0.43	0.54	1.8–3.5
1.025	6.3	65	0.54	0.67	2.5–4.2
1.03	7.6	78	0.65	0.81	3.2–4.8
1.035	8.8	91	0.76	0.95	3.8–5.5
1.04	9.9	104	0.86	1.08	4.5–6.1
1.045	11.2	117	0.97	1.22	5.2–6.8
1.05	12.4	130	1.08	1.35	5.9–7.4

Specific Gravity	Brix (wt. % Sucrose)	Sugar (g/L)	Sugar (lb/gal)	Honey (lb/gal)	% Potential Alcohol (v/v)
1.055	13.6	143	1.19	1.49	6.7–8.1
1.06	14.7	156	1.30	1.63	7.4–8.7
1.065	15.9	169	1.41	1.76	8.1–9.4
1.07	17.1	1825	1.52	1.90	8.8–10.0
1.075	18.2	195	1.63	2.03	9.6–10.7
1.08	19.3	208	1.74	2.17	10.3–11.3
1.085	20.5	222	1.85	2.31	11.0–12.0
1.09	21.6	235	1.96	2.45	11.6–12.7
1.095	22.7	248	2.07	2.58	12.1–13.4
1.10	23.8	261	2.18	2.72	12.7–14.1
1.105	24.9	274	2.29	2.86	13.3–14.8
1.11	25.9	287	2.40	3.00	13.9–15.5
1.115	27.0	301	2.51	3.13	14.5–16.3
1.12	28.1	314	2.62	3.27	15.1–17.0
1.125	29.1	327	2.73	3.41	15.7–17.7
1.13	30.2	340	2.84	3.55	16.3–18.5
1.135	31.2	354	2.95	3.69	16.9–19.2
1.14	32.3	367	3.06	3.82	17.5–19.9
1.145	33.3	380	3.17	3.96	18.1–20.7
1.15	34.3	394	3.28	4.10	18.7–21.4
1.155	35.3	407	3.39	4.24	19.3–22.3
1.16	36.3	420	3.50	4.38	19.9–23.1
1.165	37.3	434	3.61	4.52	20.1–23.6
1.17	38.3	447	3.72	4.66	20.7–24.4
1.18	40.2	474	3.95	4.94	21.7–25.9
1.19	42.2	501	4.17	5.22	22.8–27.5
1.20	44.1	528	4.40	5.50	23.8–29.1
1.21	46.0	555	4.63	5.78	24.8–30.7
1.22	47.8	582	4.85	6.07	25.8–32.2

Ingredients

"Tak sweet Margoram, harts towng Madenhair, Colts fwtt, zegrimony, bwrag, bowglas, Roasmary, Liverwortt, of eatch two handfwls walnut tree leaves" (*Book of cookery recipes*, 1640 p.55).

A witch at her cauldron surrounded by beasts, van de Velde, 1626

Understanding ingredients and finding suitable modern versions can make historical mead making feel like alchemy or magic. Basic identification of an ingredient in modern terms is only a starting point. Even an innocuous instruction such as "add yeast" has enormous complexity.

Ingredients

My current catalog of historical mead recipes dating up to 1750 includes over 330 different ingredients added to meads. Over 100 are used in the recipes in this volume. The 20 most frequent additions, for the subset of Wellcome recipes in this volume, and for the recipe catalog as a whole, in order of their overall frequency, is as follows:

Recipes this Volume	All Historical Recipes
1. Ginger	1. Ginger
2. Cloves	2. Cloves
3. Nutmeg	3. Cinnamon
4. Lemon/Lemon Peel	4. Rosemary
5. Mace	5. Nutmeg
6. Rosemary	6. Lemon/Lemon Peel
7. Egg Whites	7. Mace
8. Cinnamon	8. Thyme
9. Eglantine (Sweet Briar)	9. Egg Whites
10. Marjoram	10. Eglantine (Sweet Briar)
11. Refined Sugar	11. Marjoram
12. Thyme	12. Balm
13. Balm	13. Bay
14. Coriander	14. Refined Sugar
15. Bay	15. Sage
16. Agrimony	16. Agrimony
17. Eringo Root	17. Pepper
18. Anise Seed	18. Hops
19. Licorice	19. Hyssop
20. Angelica Root (tie)	20. Betony
Wine (tie)	
Burnet (tie)	
Raisins (tie)	

The sections below provide information on each of the ingredients used in at least one of the Wellcome recipes in this volume, including:

- Identification using modern scientific names and historical designations, with uncertainties in identification highlighted.
- A summary of use in the Wellcome recipes in this volume and in historical recipes in general.

- Additional information including flavor, perceived medicinal characteristics, and issues with use.
- Notes for obtaining ingredients that are not readily available through established sources.

After a brief discussion of how to find ingredients, the first sections cover the core mead elements of mead, honey, water, and yeast. The next section includes other sugar sources as well as citrus, which does supply sugar but is typically used more for flavor. The two longest sections present individual spices and non-spice botanicals (mostly herbs). Miscellaneous ingredients including flavors and brewing adjuncts are grouped next.

NOTE: Some ingredients called for in historical mead recipes may no longer be considered safe for ingestion. It is critical that every mead maker understand the ingredients they choose to use, and their potential health effects under the use to which they are put. Modern knowledge contradicts use of some herbs or other ingredients commonly used in the past for reasons of toxicity. For example, a number of herbs used in historical mead recipes are now known to be potentially dangerous for pregnant or nursing women, others are dangerous only in large amounts or in certain circumstances. Ingredients can become toxic if taken in large doses, over a long period of time, or under circumstances where a specific component has been concentrated. Finally, if an ingredient or herb is reviewed for use in one set of circumstances, such as for brewing a tea, but is used in a different circumstance, such as in a brewed mead where alcohol is present, different portions or amounts of substances in herbs may be extracted.

Finding Ingredients

I write within the metropolitan district of a large city in the United States, so I can readily find many unusual items. With the use of established internet resources, I can obtain almost any legal ingredient within a few weeks. In the cases where herbs must be grown from seed, a longer time will be required.

Sourcing quality, properly-identified ingredients for mead is not necessarily easy. In some cases, it is necessary to ensure the items are also food safe. For example, dried rose petals are easily obtained, but petals which have not been treated with pesticides are much harder to come by.

Title page of *Grete herball,* 1526 (Rohde, 1922)

For many ingredients, the botanical name is invaluable to cut through confusion of common names.

Of the 100+ ingredients in the mead recipes in this book, about three-quarters are readily available from a few established sources. Of the remainder, the vast majority can be obtained either from varied additional sources or grown if required. A few are illegal in the US, are not readily available but have clear substitutes, or may be difficult to acquire. As with other recipe choices, the decision of how to address hard to find (or expensive) ingredients must be addressed by the individual mead maker.

A number of resources I have used to obtain mead ingredients and have found to be responsive are presented below. Whole or cut forms are always preferred over ground or powdered for use in mead making.

- Grocery stores: Common herbs and spices can be found at most grocery stores. Specialty or ethnic food sections should not be ignored. A few of the ingredients can be found as fresh produce.
- Ethnic shops. Most larger communities have specialty shops for spices or ethnic foods. A Chinatown, Italian area, or Indian specialty store may have herbs/spices not easily found elsewhere.

Ingredients

- Organic or health food stores. Look in the bulk food/spice sections of organic or health food stores.
- Specialty spice suppliers: Some large cities have specialty herb/spice shops. These are always useful. Others retailers have online presences. In the US I have found several useful, including:
  - Penn Herb Company
  - Rose Mountain Herbs
  - San Francisco Herb Company
  - Penzey's Spices

If you search for suppliers of unusual herbs, spices, or other ingredients you will often find referrals to Amazon, eBay, and/or Etsy (here in the US). Before ordering you should ensure the ingredient has been properly identified, the supplier is generally reputable (you will be ingesting their products), all shipping or other costs are understood, and the time for shipping is clear.

Water

Bailey (1742) said of water used for brewing:

Water is of great consequence in brewing malt liquors, and ought to be both wholesome and fine; it being the vehicle by which the nourishing and pleasant particles of the malt and hop are convey'd into our bodies.

Now the more simple and free any water is from foreign particles, the better it will answer those ends and purposes.

For as it has been observ'd by Dr. Mead, some waters are so loaded with stony corpuscles, that even the pipes through which they are carried, are in time incrusted and stopp'd up by them, and are of that petrifying nature, that they breed the stone in the bladder; ...

It must be allow'd, its true, that such fluids as well waters have a greater force and aptness to extract the tincture out of malt than the more innocent and soft water of rivers; but nevertheless they ought not to be us'd but upon necessity ...

Just like today, the water available to historical mead makers in different locations varied enormously. Water differs based on the source, potential sources of contamination, and how it was stored before use. Some manuscripts may be associated with a specific location, implying a specific water source, but recipes were often freely shared, implying other waters are generally possible.

One of the earliest written recipes for mead provides specific requirements for the water used for brewing. Pliny the Elder's instructions for making hydromel dating from about 70 CE, taken from a 1601 translation by Holland, (1601 Book 14 Ch XVII) told us "some doe prescribe raine water, and the same kept five yeeres for that purpose." While this instruction requires an unusual degree of planning and preparation, requirements for rain, clean, well, spring, or running water are not uncommon. Several Roman-era meads are named for the specific water source used to make them: Thalassiomel uses sea water and Chionomel uses snow melt.

The Wellcome recipes sometimes call for specific types of water, ranging from "fair" to "running" or "spring." Two recipes call for rain water, which is notable because rain water would be much purer than ground or surface water, unless storage added minerals or other components.

Relative to historical accuracy, this variability is helpful rather than confounding, because most modern sources of water can be argued to be historically accurate to one locale or another. Therefore, the mead maker has many options to choose their preferred water source.

Honey

Honey is the essential ingredient for mead. Its core composition is fairly consistent: about 80% sugars and 20% water, with minor other ingredients. But the precise sugar mix is variable, and the breadth of variation from those minor other ingredients is enormous.

Honey is an ideal ingredient for making alcohol. It is a concentrated sugar source with widespread availability, ferments readily once diluted, and can be easily stored and transported. Based on this, it is not surprising that honey was an ingredient in the earliest documented fermented drinks, and mead is invariably seen in cultures where honey is available.

Ingredients

The process by which bees create honey from flower nectar is astounding in the sheer effort involved and the complex series of steps from flower to honeycomb. A cup of honey represents the lifetime efforts of over 500 bees and nectar from millions of flowers.

Bee keeping at Chelsea Physic Garden, London

Dublin Society in their 1733 *Instructions for managing Bees* wrote (p.40):

a good Hive when taken, will yield from Eight to Ten Quarts of Honey, and from One Pound and half to Two Pounds of Wax.

Honey is commonly distinguished into Virgin and Common Honey; the Virgin is that, which is taken the Year it is made, and the purest of these runs from the Combs upon breaking, without any Pressure; but that which is obtained by Pressure, hath some bits of Combs and Sandrack, or other Foulness mixed with it

The nature of beekeeping during the period of the Wellcome recipes meant that hives were typically destroyed for collection of honey. This had three significant effects relevant to mead:

1. Collection of monofloral honeys, such as thyme, lavender, apple, or orange, was generally not a practice.
2. Hives could be left for several years before honey was collected, resulting in honey of highly mixed character.
3. Honey was likely to contain significantly more refuse from collection and processing. These materials are potential yeast nutrients.

Ingredients

Some historical honeys are described with the names of specific plants, but it is likely even these honeys were, in the end, more multi-floral in nature. With a typical foraging distance up to two miles, extensive monoculture is required to ensure bees are primarily exposed to a single crop for nectar collection, and such monoculture is atypical in historical periods. In addition, immediate honey collection is required to prevent adulteration of monofloral honey from the next plants to flower, and such specific timing of honey collection is not indicated by documents detailing honey collection methods. As a note, modern rules typically require 45% or more of pollen from a single plant species for honey to be given that name, so even modern monofloral honey can be majority mixed flower.

Historical descriptions indicate that honeys varied in color and flavor. Even with mixed floral sources, spring honey and fall honey differ, as will honey from a field hive as opposed to a forest hive. Similarly, the modern 'wildflower' honey I buy from a local apiary varies significantly from batch to batch in color, flavor, and tendency to crystallize.

The Wellcome recipes add some specification to the type of honey in about one-quarter of the recipes. Most of these clearly designate quality, such as "pure", "best" or "white." Others specify origin as "English" or "Hampshire", relevant because import records of the period indicate that honey was traded internationally. A few call for honeycombs as a starting point. Finally, one recipe, in two incarnations, calls for stone honey, which appears to be honey that has crystallized.

While the reader is encouraged to make their own choice of honey, raw wildflower honey is probably the best readily-available modern analog for historic honey. The diverse nectar sources and relatively unprocessed nature of this product are the closest match to what is known of historic honey-production processes. If the mead maker has access to unprocessed comb, breaking combs and collecting honey by gravity is closer to historical practices. Those interested in the range of flavors and character of modern varietal honeys can move away from historical accuracy to pair them with the wide spectrum of flavors used in historical recipes to add a modern twist to the flavor of the resulting drink.

Yeast

Yeast for historical recipes is an enormously complicated topic, and one where the knowledge base is rapidly changing. The core products from metabolism of sugar by *Saccharomyces cerevisiae* and related yeasts are, and always have been, ethyl alcohol and carbon dioxide. But the variety of yeast strains, historically and in the modern day, is extremely large. Modern mead makers can readily access hundreds of yeast strains. Historical mead makers, over time and geography also would have used hundreds or thousands of yeast strains, and data strongly indicates many were not *Saccharomyces*. Side products of metabolism for different strains vary greatly, as does their response to differing fermentation conditions. Yeast cultivation, brewing, and fermentation conditions in many historical recipes allow, and even promote presence of organisms other than the core fermenting strain, which will have significant effects on the results of fermentation.

It is of critical importance to understand that every yeast strain that is currently commercially available is separated from the yeasts used in the Wellcome recipes by hundreds of years of adaptation and mutation, and hundreds of thousands of potential yeast generations. Given this, there is no reason to believe that any yeast strain today, even one with an unbroken lineage, operates in any given way comparably to its 270 or more year old counterpart, other than in the core production of ethyl alcohol.

To frame and work through this multifaceted topic, three threads are critical:

- Understanding what the historical mead maker using the Wellcome recipes knew about yeast and what the yeasts they were using were like.
- Summarizing the current knowledge driven by very technical modern scientific study of yeasts as well as the burgeoning experimental archaeology field as it studies historical fermentation.
- Compiling this information into a sensible rationale for addressing yeast applicable to modern mead makers using historical recipes.

Yeast: What They Knew

It is easy to think that our historical mead makers, because they knew nothing of the existence of yeast as a micro-organism, had no care for the source of their yeasts. But this could not be more untrue. By the time of the Wellcome manuscripts, yeast was generally recognized as a substance with defined sources, differing characteristics, and a notable effect on the resulting mead. This is seen in the details of the recipes themselves, and in other discussions in printed and manuscript texts. The following excerpts provide an outline of some of the understood parameters over time.

A 1576 mead recipe called for addition of "six onces de levain, ou de biere, ou d'ale" (Estienne, 1576, p.143b) , giving us three yeast choices, beer yeast, ale yeast, or levain. Levain is a mixture of flour and water that is colonized by yeast and other microorganisms, then maintained continually (think sourdough, but without the same flavor connotations).

Glauber, 1651 p. 198 wrote:

Of the fermentation of Honey.

Neither hath honey any need of a singular Art in its fermentation, because being mixed with 6, 7, 8, 10 parts of warm water, it is dissolved, and unto the solution is added ferment, as hath been spoken concerning malt, which afterward is left covered in some heat for to be fermented, being fit for distillation when it becomes to wax hot. Now know that too great a quantity of honey makes a very slow fermentation, *viz.* of some weeks and months; wherefore for acceleration sake, I advise that a greater quantity of water bee added

---

Antony van Leeuwenhoek on June 14, 1680 wrote a letter to Thomas Gale of the Royal Society in London which contains the first description of yeast observed under the microscope. DBNL – De Digitale Bibliotheek voor de Nederlandse Letteren translated the Dutch to English as, "I have made several observations with regard to the yeast formed by beer and have constantly seen that it consists of globules floating in a clear substance, which I took to be beer. I also saw quite distinctly that each globule of yeast in its turn consisted of six distinct globules, and that it was of the same size and form as the globules of our blood" (van Leeuwenhoek, 1948, pp.245–249).

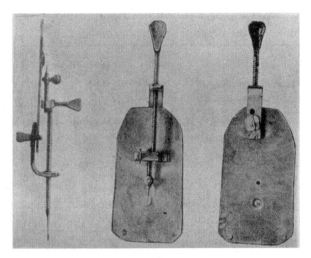

Leeuwenhoek's first microscope

Markham (1695) in his book *The husbandman's jewel* pp.22–23 wrote in a note to a recipe for mead:

if you work it with yeast, have a great care to draw it into Bottles; presently after the working is over, as in 14 or 18 Days; for Working it with Yeast, makes it soon grow stale, sower and dead, before you are aware; but if you singly work it of it self, and by the Suns help, or a gentle Sand-heat, or B. M. without adding Yeast or Leaven, it will keep 12 Months

Bailey (1742) stated on yeast:

YEAST or BARM, is of extraordinary use to excite fermentation in liquors, as wort and other fermentable liquors.

The yeast on the top of wort is the flower of ale, a great number of the spirituous particles, wrapp'd up in a viscid, light body, is crisp, rare, and feculent, swims at the top; and after the drink is fermented and settled, it gradually condenses and subsides or sinks to the bottom; and if the drink be shaken or moved, or the air contain'd in it be rarefied, the subtilty, fineness and smalness of those spirituous particles, that were lock'd up in the viscid body, which is also light, cause the yeast again to mix with the ale, mount up to the head, and put it again upon the fret.

Again yeast is also of singular use in making bread, for without it wheat flour would make the heaviest bread of all grain ...

Yeast is called for in the Wellcome recipes in a number of different forms. The form called for can be used to narrow possible modern yeast varieties and determine the treatment of the yeast starter before it is pitched into the must. It is important to note that when yeast is added as beer or wine lees, the amount added may be enough to have a noticeable effect on the flavor of the resulting drink.

Historical recipes also call for yeast in ways that the historical mead maker would not have understood to be yeast sources. Leaving must open after boiling will collect wild yeast particular to the locale. Use of a barrel or cask that had been used for wine or beer would provide residual yeast.

Yeast: What we Know

In 1996, the complete genome a strain of *Saccharomyces cerevisiae* was sequenced. At the time this was a herculean task (Dujon, 2017). Twenty years later, Peter (2016) used data from the complete genome sequences of over 1,000 isolates of *S. cerevisiae* to postulate an ultimate origin of the species to China and multiple independent "domestication events." Another article printed the same year (Gallone, 2016) concluded that Belgian/German, United States, and United Kingdom groups of beer yeast strains diverged between 1574 and 1604.

A 2019 paper detailed extraction of yeast cells from a number of ceramic vessels from Israeli archaeological digs, each 2000–5000 years old. When used to produce beer, three strains produced beer that was "aromatic and flavorful" while one another was "drinkable but had a slightly spoiled off-taste." Only one of these four strains was *Saccharomyces cerevisiae*. None of these strains are currently available to the mead making public (Aouizert, 2019).

Yeast strains are commercially available which have been used or preserved continuously for many years, such as kviek yeasts from Nordic areas or yeasts used in old breweries in Europe. These are philosophical close kin to historic yeasts, but we still cannot speak with any certainty how close they are in response to specific fermentation conditions to their pre-1750 ancestors.

Those who prefer use of wild yeasts have the same issues of multiple generations, plus the complication that a change in locale from where a recipe was written will affect available yeasts.

We know an incredible amount about the specific response of yeasts to fermentation conditions. We understand the metabolic pathways and production of energy, cell material, and specific side-products. But current information does not provide any notable detail on operation of specific yeasts actually used in historical mead recipes.

This leaves the historical mead maker with an essentially unsolvable problem. What yeast can be used for historical meads? We don't know the technical specifications, we expect the strains have changed significantly in the intervening years, and physical samples are unavailable.

Yeast: What to do about it?

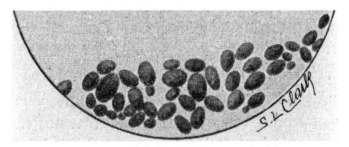

Yeast cells. *Saccharomyces cerevisiae*

Based on the current level of knowledge, the simple answer to the question of what yeast to use is both liberating and non-specific. Almost anything goes within the strictures set by the recipes themselves.

About three-quarters of the Wellcome recipes call for a specific yeast source, and for some that do not, the other ingredients or the fermentation vessel provide an obvious yeast type. But specific species or strains of yeast are never identified, and the specifics of attenuation, flocculation, alcohol tolerance, and production of by-products for any given yeast are almost completely unknown.

My choice when trying to emulate historical brewing processes has been to use basic yeasts which are not purposefully manipulated for specific characteristics because that level of scientific breeding was unknown to our historical mead making forebearers. Basic wine yeast, beer/ale yeasts and, when called for, bread yeast are the staples of my historic brewing. When a sack cask is called for, I will use a wine yeast, and when ale barm is in the recipe, a beer/ale yeast.

Others may choose to use a yeast with a particular lineage that resonates with their goals. For instance, the mead maker re-creating historical farmhouse brewing may use one of the yeasts preserved within that tradition, even though it has almost certainly changed over time. Similarly, when making a Wellcome recipe calling for a beer/ale yeast I use Nottingham or Windsor yeasts, their English pedigree matching that of the recipe.

The mead maker who chooses to use yeasts tailored for specific characteristics is using their scientific knowledge to manipulate the process in a fashion that could not be achieved by the original recipe makers. However current information cannot support a conclusion that their result with the tailored yeast will be closer or further from the result achieved by long-ago mead makers than or from results from using the most generic brewers (or even bread) yeast.

Sugar Sources Other than Honey

Other than honey, sources of sugar in the Wellcome recipes are discussed together here. Each of these reflects a unique historical narrative and pattern of use in historical mead recipes.

Citrus is included here as a sugar source, not because it is expected to add significant sugar in the recipes where it is used, but because it is a better fit in this category than others. Wheat flour and toasted bread are included with miscellaneous ingredients as their use in small quantities appears to be as a fermentation adjunct rather than as a sugar source.

Ingredients

Apples

Apples were domesticated in central Asia as much as 10,000 years ago. Modern apples have incorporated genetic material from several other primordial apple species on the way to becoming the most prominent temperate fruit crop.

Dodoens (1578) p.701, stated that the many kinds of apples could not be enumerated. "sweet, sower, rough, astringent, waterish apples, and apples of mixt temperature, as betwixt sweete and sower, &c." Hogg's 1851 *British Pomology* described 942 apple varieties in Great Britain.

The modern mead maker asking for a cyser in 17th or 18th century England might be surprised to be served plain hard cider. The word has been adopted by the modern mead making world to mean a mead made with apple juice, but historically was an alternate term for hard cider.

The Wellcome mead using apples calls specifically for "pippins." Worlidge (1678) in a list of dozens of types of English apples indicated:

> *Pippins*, which are of several sorts, take their name from the small spots or pips that usually appear on the sides of the Apple. Some are called *Stone-Pippins*, from their obdurateness. Some are called *Kentish-Pippins*, because they are a Fruit that agrees well with that soyl; others are called *French-Pippins*, having their original from *France*; the *Holland-Pippin* from the same cause, and the *Russet-Pippin* from its Russet hew. They are generally a very pleasant Fruit, and of a good Juice, fit for the Table, Conservatory and Kitchin; but not so fit for our Plantation for *Cider*, p.202–215

This suggests that apples for this recipe could be a general-purpose apple like a Macintosh or Cortland if a true pippin cannot be obtained.

Apples are a relatively common addition to historical meads. Apples are called for in one of the Wellcome recipes in this volume, White Meade MS 3009, which has an alternate recipe adding brandy.

A new orchard and garden (Lawson, 1623/1858, p.19)

Barley

Barley is included in several of the Wellcome manuscript recipes as ale or ale wort in order to make a braggot. Barley is also added to many recipes through small additions of ale barm to provide yeast, but not in amounts that are expected to affect flavor. The six braggot recipes are as follows:

- Meath Lemons MS 1806, Meath Oranges MS 1806: "2 quarts of Barm" added to about 5 quarts of honey wort.
- Braggat MS 2954: "good ale, & when it is 3 dayes ould ... worte or new Ale"
- Another Braggat MS 2954: "ale about a weeke old & draw it of the crepes ... new ale and barme"
- Braggat MS 4054: "good Ale, and when it is 3 days old ... worte or new Ale"
- Braggot MS 8097: "old alle"
- Chosin's Malt Drink MS 8903: "good Ale when it is 3 days old ... wort or new Ale"

Ale/beer making in England in the period of these recipes was a well-defined process and standard variances in the beer making process could affect the strength and composition of the wort or fermented drink. Beer/ale recipes could vary by the specific grains used, whether the drink was full strength or a small beer, and what additives (hops, etc.) were used.

Ingredients

Choice of an ale wort to make braggot is therefore somewhat open to interpretation. The recipes above generally call for 'good' ale, indicating wort from the first running and not small ale. Ale is called for in all cases, which should refer to an unhopped drink, although terminology in this time period was often applied in inconsistent fashion. The ale called for could also contain grains other than barley in some cases. The grain varieties used in 17th and 18th century Britain will vary from modern ones, and may include wheat, oats, and occasionally beans.

Interestingly enough, all but one of the Wellcome recipes appear to use both ale that has already been partially fermented and new, unfermented ale. This is not as common historically as is suggested by the recipes in this book. In the modern day this could be modeled by refrigerating a portion of a batch to prevent fermentation while another portion is fermented.

Birch Sap

Like the better-known maple sap, birch sap is collected in the spring when the tree reawakens from the winter. The sap flows out through a tap from a hole bored in the trunk. It contains about 1% sugar (mostly fructose and glucose) and is clear and slightly sweet as it flows from the tree.

As early as 921 CE, Ahmad ibn Fadlan, traveling along the Volga River, noted the Bulgars drank a fermented drink made from birch sap (Svanberg, 2012). Use of birch sap appears to have been prevalent in northern, central, and eastern Europe, where it was drunk straight, fermented by itself, used as a base for ale, and used in food. In locations such as Latvia and the Ukraine, birch sap is a commercial product in the modern day.

Specific methods or recipes for producing fermented drinks from birch sap are elusive until the later 17th century, when they appear as a class of drinks in English writings. There is no known evidence showing a direct relationship between these English recipes and the Eastern European traditions using birch sap.

Floyer (1687) on p. 102 said of the birch tree: "the fresh Juyce of the wounded Tree is Sweet, which will turn sowre: It will make a good Wine for the *Stone* with Spices."

Birch sap is an uncommon addition for mead. Two recipes in this volume use birch sap: Evelyn's Birch Wine MS 7892, and Worlidge Birch Wine MS 7892.

Other than the obvious source of birch trees in the spring, birch sap may be obtained as a specialty drink, although many such drinks add additional ingredients.

Citrus: Lemons, Citrons, Oranges

Dodoens, 1578 wrote "Of Orenges / Citrons / and Limons" that the trees do not often bear in England due to cold. On p.704 he detailed:

> The Orenge is round as an apple, with a thicke pyll, at the first green without, but after when they be ripe, of a faire red or pleasant tawnie colour … The Citron is long almost lyke a Cucumber, or somwhat longer and rugged, or wrinckled, the rind or pil is thicke, yellow without, & white within. … The Limon in fashion is longer than the Orenge, but otherwayes not muche unlike, saving that the outsyde of the Limon pill is paler and smother

Blackwell, 1737 said of the orange, "the Peel is accounted good to strengthen and warm the Stomach, prevent Nausea & Vomiting, and ease the Collick." Under the humor theory of medicine, the peel is characterized as hot and dry and the pulp and juice as cold and dry.

Citron (*Citrus medica*) is one of the three ancestral citrus species. The closely related bitter orange (*Citrus aurantium*) and sweet orange (*Citrus sinensis*) are both descended from the other two ancestral species, pomelo and mandarin. Lemons (*Citrus limon*) are descended from citron and bitter oranges.

Types of citrus used in the Wellcome recipes include lemon, citron, and orange. Forms include juice, peel, syrup, and whole fruit. "Peel" is ambiguous, it is not clear in many uses whether it means the entire peel or just the colored zest. I typically use zest.

Overall, citrus was a common ingredient in meads after about 1600, but has not yet been documented in recipes prior to that date.

Ingredients

Citrus in some form is used in 45 of the Wellcome recipes in this volume, about one third. This is a slightly greater proportion than expected for the overall time period of these recipes. The most common form is lemon peel, used in 33 recipes. Lemons, usually whole but sometime just the juice, are used in 24, of which many also call for lemon peel. Orange juice and orange peel are used in one recipe. Syrup of lemon or syrup of citron is used in six recipes.

The meads containing lemon also show a specific correlation with meads containing sugar. Of the 24 recipes containing whole lemons or lemon juice, and the 20 recipes using sugar, 14 contain both.

It is notable that a typical way of adding citrus in the Wellcome recipes is adding it to the must after boiling but before cooling. Maide MS 1808 gave an indication of the reason for this "You must not boyle your lemon peele that will make it bitter but pour your Liquor scalding hot on it."

Modern citruses are likely to vary somewhat in flavor and acidity/sweetness from their 300-year old predecessors.

Currants

The term currant was used during the time of the Wellcome manuscripts for both dried small grapes (Zante currants) and for the tart berries from the currant bush (including red or white currants – *Ribes rubrum* and black currants – *Ribes nigrum*). Zante currants are readily available and are known for the intensity of their flavor. Fortunately, the context almost always makes it clear what type and color of currants is meant.

The four Wellcome recipes in this volume which use currants all refer to the dried grape version, which are an uncommon addition to historical meads. These recipes are all variants of the same core recipe, where currants are used in conjunction with raisins.

Hawthorn Berries

Whitehorn is an uncommon name for several hundred species in the *Crataegus* genus, commonly called hawthorns. Other names include thornapple, May-tree, hawberry, and quickthorn. *Crataegus* grows as a shrub or small tree, and usually has thorns. The young leaves and flower buds are edible, but the most commonly used part of the plant is the berry, or haw, from the Old English for hedge or enclosure. Fruits of Chinese hawthorn are red while other species have yellow or black fruit.

Hawthorn has a history of being used in charms against witchcraft and the Serbians held a hawthorn stake the best to slay a vampire.

Hawthorn berries are rare in mead recipes and are used in one recipe in this volume: Welsh Wine MS 7849. The berries can be found dried. Their flavor is characterized as a mixture of sweet and sour, and the juice is more often characterized as sweet.

Raisins

The use of raisins in historical meads is relatively common. They appear to primarily be used both for fermentable sugars and for flavor. In some cases, they appear to be used to provide color. The persistent but false belief that raisins should be added to mead as a source of yeast nutrients is not reflected in the Wellcome recipes or in other historical mead recipes.

Raisins are often called to be stoned, or sliced and stoned. This reminds us that unlike today, raisins of the period were not made from seedless grapes. Removal of the seeds is important because undesirable flavors in the seeds may be extracted during boiling and fermentation.

The choice of commercial modern raisins for use in these recipes is an obvious one, but must be made with the knowledge that the exact grape varieties producing raisins in the 17th and 18th century were probably somewhat different in flavor from their modern counterparts.

Raisins are used in seven recipes in this volume, five of which are variants of the same core recipe.

Refined Sugar

The earliest cataloged mead recipe using refined sugar which can be assigned a definitive date is from 1604, where Helbach presents a recipe that uses both honey and sugar in a medicinal mead.

At the time of the Wellcome recipes, trade in refined sugar was rapidly increasing, and sugar was manufactured and sold in round-top conical sugar loaves. The smallest of these were generally made of the whitest and purest sugar, and the largest, up to 35 pounds, were less pure. When sugar was needed, it was cut from the loaf with sugar nips.

The Wellcome manuscript meads include a number that use sugar in addition to honey. The prevalence of these recipes increases greatly in the second half of the 17th century. Fewer than two percent of the recipes dating before Digby include sugar, while almost 12% of the recipes from 1670–1750 use it. Citrus is used at a much higher rate in recipes using sugar than in the entire group of recipes from the same time.

While about 15% of the Wellcome recipes add sugar, none of the plain mead recipes use it. This holds true for recipes from other sources as well. This omission suggests that sugar was considered a second class or filler ingredient, suitable when other flavors were being added, but not appropriate for a plain mead.

Meads with sugar added appear to be much more common among manuscript recipes than in recipes from printed texts. The Fettiplace manuscript, dated to 1604 (Spurling, 1987) includes a recipe for lemon mead using honey and sugar, with the notation that the sugar can be replaced with more honey. Given the use of both lemon and sugar, I believe this recipe dates from later than the given 1604 date for the manuscript.

The reasons for the frequent use of sugar in manuscript recipes but not in printed recipes is unclear, but possible explanations include:

- The samples of printed and manuscript recipes reviewed to date are not representative.
- Printed mead recipes represent an ideal with no sugar versus a practical represented by the manuscripts, where sugar is used.
- The use of sugar is a cost-saving device.
- The manuscript recipes may represent a "trendier" group of mead making practices.

Seventeen of the twenty Wellcome recipes in this volume that contain refined sugar use it in primary fermentation, three at bottling. The texts do not specify if this was for carbonation, to back-sweeten, or a combination of the two purposes. The context within the recipes makes any of these possible.

The form of the sugar used in the Wellcome recipes is usually loaf sugar. "Lump", "fine", "beaten", "refined", and "double refined" sugar are each called for in at least one recipe.

When sugar is called for in a recipe, the modern mead maker can use commercial white sugar, although raw sugar may be a better choice as much of the sugar of the time was less processed than modern sugar. They may also choose to replace sugar with honey.

Sloes

The sloe is a type of plum. While Dodoens, 1578 (and Pliny) called the sloe tree *Prunus sylvestris*, the modern name is *Prunus spinosa*. The plant and fruits are both called sloe or blackthorn. Sloes grow as a large shrub or small tree, with stiff, spiny branches (thus the spinosa and blackthorn names). The plant grows across most of Europe, and has been used in Britain to create hedges

Sloe or blackthorn c.1759

to contain cattle. The *Prunus* genus also includes cherries, apricots, peaches, nectarines, and almonds.

The sloe is traditionally harvested after the first frost has sweetened it, though it is still characterized as too bitter to eat raw. The recipe containing sloes in this volume (Welsh Wine MS 7849) is the only cataloged historical mead recipe calling specifically for sloes. Recipes calling more generically for plums are rare.

The most notable historical use of sloes, in sloe gin provides an example of how a confluence of changes in 17th and 18th century Britain caused significant effects in many areas.

Sloes became common in England in the 17th century as the shrubs were used to create agricultural enclosures. These enclosures were enabled by acts starting in 1604 that were part of shifting land control in rural

England away from small landholders and common use towards large landowners. Enclosures made rural life more difficult for the masses, driving migration to cities, and greatly increasing urban populations. London's population went from an estimated 200,000 in 1600 to about 600,000 in 1700.

Across the 16th and into the 17th centuries distilled drinks became more common. Use of distillation became prevalent commercially and in well-to-do households and the use of the products shifted from almost exclusively medicinal to recreational. Gin, named for its juniper berry flavoring, "genever" in Dutch, was initially noted for the numerous and remarkable health effects attributed to the berries, but then became a recreational drink. The Dutch head of state, William III, became William II of England in 1689 and the popularity of gin in England rose.

In the late 17th and early 18th century England placed a heavy import tax on distilled spirits but freely allowed domestic gin production. This was largely to discourage use of brandy because of the religious and political animosity between France and England. The increased population in London found English gin cheap and plentiful. This ready supply of strong drink in a time of political, economic, technological, and social change led to the gin craze of the first half of the 18th century. But much of the gin was of poor quality, thus sloes and sugar (also becoming much cheaper and more available from the West Indies slave-labor sugar plantations) were added to gin to make it more palatable.

Sloes can be purchased dried. Use of a sour plum such as a damson might also be a good substitute.

Spices

"Cinnamon and ginger, nutmeg and cloves, and these gave me my jolly red nose", are words from a nursery rhyme first printed in 1609.

Spices are technically defined as seeds, fruits, roots, barks, or other plant substances used for flavor. Herbs are leaves, flowers, or stems of plants used for flavoring or garnish. These technical definitions result in groupings that do not always make sense to the average person. The technical definitions of herb and spice also do not conform well to how the terms are used in historical mead recipes. The recipes themselves indicate a group of "spices" that is relatively limited and excludes many flavorings that are technically spices. "Herb" is used more generically.

I use a functional definition for historical mead spices, specifically those flavorings the recipes themselves define as spices and group together. Under this definition, almost all other flavor additions are grouped together and I often simply refer to them as herbs, even though that is somewhat of a misnomer. The "herbs" group includes herbs as well as flowers, roots, barks, fruits, and seeds – even when they are technically spices by modern definitions.

Several flavorings could be included in either group:
- Coriander is not classified as a spice. Despite being identified as a spice in several recipes, it is most commonly grouped with other seeds such as caraway and fennel, and therefore is not a spice in the context of historical mead recipes.
- Galangale is included as a spice because it generally appears embedded in a list of spices.

Regarding the form in which spices are used historically in meads, spices are typically added sliced and or bruised (partly crushed). *The whole duty of a woman* (Lady, 1737, p.682) made it clear, "The next Morning you may barrel it up, putting in an Ounce of Cinnamon, of Cloves and Mace, each an Ounce and a Quarter, all grosly pounded; for if it be beat fine, it will always float in the Metheglin and make it foul, and if the Spices be put in while it is hot they will lose their Spirits."

About two-thirds of the time spices are added to mead must during the boiling step, but are also commonly added to fermentation (over one-third of the time). Spices can also be added to the boiling and then transferred into fermentation (about 10%), and are occasionally added during the must cooling step.

Ninety-nine of the Wellcome recipes and variants in this volume use spices.
- The maximum number of spices used is seven.
- The average number of spices in recipes using them is 2.7.
- The median number of spices in recipes using them is three.

- It is not uncommon for mead recipes to instruct the user to add spices "as desired", either for quantity or selection of the specific spices. Overall, about one in eight historical recipes which call for spices instruct the user to use the spices they wish. Meade MS 3087, Artificial Malmsey MS 4759, Mead MS 7850, and the four variants of White Metheglin MS 8687 simply instruct the mead maker to add spices as desired.
- Nutmeg and mace appear together frequently, often accompanying two to three other spices.
- Ginger and cloves are often together, and 11 of the 18 meads with only two spices have these two. Since ginger and cloves are also the two most common spices, this could be coincidence.
- The recipes in this volume do not generally have mace or nutmeg as a spice in recipes with two spices, which is surprising based on the overall frequency of their use.
- Of the seven recipes with five spices (including one variant recipe and one duplicate) all use cinnamon, cloves, ginger, mace, and nutmeg. The majority of the recipes with four spices omit one from that list.

The table below details spice use in the Wellcome recipes in this volume, which is ordered with the most common spices first and to show patterns of spice usage and combinations. Spices with low frequency are listed in the "Other" column, which includes A - allspice, G – galangale, LP – long pepper, P – pepper, and S – Saffron. The number of herbs used in each recipe is noted as an indication of recipe complexity.

Recipe	Ginger	Cloves	Nutmeg	Mace	Cinnamon	Other	HERBS
Another Mead MS 144	X						1
Small Mead MS 1795	X						1
Small Meth MS 2323	X						2
Another Mead MS 8097	X						2
Another Mead w Rosemary MS 8097	X						3
Mrs. Heath's Mead MS 2535	X						3
Meade MS 7721	X						5
Mead MS 7102; Superfine Mead MS 7102		X					
Evelyn's Birch Wine MS 7892		X					
Bottled Small Meade MS 3582		X					3

Ingredients

Recipe	Ginger	Cloves	Nutmeg	Mace	Cinnamon	Other	HERBS
Lady Parkhurst Mead MS 3009; Lady Parkhurst Quick Mead MS 3009			X				
Mead II MS 3009; Mead II w Lemon MS 3009			X				
Mead MS 7721			X				
White Meade MS 3009; White Meade w Brandy MS 3009			X				1
Strong Mead MS 7788				X			
Mead like Sherry MS 144					X		1
October Strong Mead Saffron MS 8002						S	
Cleare Mead MS 1127	X	X					
Meade MS 1794	X	X					
Mead MS 1803	X	X					
Mead Any Time MS 4759	X	X					1
Aunt L. Mead MS 7721	X	X					1
Small Mead MS 7979	X	X					1
Mrs. Michael's Mead MS 8903	X	X					1
Mrs. W Mead MS 7892	X	X					1
Mrs. Wig Mead MS 7892	X	X					1
Mrs. Wig Mead w Herbs MS 7892	X	X					3
Small Mead MS 1796	X	X					2
Neece Green's Mead MS 3082	X			X			4
White Methiglin MS 1794	X				X		2
Braggot MS 8097	X					A	5
Chosin's Malt Drink MS 8903		X	X				2
Delicate Metheglin MS 1511			X		X		
Worlidge Birch Wine MS 7892				X	X		
Mead MS 1325				X	X		2
Lady P Small Mead MS 1799	X	X	X				3
Mrs. Salendines Metheglin MS 3582	X	X	X				4
Mead MS 4047	X	X	X				5
Spiced Spanish Methegline MS 7892	X	X	X				12
Mead MS 3009; Mead from Combs MS 3009	X	X		X			
Chumley White Mead MS 8903	X	X		X			4
Small Meade MS 7787	X	X			X		1
Metheglin w Spice Boil MS 4759; Metheglin w Spice Ferment MS 4759	X	X			X		7+
Mead MS 1321	X	X				A	
Metheglin MS 8097	X	X				G	1
White Mead MS 4683	X		X	X			3

68

Ingredients

Recipe	Ginger	Cloves	Nutmeg	Mace	Cinnamon	Other	HERBS
White Mead MS 4759	X		X	X			3
Sussex Metheglin MS 1511	X		X		X		1
Meath for Stomach & Liver MS 2477	X		X		X		2
White Metheglin MS 3828	X		X		X		
White Metheglin MS 8450	X		X		X		
Strong Mead MS 8002	X				X	S	3
Smale Mead MS 8097		X	X	X			
Mead MS 6812		X	X	X			5
Braggat MS 2954		X	X			P	2
Braggat MS 4054		X	X			P	2
Mead Stronger Flavor MS 3009; Mead from Combs Stronger Flavor MS 3009	X	X	X	X			
Mrs. Pyke Strong Mead MS 1343	X	X	X	X			
Strong Mead MS 3098	X	X	X	X			
Strong Mead MS 4759	X	X	X	X			
Mrs. Pyke Strong Mead w Rosemary MS 1343	X	X	X	X			1
Strong Mead w Rosemary MS 3098	X	X	X	X			1
Strong Mead w Rosemary MS 4759	X	X	X	X			1
Mead MS 3082	X	X	X	X			1
Mead MS 3547	X	X	X	X			2
Methegling MS 4683	X	X	X	X			3
White Metheglin MS 1511	X	X	X	X			4
Maide MS 1808	X	X		X	X		1
Mead of Citron MS 1407	X	X		X	X		2
Mead MS 3498	X	X		X	X		5
Mead MS 3539	X	X		X	X		5
White Mead MS 4054; White Mead w Citron MS 4054	X	X		X	X		5
Methegling MS 3769		X	X	X	X		
Mead MS 3008; Newer Mead MS 3008		X	X	X	X		2
White Mead MS 1026		X	X	X	X		21
Another Braggat MS 2954	X	X	X	X	X		
Mead MS 144	X	X	X	X	X		1
Mead w Herbs MS 144	X	X	X	X	X		5
Methegling MS 1792	X	X	X	X	X		5
Metheglin MS 5431	X	X	X	X	X		5
Another White Metheglin MS 3828	X	X	X	X	X		8
Metheglin MS 3009	X	X	X	X	X		11
Metheglin for Liver & Spleene MS 7391	X	X	X	X	X	G, LP	30

Ingredients

All of the spices used in the Wellcome recipes in this volume are relatively easy to come by. They should always be purchased in whole or cut form rather than powdered. Many recipes call for them to be bruised or lightly crushed before using and/or placed in a bag for easy removal.

Flavors typically ascribed to each of the spices above are:
- Allspice: Pungent, sweet
- Cinnamon: Sweet, earthy
- Cloves: Bitter, warming
- Galangale: Earthy
- Ginger: Pungent, zesty, sharp
- Long pepper: Spicy, stronger and more aromatic than black pepper
- Mace: Bitter, more subtle than nutmeg
- Nutmeg: Sweet, slate, aromatic
- Pepper: Bitter, sharp, hot, burning
- Saffron: Earthy and floral

Allspice (Berry)

Allspice (*Pimenta dioica*) is almost certainly the spice referred to in Christopher Columbus' journal entry for Sunday November 4, 1492 where he stated, "The Admiral showed the Indians some specimens of cinnamon and pepper he had brought from Castille, and they knew it, and said, by signs, that there was plenty in the vicinity" (Columbus, 1893 p.67). The spice is commonly reported to have reached England in 1601 and was at that time often called Jamaican Pepper.

Berries from the allspice tree are picked green and dried before use. The flavor resembles a combination of the flavors of many other spices, thus the modern name allspice.

The first cataloged appearance of allspice in a mead recipe was in MS 1321, dated to c. 1675, where it appears with ginger and cloves (see p. 216). It is an uncommon additive in historical mead recipes. It is used in one other Wellcome recipe in this volume.

Ingredients

Cinnamon (Bark)

Cinnamon is native to Myanmar and Southern India to China. The spice is tree bark. The stick form, called quills, where the bark is rolled and dried, almost always comes from one of two tree species. Cassia cinnamon, which is thicker and has a sharper flavor, is *Cinnamomum cassia* and is more common. *Cinnamomum verum*, also called Ceylon or "true" cinnamon, has a bark with multiple thin leaves and is typically characterized as sweeter and more aromatic. Related tree species also produce the spice. Powdered cinnamon, which should not be used in brewing, is often from one of these other tree species.

Cinnamon has had many tales told about its origins. One of the more enduring relates that the Cinamologus Bird nests in the top of cinnamon trees. To harvest cinnamon, a brave soul throws rocks at the nest and the cinnamon sticks will fall down. Another species builds its cinnamon stick nests on cliffs, from whence they can be knocked down and harvested.

Most historical mead recipes do not clearly specify the type of cinnamon used, providing the option for the mead maker to choose which they prefer. Where "cassia" is named, it is most likely that cassia cinnamon is meant, but confusion between the types can be expected to have been as widespread historically as it is today.

Although cinnamon is the third most common additive for cataloged historical mead recipes, it is the 8th most common ingredient in the Wellcome recipes in this volume. This is not because cinnamon became less common, but because other ingredients became more common.

Ingredients

Cloves (Flower)

The English name for cloves comes from the Latin "clavus" for nail or spike. The trees flower from September to January, earlier at lower altitudes and later at higher. When the flower buds begin to turn pink, they are picked and dried; if allowed to open they are not useable.

Pomander c.1610

The proper scientific name for the clove tree is *Syzgium aromaticum*. *Eugenia caryophyllis* is sometimes used as an alternate name.

In addition to their many culinary and medicinal uses, cloves have been commonly used for their scent. Pomanders, such as the example from the Wellcome collection illustrated above, were filled with wax mixed with aromatic substances such as cloves and carried by both men and women against the "corruption in the air."

Cloves are, after ginger, the most common additive to historical mead recipes. This frequency is continued in the Wellcome mead recipes in this volume, where they appear in almost half the recipes.

As discussed with the recipes, some of the Wellcome recipes add cloves in amount far in excess of what would be considered wise today.

Galangale (Root)

Galangale (galangal) can refer to any one of four species, all of which are in the ginger family, and each of which has a slightly different flavor. The rhizome, fresh or dried, is the portion typically used. It is aromatic and has a spicy flavor. *Alpinia officinarum* (lesser galangale), is darker in color than ginger, native to China, and is the version most often found dried in the US. Greater galangale (*Alpinia galangal*), is about the same color as ginger and is native to Indonesia. It is prevalent in Thai and Indonesian cuisine. Other less common species are *Kaempferia galangal*, confusingly also known as lesser galangale, and *Boesenbergia rotunda,* Chinese ginger or fingerroot.

Ingredients

Orta confirms this in his 1563 tome on simples and drugs of India (Orta, 1913, pp.208–212) where he stated, "There are two kinds of what we call GALANGA, one small with a strong scent, which is brought from Chine ... There is another larger which is found in Java ... It is larger and not with so strong an aromatic smell as the first." According to Dodoens (1578 p. 346), galangal is hot and dry in the third degree, both the herb and the roots are used, and it is good against poison and to "provoke urine."

Galangale is one of the less common spices in historical meads, but is somewhat common among mead additives overall. It appears in two of the Wellcome meads in this volume.

If the mead maker chooses to use dried galangale it is likely that lesser galangale is most readily obtained. If using fresh galangale, which is available in many Asian markets, other species may also be available. Use of fresh rather than dried galangal will introduce slightly different flavors, with dried being characterized as more subtle and earthy than fresh.

Ginger (Root)

Ginger belongs to the over-arching Zinziberaceae family of aromatic perennials with rhizomes which are native to Africa, Asia, and the Americas. Spices in this family include cardamom, galangale, grains of paradise, and turmeric. Ginger (*Zingiber officinale*) originated in south-east Asia, but despite its preference for warm climates has been grown in many temperate areas, including the United Kingdom.

Culpepper (1665, p.6) said of ginger, "[It] helps digestion, warms the stomach, cleers the sight, and is profitable for old men, heats the joynts, and therefore is profitable against the Gout, expels Wind, it is hot and dry in the third degree."

Ginger is the single most common addition to mead recipes across all time periods after 1600. In earlier recipes it was edged out slightly by cinnamon. It is also the most common ingredient by a slight margin over cloves in the Wellcome recipes in this volume, appearing in almost half.

Ginger is readily available both fresh and dried. Most historical mead recipes do not specify which form is used, which leaves the decision to the mead maker. Choosing fresh versus dried when a weight addition is specified can significantly affect the flavor of the resulting drink.

Long Pepper (Fruit)

Long pepper (*Piper longum*) is grown for the fruit, which is cylindrical in shape. Like its close cousin black pepper, it is dried and used as a spice. Knowledge of this spice in the European sphere goes back to the 5th century BCE. In the middle ages, spherical black pepper began to displace long pepper and by the time of the Wellcome recipes long pepper was an uncommon spice.

Long pepper is quite similar in taste to black pepper, but is both stronger and more aromatic. Some characterize the taste as having elements of citrus as well.

Overall long pepper is an uncommon spice in meads historically, and is more common in earlier recipes. It is used in one recipe in this volume. It appears more consistently as an ingredient in hippocras, or spiced wine.

Mace and Nutmeg (Fruit)

Dela Nuez Moscada.

Nutmeg (Acosta, 1578, p.35)

Mace and nutmeg are the fraternal twins of the spice world. Nutmeg is the pit of the fruit of the *Myristica fragrans* tree, an evergreen tree up to 40 feet tall, native to the Spice Islands (modern Indonesia). Nutmeg is surrounded by a lacy aril, which is mace. Mace is generally held to have a stronger and more bitter flavor than nutmeg. The weight of a nutmeg is about 100 times the weight of the surrounding mace aril.

A 1737 herbal stated, "Nutmegs are heating, drying and carminative, good to strengthen the Stomach and Bowels, stop Vomiting, help Digestion, comfort the Head &

Nerves, prevent Swooning, & Miscarriage. The Mace has much the same Qualities but more penetrating; & is also accounted good for the Sight & to strengthen the Memory." (Blackwell, 1737, Plate 353).

Mace and nutmeg are common spice additions to historical mead. Nutmeg appears in 47 recipes in this volume, mace in 41. They appear together in 28.

There is reasonable confusion about how much of the aril makes up a "blade" of mace. Most agree that it is only a portion of the aril. I use a 'blade' of mace to mean about 20-25% of a full aril.

Pepper (Fruit)

Pepper is recognized as the world's most commonly used spice. Its popularity can be proven as far back as the Roman empire where Apicus' famous cookbook makes extensive use of it. This prominence has continued to the modern day.

Pepper plant (de Bruin, 1706)

Pepper berries grow in a group along a stalk on the flowering vine of *Piper nigrum*. They are collected for drying as soon as the fruits at the base begin to turn red. Black, white and green pepper are different forms of the same fruit. Pink pepper comes from the South American plants *Schinus molle* or *Schinus terebinthifolius*.

Pepper is heating and drying, good to expell Wind, & ease the Collic: it strengthens the Nerves, Head, and Sight. Pepper should never be powdered fine, but grossly broken, when it is eaten with Food or used to Season it. (Blackwell 1737, Plate, 348)

Dodoens said it is hot and dry in the third degree (1578, p.635).

The culinary popularity of pepper is reflected to a lesser degree in historical mead recipes. It is one of the top 20 additions to historical meads, although its use in meads of the later 17th and early 18th century appears to have dwindled somewhat. The spice is used in only two of the Wellcome meads in this volume, both braggots.

Saffron (Flower)

Saffron is currently, and has historically been, the world's most expensive spice. Saffron is the dried stigmas of *Crocus sativus*, the saffron crocus. At one pistil with three stigmas per flower, it takes roughly 100 flowers to produce one gram of dried saffron. Unlike many other spices, crocuses can be grown in a wide variety of climates.

In his *Dictionarium domesticum*, Nathan Bailey stated, "The *English* saffron is justly esteem'd to be the best in the world, is of an opening and digestive quality; an extract of the flowers fortify the heart, purify the blood and expel poison, and being eaten or drank promote spitting, urine and the *Menses*, but if used too much it offends the head." (Bailey, 1742)

Saffron is somewhat uncommon as an addition to historical meads overall. In many of these meads, it is unclear whether it is added for flavor, color, or both. It is a far less frequent ingredient in the later 17th and 18th centuries and is used in two of the Wellcome meads in this volume.

Herbs, Roots, Barks, Seeds, Berries, Flowers

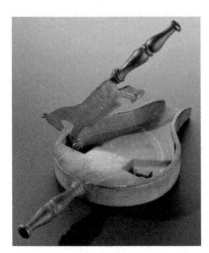

Spanish herb cutter 18th c.

The short list of historical mead spices is complemented by a much longer list of additions that includes herbs, roots, barks, seeds, berries, and flowers. In many cases more than one part of a plant is used.

These non-spice additions are grouped together here and are often generally called "herbs" even though that term is not strictly accurate. This reduces repetition where multiple portions of one plant are used, and also reflects how these ingredients are grouped together in the recipes.

Ingredients

About 60% of the Wellcome meads in this book contain one or more ingredients in this group. The group includes about 43 herbs, 15 roots, nine flowers, five seeds, two berries, and one bark. Five primary recipes and two variants call for the mead maker to add herbs as desired, although several of these limit the allowable list.

Of the 75 different ingredients in this category, 33 appear in only one recipe. And of those unique appearances, 20 are in the two recipes with the most ingredients in this category, which each contain over 20.

The average number of additions in this category to a mead using them is 3.9 and the median three. This data is skewed by five recipes that each contain 11–30 ingredients. Without these, the average is three and the median is also three.

Herbs are almost always added to mead must during the boiling step, occasionally (about 10%) during fermentation, and rarely during cooling after boiling.

Herbs in particular may present toxicity issues which were not known when the recipes were written, but which are better understood today. The mead maker should always ensure they understand safety concerns for all ingredients they are using.

I briefly discuss each of the ingredients in this category below.

Agrimony (Herb)

Agrimony eupatoria, a member of the rose family, is the species known to Dioscorides as Eupatorium, and commonly known as agrimony. Other historical names include Churchsteeples as well as Cockleburr and Stickwort for the burrs on the seeds. It grows widely in temperate areas around the world. Dodoens (1578) says the herb should be gathered and dried in May for medicinal use, before it flowers. The taste is typically characterized as astringent or bitter and slightly sweet.

Agrimony has also been called liverwort (see p.98), but it appears that most of the uses of liverwort in historical meads are not agrimony.

Ingredients

Both the leaves/stems and seeds of agrimony have been used medicinally but the leaves and stems appear to dominate. Historically, varied medicinal uses have been attributed to the herb, primarily against liver problems, but also the ability to cleanse and purify the blood. The herb is characterized as hot and dry. Culpepper (1725) places the herb under the planet Jupiter and the sign Cancer.

Agrimony is a common additive for historical meads and for the Wellcome recipes in this volume. It appears in 11 recipes. Agrimony is slightly more common in 17th and 18th century meads than in earlier ones.

Angelica (Herb, Root)

Angelica as a genus contains about 60 species; the one of interest for mead is *Angelica archangelica,* also called *Angelica officinalis,* garden angelica, and wild celery. The family also includes carrot, celery, and parsley. It is closely related to fennel, anise, dill, cumin, and lovage, but is also related to toxic plants such as water hemlock.

The seeds and roots are commonly used as flavors. The leaves are also used, more commonly in culinary applications than in medicinal. The flavor of the leaves and stems is generally identified as bitter. Angelica is characterized as hot and dry in almost the third degree.

Overall, angelica is a somewhat common additive for historical meads. Its frequency of use appears to increase in the later 17th and the 18th centuries compared to earlier periods. Angelica herb is used in two of the recipes in this volume, and the root is used in seven.

The root is available from well-supplied herb stores. The herb is difficult to find, and may be most readily obtained by growing from seed.

Anise (Seed)

Anise, *Pimpinella anisum,* is native to southwest Asia and the eastern Mediterranean. The seed is used medicinally and in cooking, it also has a long history of use as a flavoring in distilled beverages. The term "anise" is often used to describe licorice flavor.

According to Dodoens (1578, p.271), "Annise seed plentifully eaten, stirreth up fleshly lust."

> The Seed is one of the four greater hot Seeds; and is esteemed good to expel Wind out of the Stomach and Bowels, either taken at the mouth or applied as a Glyster. It is also used for cold affections of the Lungs, Difficulty of Breathing and Asthma. (Blackwell, 1737, Plate 374)

The four greater hot seeds are anise, cumin, fennel, and caraway.

Overall, anise seed is a relatively common additive for historical meads and for the Wellcome recipes in this volume. It has an apparent peak popularity in mead in the early 17th century. It is used in nine of the Wellcome recipes in this volume, four of which are braggots.

Ash tree bark (Bark)

Ash trees are flowering trees in the same family as olive and lilac. European or common ash (*Fraxinus excelsior*) is found across Europe. The tree is often mis-identified as Yggdrasil, the Norse tree of life that holds and connects the cosmos. However, modern scholarship, looking at the etymology of this word, identifies Yggdrasil instead as a yew tree.

The bark was characterized by Floyer, (1687, p. 127) as "Bitter, Astringent, and of a *Laurel*-Bitter Taste."

The first appearance of ash tree bark in mead is in Digby (1669), where it appears in three recipes and one variant. It appears in one recipe in this volume. All of the recipes cataloged with this ingredient appear to be related, with similar instructions, the same four spices, and 19 to 23 additional ingredients with significant overlap.

Asparagus/Sparrow Grass (Flowers, Root)

Whatever image "sparrow grass" first brings to mind, it is unlikely to match the herb's true identification as asparagus (*Asparagus officinalis*). This common name is a corruption of the classical Latin name and was commonly used in the 17th and 18th centuries before fading away again.

Asparagus appears in meads historically as asparagus flower and as asparagus root. The entire stalk we use as a vegetable transforms to the flower as the plant grows. Floyer (1687, p.98) noted, "The Roots have a *Pea*-taste, Bitterish, Watry, and Acrid" and ascribes a pea taste to the grassy leaves and a sweet taste to the berries, but does not mention flowers.

Ingredients

Another White Metheglin MS 3828 uses asparagus root, Metheglin for Liver & Spleene MS 7391 calls for asparagus flowers.

Asparagus root is available, but may be difficult to find. Wild asparagus root (*Asparagus cochinchinensis*) is used in Chinese medicine and is a different species. If asparagus flowers are desired, it may be necessary to grow them; the female asparagus plant will grow both flowers and berries, while the male will only grow flowers.

Balm (Herb)

The term "balm" can be used widely to refer to a number of substances. *Melissa officinalis,* commonly called lemon balm and unsurprisingly known for its lemon character, is the plant most typically meant when balm is referenced. Bastard balm (*Melittis melissophyllum*), bee balm (*Monarda didyma*), bergamot (*Monarda dudyma*), and lesser calamint (*Clinopodium nepeta*) are other herbs using the name. Balm can also refer to the resin from trees such as balm of Gilead, balm of Mecca, or balm fir. My recipe interpretations assume balm means lemon balm; it is expected that if other definitions were meant, they would be specifically noted.

Balm is a fairly common addition to historical meads. The herb is more common in 17th and 18th century recipes than in earlier ones. Balm is found in 16 of the Wellcome meads found in this volume.

Lemon balm is easy to obtain as a garden plant, and also can be bought from well-stocked herb sources. As a plant it is easy to grow, like many others in the mint family.

Bay (Herb, Berry)

Bay laurel, *Laurus nobilis,* is a tree with a long and notable history, having been used for ceremonial, medicinal, and culinary purposes. The laurel (bay) leaf crown has been associated with victory and kingship in Western cultures for close to 3000 years.

While there is no evidence confusion existed at the time of the Wellcome recipes, in the modern day bay may refer to multiple species, some from different taxonomic families. Bay most commonly is *Laurus nobilis,* but the California bay (*Umbellularia californica*) is also used culinarily and is noted as having a stronger flavor. Several Indian and Indonesian herbs from the Laurel and Myrtle families are also called bay. One of these, Indian Bay leaf (malabathrum, *Cinnamomum tamala*) is specifically called for in one 17th century mead recipe.

Bay leaf is a common ingredient in historical meads. It is significantly more common in later recipes than in earlier. It is used in 11 recipes in this volume.

Bay berry is slightly less straightforward. Most of the cataloged recipes using bay berries appear to be related, and earlier versions call specifically for fruit of Laurel; the earliest appearance in a 1623 German recipe uses an unambiguous German name. The bay laurel berry was characterized by Floyer (1687, p. 236) as "Bitter and Acrid, and of a hot Aromatick Smell and Taste." Edible fruits called bayberry in the modern day also come from *Myrica rubra*, the Chinese bayberry (yang-mei, or in our more marketing-focused day, "yumberry"), and from *Myrica pensylvanica* and related species; these are not the bay berry of historical mead recipes.

Bay berries are historically a rare addition to mead. Bay berries are used in only one of the Wellcome recipes in this volume, Braggot MS 8097.

Betony (Herb)

Betony

The modern botanical name for betony, *Stachys officinalis,* is quite different from the old botanical name of *Betonica vulgaris*. This species has a variety of alternative common names including wood betony and bishopwort. *Veronica officinalis*, also called veronica, speedwell, and Paul's Betony, is potentially confused with betony.

Using betony in a maceration rather than a fermentation, Dodoens (1578, p.291) noted, "The leaves of Bettayne dried, are good to be given the quantitie of a dram with Hydromel, that is to say, Honied water, unto such as are troubled with the Crampe, and also against diseases of the Mother or matrix. [The matrix is the womb] … The same taken with Hydromel or Meade, looseth the belly very gentlily,

81

and helpeth them that have the falling sicknesse, madnesse, and head ache."

Betony is a somewhat uncommon addition to historical mead recipes and its frequency appears to increase slightly in later recipes. It appears in five of the Wellcome recipes in this volume.

Borage (Herb)

Borage (*Borago officinalis*) is native to the Mediterranean area but, like many plants, has spread to the majority of Europe, including England. Its flavor is characterized as cucumber-like.

Dodoens (1578, p.11) calls it *Buglossum verum* and characterizes it as hot and moist. He indicates that the leaves and flowers are used to drive away melancholy, and that the root and seed are also used medicinally.

Borage is an uncommon addition to mead recipes. It appears to be more common in later recipes and is found in two of the Wellcome recipes in this volume. The form of borage used is not specified, which typically suggests using the herb (leaf).

Bucks Horn Plantain (Herb)

Buck's horn plantain
Plantago coronopus (1774)

The bucks horn plantain is *Plantago coronopus* and is also called minutina or erba stella. It is under the last name that it has more recently become a specialty ingredient in high-end salad mixes. It is in the same family as Ribwort, discussed on p.104.

Salmon in his 1710 Herbal (p.52) wrote on the plant that it, "comes up with some of its Leaves jagged or sprouting out at the sides, like the Horns of a Buck …This is a kind of Plantane different from some others, and has a quality of binding and drying."

Salmon (p.876) also stated *Plantago coronopus* is like *Plantago major* or common plantain. Although *Plantago coronopus* is not readily available, *Plantago major* herb can be bought as an alternative.

The one recipe in this text which calls for bucks horn plantain names it hartshorn. Harts horn, or deer horn, is also an ingredient in medicinal and culinary recipes of this era. In this case we know the herb is called for because harts horn is included in a list of other herbs. Metheglin for Liver & Spleene MS 7391, calls for almost 40 additions, and a number of them are not seen in other recipes.

Bugloss (Herb, Flower)

Bugloss is in the borage family and its characteristics are similar to borage, according to Tournefort (1719a, pp.165–170) and Culpepper (1651, p.15). Bailey, 1742 stated, "Bugloss, is in quality much like borage, but something more astringent; the flowers of both, with the intire plant; are greatly restorative, being preserv'd." Roots, flowers, and leaves are the portions specifically used, but much like Borage above, the leaves (herb) appear to be most prevalent.

The name, bugloss, is somewhat ambiguous. Plants in the *Anchusa*, *Echium*, and *Petaglottis* genera are all called bugloss. Viper's bugloss (*Echium vulgare*, wild bugloss) is the most common medicinal form of bugloss. *Anchusa officinalis* (common bugloss, true alkanet, ox tongue, langue de bouef, garden bugloss) is another form of the herb, which Tournefort credits with being the most common. The root of *Anchusa officinalis* can be used to make a red dye. These two are the best candidates to be the bugloss of historical mead recipes.

Bugloss is an uncommon addition to historical meads. It is much more frequent in recipes of the era of the Wellcome manuscripts than earlier. Bugloss herb is used in three of the Wellcome meads in this volume, and bugloss flowers in one.

Both *Echium* and *Anchusa* are available as an herb from a few sources. Seeds for both can also be used to grow both herb and flower.

Ingredients

Burnet (Herb), Saxifrage (Herb, Root)

Burnet and saxifrage present an excellent example of the challenges of identifying herbs named in historical recipes. While we can usually decipher the words of the recipe, connecting those words to a specific modern ingredient can be speculative.

Discussing *Saxifraga granulata*, Miller (1807, under "Weeds") stated, "From a want of sufficient distinction in English names, much confusion has arisen between Meadow Saxifrage (*Peucedanum Silaus*), Burnet Saxifrage (*Pimpinella Saxifraga*), Burnet (*Poterium Sanguisorba*), and this White Saxifrage." This gives us four plants in four different genera to consider.

Researching these names, modern pictures, and historical woodcuts leads me to the following conclusions:

- The burnet of historical mead recipes is most often *Poterium sanguisorba*, however individual references to burnet could be to Pimpinella, because the naming is inconsistent and ambiguous.
- The saxifrage of historical mead recipes is probably *Pimpinella saxifraga*. Floyer (1687, p.166) said it is "Sweet, Aromatick, Hot."
- *Peucedanum silaus* is a possible option as well. Floyer (1687) p.181 said it is "Sweet and Hot"
- *Saxifraga granulata* is not a historical mead addition. Floyer (1687, p.181) said it is "Bitterish, Astringent"

Saxifrage (*Pimpinella*) is an uncommon addition to historical meads which appears throughout the history of these recipes. It is used in three of the Wellcome meads in this volume, twice as an herb, and once as a root.

Burnet/saxifrage (*Poterium*) is also an uncommon addition to historical mead recipes. Its earliest appearance in cataloged recipes is in the 1650's, and it appears in three of the Wellcome recipes in this volume and the variants of each of those recipes.

Poterium herb or seed to grow the plant is available from specialty outlets. *Pimpinella* root is available from specialty outlets, the herb may need to be grown from seed.

Ingredients

Caraway (Seed)

Caraway (*Carum carvi*) has a long and diverse history of culinary and medicinal use. It is a member of the carrot family and the so-called seed is actually a fruit. In 2011, Finland claimed to have a 31% share of the world caraway market.

In the medical humor theory, caraway is one of the four greater hot seeds along with anise, fennel, and cumin.

Culpepper (1725, p.75) said of caraway, "This is also a Mercurial Plant. Carraway-seed hath a moderate sharp Quality, whereby it breaketh Wind, and provoketh Urine, which also the Herb doth. The Root is better Food than the Parsnip, is pleasant and comfortable to the Stomach, and helpeth Digestion. The Seed is conducing to all the cold Griefs of the Head and Stomach, the Bowels, or Mother, as also the Wind in them, and helpeth to sharpen the Eye-sight."

Caraway seeds are an uncommon addition to older historical mead recipes, but appear to become more common over time. They are present in five of our recipes.

Centaury (Herb)

One of the oldest names for centaury is chironia, for Chiron, called by Homer the "wisest and justest of all the centaurs." Chiron was known for his knowledge of botany and skill at medicine as well as for teaching Greek heroes. Chiron is reported to have used this herb to heal himself of a poisoned arrow wound.

Centaury, also called common centaury and lesser centaury is *Centaurium erythraea*. It is in the Gentianaceae family, but is in a different genus from Gentian, the root of which is also used as a liver treatment.

The stems and leaves of centaury are used as a tea, which is credited with helping digestive and liver health. It is noted as being extremely bitter.

Centaury is a relatively rare addition to historical meads. It is present in one of the meads in the Wellcome recipes in this volume, Metheglin for Liver & Spleene MS 7391.

Ingredients

Chicory/Succory (Herb, Root)

Cichorium intybus has a host of other names: common chicory, coffeeweed, succory, wild bachelor's buttons, cornflower, horseweed, ragged sailors, blue dandelion, and *Intubum sativum*. The blue and white flowers, which are similar to bachelor's buttons, turn to the sun, leading to another of the common names of turnsole. Turnsole as a common name has been used for a variety of plants, leading to great confusion.

The root of the plant has a long history of use as a coffee substitute and adulterant. Its leaves are noted for their bitter taste.

Chicory's historical roots are as an English roadside plant. The modernized hybrid is typically called salad chicory or endive and is also known as radicchio, sugarloaf, large-leaf chicory, and escarole and is a staple of modern salads.

Dodoens (1578 p.563) characterized it as cold and dry almost in the third degree. He says it comforts the stomach and cools hot stomachs.

Chicory is a rare ingredient in historical meads. It is used in three of the Wellcome meads in this volume. Two of these recipes explicitly use the root. The third recipe does not specify form, but chicory is listed with herbs and not roots, so the herb form is assumed.

China (Root)

Smilax china, known as China root, or simply, china, is a hardy climbing shrub native to east Asia, including China. The root is eaten by itself, can be used to make a brown or yellow dye, and is used medicinally.

China root is relatively rare in historical mead recipes, and all of its appearances can be traced to two core recipes, both 17th century in origin. It appears in five Wellcome manuscript recipes in this volume, all of which are variants of a single recipe.

This recipe using china root is attributed as good against a cough or consumption. *Medical and Cookery Recipes* (1670–1700) said of china root, "The Root resisteth putrifaction, it strengthens the Liver and is commonly used in Diet Drinks." Floyer (1687, p.217) noted that china root, "is of a dry Taste, a little Warm or Acrid."

Ingredients

While not as common as mead recipes, diet drinks are frequent in manuscript cookbooks. These drinks are almost always ale or beer prepared with herbs, the herbs being incorporated into the wort prior to fermentation. Like herbed meads, some contain only a few herbs and others contain a long list. The term "diet" in the drink name appears to be a reference to what is eaten rather than the modern term associated with weight loss.

China root does not appear to be readily available. The much more available sarsaparilla root is considered a substitute (as is china for sarsaparilla), indicating it is a good potential substitute. Sarsaparilla can come from any one of a number of *Smilax* species.

Clove Gilliflower (Flower)

Gilliflower is a general name for Dianthus – carnations. This is a very large group of flowers and the clove gillyflower (*Dianthus caryophyllus*), named for its scent of cloves, is one type. Gilly flower is an adaptation of the term "July-flowers" for the month in which they begin to flower.

Use of clove gilliflowers in meads appears to start at the same time as use of the flowers with sugar to make wine. Several dozen recipes for wine made from clove gilliflowers have been found in 17th and 18th century books and manuscripts, typically using sugar rather than honey.

Floyer (1687, p.216) indicated, "The Flowers taste Bitterish, Sweet, and Acrid on the *Throat*" and characterized the smell as "grateful."

Clove gilliflowers are an uncommon addition to historical meads and do not appear in cataloged meads before 1600. They are used in three variants of one of the Wellcome meads in this volume White Metheglin w Gilliflowers MS 8687 as a coloring agent.

Gilliflowers are available as seed. Commercial carnation plants are less

A carnation and hollyhock by Robert, c.1660

suitable for use as most are grown with pesticides unsuitable for use in food. An easier-to-find choice for coloring might be hibiscus, although that would add different trace flavors.

Colts foot (Herb)

Tussilago farfara is currently the only species in the *Tussilago* family. The common name, colts foot, is for the shape of the leaves. The name tussilago comes from the Latin word for cough, "tussis." Other names include coughwort, foalswort, and "son before the father", this last because the flowers bloom and seed before the leaves appear. The flowers and seeds are very similar to dandelions in appearance.

Coltsfoot contains alkaloids, which are a liver toxin. Most sources recommend avoiding all internal use, making it unsuitable for use in modern mead making. A varietal called *Tussilago farafar* 'Wien' has been developed which does not contain these alkaloids. The taste of the leaves is reported to be bitter.

Dodoens (1578, p.20) said it grows in wet places and calls it foalfoot, horse hoove, Bechion, and Tussilago. The leaves and roots are used fresh or dried; "The greene and fresh leaves are moyst, but whan they are dry they become sharpe or sower, and therefore are of a drying nature." It is reported to heal inflammation of St. Anthony's Fire and help with shortness of breath. St. Anthony's Fire is ergotism, an illness causing hallucinations and madness which is caused by eating alkaloids produced from contamination of rye with the ergot fungus. This illness was common

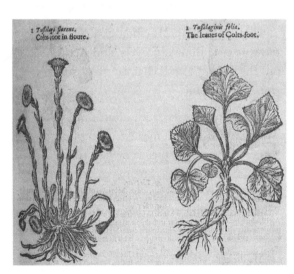

Colt's Foot (Gerard, 1636, p.811)

historically and the symptoms are believed by some to be the cause of accusations in the Salem witch trials. It is ironic that a plant containing poisonous alkaloids was recommended as a treatment for an alkaloid-caused disease.

Colts foot is an uncommon addition to historical mead recipes, and is present in four of the Wellcome recipes in this volume, all of which are variants of a single core recipe.

Coriander (Seed)

Coriandrum sativum, or coriander, is used to refer to two distinctly different materials from the same plant. The first of these is the herb, the green stems and leaves, which are currently known as cilantro in North America. The dried seed, also known as coriander, is used as a flavoring.

The leaves are characterized as tart, with a citrus character, but a certain percentage of people have a genetic disposition to dislike the taste. The seed is characterized as warm with many aromatics, including nutty and citrus flavors.

Coriander is a relatively common ingredient in historical meads, but is much more common in the 17th and 18th centuries than in earlier recipes. It is used in 16 recipes in this volume, but its apparent frequency is increased by appearances in variant and duplicate recipes.

These recipes solve the potential confusion of whether seed or herb is meant, each one unequivocally calls for use of the seed.

Cowslip (Flower)

Cowslip (*Primula veris*) is a perennial in the primrose family with flowers that are predominately yellow and have a shape somewhat different from that associated with the better-known primroses. It is well-known as an English roadside plant.

Cowslip
(Brunfels, 1532, p.96)

In the accompanying illustration from the 1530's it is called *Herba paralysis* for its reputation as an anti-paralytic.

Cowslips are one of the more common flowers used in historical mead recipes, although flowers are somewhat uncommon as ingredients. They are not used in meads prior to the 17th century, and become more common in the later 17th and 18th centuries. In this same period, cowslip wine (almost always made with refined sugar) also became popular in England. They are used in one of the meads in this volume.

Dock (Root)

The numerous docks are all in the genus *Lapathum*. The modern genus is *Rumex*, it is closely related to rhubarb. Floyer (1687, p.144) recognizes four kinds of dock, and indicates that all are bitter and astringent or rough in character, and are typically good for itch or as purgatives. Miller (1740) recognized 14 varieties, and noted, "The first and third Sorts are directed by the College of Physicians, to be used in medicine; but the People who supply the Markets, take the Roots of all the Sorts promiscuously as they find them." It is not evident which type of dock is used in historic mead recipes.

Dock is a very rare addition to historical meads. The only cataloged recipe in which it appears is Metheglin for Liver & Spleene MS 7391.

Rumex crispus, yellow dock, is the type most available commercially.

Ingredients

Docus/Carrot (Seed)

Docus derives from daucus, and *Daucus carota,* the plant most commonly known as Queen Anne's Lace, but also called wild carrot, bishop's lace, and bird's nest. The leaves and flowers are noted to be edible, and the root, noted as having a carrot smell, can be eaten while the plant is young, but becomes too woody to eat as the plant ages.

The entire variety of cultivated carrots in their varied colors and flavors, are a subspecies of this wild carrot. Cultivation of carrots goes back about 5000 years (Stolarcyzk and Janick, 2011). Tournefort's *Compleat herbal* (1719b, pp.82–84) combines the wild and cultivated into a single entry where he stated, "It is easy at first sight to distinguish betwixt *Wild* and *Garden Carrot*: For the Root of the former is smaller and more acrid."

This identification of docus with *Daucus carota* does not help the mead maker decide whether wild or domesticated carrot seeds are intended. The seed of both wild and cultivated carrots have been used medicinally. While the character of both can be expected to be quite similar, there is no concrete evidence to choose one over the other.

Carrot seed is a rare addition to historical mead recipes; its appearance in Braggot MS 8097 is currently one of only four cataloged. The earliest of these dates to the mid-17th century.

Eglantine / Sweet Briar (Herb)

The eglantine or sweet briar rose (*Rosa rubiginosa*, also *Rosa eglanteria*) grows simple pink flowers. In the language of flowers, the sweet briar conveys the message that there is a wound to heal.

Recipes calling for eglantine/sweet briar are often indeterminate in the form of the plant being added. The recipes here typically include it with a list of other herbs, implying that the leaves are the portion used. I believe that flowers or hips would have been specified if they were desired, although both flowers and hips are commonly used.

Sweet briar is a common addition to historical mead recipes with a notably higher frequency in late 17th and 18th century meads than in earlier ones. Its presence in 25 of the Wellcome recipes in this volume is in keeping with its overall frequency in recipes from the same period.

Ingredients

Eglantine leaves do not appear to be commercially available.

Elcampane (Root)

Elcampane (*Inula helenium*) is also called elecampane, elfdock, horse-heal, helenium, inula, and enula campana.

Culpepper (1665, p.4) said elecampane root, "Is hot and dry in the third degree, wholesome for the stomach, resists poison, helps old Coughs, and shortness of breath, helps Rupture, and provokes lust; in Oyntment, it is good against scabs and Itch." In his 1725 *English Physician Enlarged* Culpepper (p.125–126) indicates it is under the dominion of Mercury, the root can be gathered in spring, autumn, or winter, can be used fresh, dried, or candied, and has a wide variety of medicinal uses. Elecampane leaves are used in addition to the roots, but the roots are the portion called for in the cataloged mead recipes.

Elcampane root is a less common ingredient in historical mead recipes and appears in relatively fewer Digby and post-Digby recipes than earlier ones. It is found in one of the Wellcome recipes in this volume.

Eringo/Oringo (Root)

Eryngium is a genus with a number of species collectively known as eringo. Common forms called for in mead recipes include *Eryngium maritimum* (sea holly or seaside eringo) and *Eryngium campestre* (field or wild eringo). Many receipt books include recipes for candied eringo root, most likely popular for its reputation as an aphrodisiac.

Culpepper (1665, p.3) said, "of *Eringo*, or *Sea-holly*: the roots are moderately hot, something drying and clensing, bruised and applied to the place, they help the *Scrophula*, or Disease in the Throat called the Kings Evil, they break the stone, increase seed, stir up lust, provoke the Terms, &c."

The King's Evil, or Scrofula, is a mycobacterial cervical lymphadenitis most often caused by a tuberculosis (TB) infection. Scrofula is a painless, bluish-purple mass on the neck that grows over time. It is called the King's Evil based on the belief that the "royal touch", a skill claimed by or for the kings and queens of England and France from at least the 11th century, would cure the illness.

Ingredients

Eringo root is a less common ingredient in mead recipes. It does not appear in any cataloged recipes prior to 1600 and is particularly common in Digby where it is in close to 10% of the recipes. It appears in 10 of the Wellcome recipes in this volume. Its apparent frequency is increased by inclusion in a number of variant recipes.

Eringo seeds are available to grow the plant; the root may be available from specialty sources.

Eyebright (Herb)

Eyebright (*Euphrasia officinalis*) is medicinally associated with treating diseases of the eye. Tournefort (1719a. pp.267–268) indicated, "It is a little plant about a Span high, ... The small flowers come single out of the single Wings of the Leaves, ... being very Beautiful and Milk-white, striped within with purple Lines, with a lip divided into three Jaggs, each of which is again divided into two, and marked with a yellow Spot in the Middle."

In speaking of the herb's uses, Tournefort voiced concerns central to medical practices of his day, "But if it conduces to remove the Dimness of the Eyes, it does not effect this by its Heat and Dryness (for many Things that are hot and dry are of no Service to the Eyes) but by a Subtilty of Parts, and a certain specific Property."

Eyebright is a less common ingredient for historical meads and appears across all time periods. It is found in one of the Wellcome meads in this volume.

Fennel (Herb, Seed, Root)

Foeniculum vulgare, commonly known as fennel, is a member of the carrot family. The bulb, leaves, and stalk are all edible, but the seeds (actually a fruit) are the part most often used.

Bailey (1742) stated, "The leaves and seeds of fennel, are good for strengthening and clearing the sight, increasing nurses milk, strengthening the stomach, and for allaying prickings in the breast; the seeds taken after meals, expel wind, help digestion and being chew'd sweeten the breath." According to Dodoens (1578, p.269), it is hot in the third degree and dry in the first.

Ingredients

The flavor of fennel is often characterized as similar to licorice or anise. This flavor is strongest in the herb, but the is present in all forms of fennel. The root is characterized as having a crisp and slightly sweet flavor. The seeds are noted to contain nutty flavors.

Fennel in its various forms is a common ingredient in historical meads. Its earliest appearance is in the 15th century. Fennel is used in eight of the recipes in this volume: two use the herb, two use the seed, five use the root, and one uses both the root and seed.

**Common fennel
(Gerard, 1633, p.1032)**

Hart's Tongue (Herb)

Hart's tongue is a fern named for the shape of its fronds, which supposedly resemble the shape of the tongue of a hart (an adult male deer, typically a red deer). Its Latin name, *Asplenium scolopendrium,* provides a different animal reference. Scolopendrium is Latin for centipede and describes the pattern of the spores on the fronds, arranged in many rows perpendicular to the main shaft of the frond.

According to Dodoens (1578, pp.405–6), the plant grows in shadowed places near wells and on walls. It is dry and astringent; the leaves are used in a decoction against serpent bites.

Hart's tongue is a moderately common ingredient throughout the time period for which mead recipes have been cataloged. It appears in one of the Wellcome recipes in this volume.

Hart's tongue is not readily available as an herb. The plant can be purchased, but care should be taken to ensure it is the correct species.

Ingredients

Hops (Flower)

Humulus lupus, hops, need no introduction to most brewers. The aromatic cones are clusters of female flowers. The male vines are not planted near female so that the cones do not grow seeds. They were considered to be hot and dry in the second degree (Dodoens, 1578, p.400).

Bailey (1742) writes in detail on hops, indicating they are "compos'd of a spiritous part and an earthy phlegmatick part," and that, "At times when hops have been dear, many have us'd the seeds of wormwood, and others the wholsom herb horehound and others *daucus* or wild carrot seed." This statement invites experimentation.

The modern mead maker looking at hops for a historical recipe should consider the old German noble hop varieties such as Hallertau, Saaz, and Tettnager, or the English Goldings, all of which are of very old pedigree. Many modern hops have been hybridized to emphasize specific characteristics and are less representative of historical hops.

Hops are a relatively common addition to mead and appear across all time periods for which we have recipes. Hops are used in two of the Wellcome meads in this volume.

Horehound (Herb)

The long-standing use of horehound as a cough treatment is attested by a discovery at the ruins of a Roman fort near Carpow, Scotland (home of the VI legion). A piece of a large wine storage jar labelled with the Greek "prasion" (horehound) was found, indicating the use of horehound wine.

The horehound genus *Marrubium* contains a number of species. White or common horehound (*Marrubium vulgare*), is one of the most prevalent. Black horehound is currently identified as *Ballota nigra*, having been renamed from *Marrubium nigra*.

Historically, both the herb and the root have been used medicinally, and it is not always clear in recipes which portion is intended. Similarly, the distinction between white and black horehound plant is not always made.

Horehound is a somewhat rare addition to historical meads. It appears to be more prevalent in earlier recipes. It appears in one of the Wellcome Meads in this volume, the herb seems most likely in context.

Ingredients

Horseradish (Root)

One of the unexpected mead additions is horseradish root (*Armoracia rusticana*). The pungency of horseradish sauce derives from an evolutionary adaptation of the plant to discouraging animals from eating the roots. When the roots are crushed, an enzyme is released which creates allyl isothiocyanate, the strong and pungent horseradish flavor.

While the root is the most commonly used portion of horseradish, the leaves are also sometimes used. The root is best harvested after a single growing season and after frost kills the leaves. It is estimated that over half of the world's production of horseradish comes from the "American Bottoms" a floodplain area next to the Mississippi River and near St. Louis.

Horseradish root is a rare ingredient in historical mead recipes. Its earliest cataloged appearance is in the 1670s, and all the appearances cataloged to date use the same core recipe. The ingredient appears in one of the Wellcome recipes in this volume.

Hyssop (Herb)

Hyssopus officinalis, or hyssop, is a member of the mint family. The flavor is characterized as minty and spicy and somewhat bitter. Both the herb and the dried flower are used.

Tournefort (1719a, pp.359–361) noted, "Hyssop is hot and biting, and has a burning Taste ... Its chief Use is in the tartarous Affections of the Lungs, Cough, Asthma, &c. The Syrup is of excellent Use in the inveterate Distempers of the Breast of long continuance." It is noted as being a very good topical remedy for a black eye, or for any type of bruising.

Hyssop is a common ingredient in historical mead recipes. It appears at a relatively consistent frequency across the time period of the mead recipes cataloged. It appears in four of the Wellcome meads in this volume.

Juniper (Berry)

The juniper "berry" is actually a cone that matures on the *Juniperus communis* plant over a 2–3-year period. At any time, the berries on an individual plant are at all stages of ripeness. It is important to note that some juniper species have toxic berries.

Juniperus communis
David Blair

Use of juniper in combination with alcohol goes back at least as far as Dioscorides (about 70 CE), who recommends steeping them in wine as a treatment against breathing issues. One of the best-known uses of juniper berries in alcohol is in gin. In the 16th and 17th centuries juniper berries were given the status of a miracle cure, particularly in Germany.

Juniper berries are a somewhat rare ingredient in mead recipes. Their earliest appearance is in a 1555 recipe attributed to northern regions. They are used in one of the Wellcome meads in this volume: Braggot MS 8097.

Licorice (Root)

Licorice (*Glycyrrhiza glabra*) is a herbaceous perennial. Its primary characteristics are sweetness derived from glycyrrhizin, which also is the source of many of licorice's medicinal effects, and flavor from glycyrrhizin and anethole. Anethole is also a major flavor component in anise and fennel, and these three ingredients are often used together. There is often confusion about the subtle flavor differences between fennel, anise, and licorice.

Licorice has a long history of medicinal use, going back 4000 or more years in China, and it is mentioned in Hippocrates' writings from about 500 BCE. It has long been noted that excess consumption of licorice can be medically dangerous. Dodoens (1578 p.694) notes that licorice is temperate in heat and moisture.

Licorice root is an uncommon addition to historical meads. It appears in eight of the Wellcome meads in this volume. Most of those appearances are from a series of closely related recipes.

Liverwort (Herb)

Liverwort has been menioned as an alternate name for agrimony. In cases where both agrimony and liverwort appear in one recipe it is likely both were meant.

Liverworts are a group of about 9000 plants, typically growing small and low to the ground, and are somewhat similar to mosses.

Dodoens (1578, p.411) speaks of stone liverwort. It grows in moist ground and stony places in shadow. It is called Lichen in Greek and Hepatica in shops. It is cold and dry and is good for the liver.

Liverwort is an uncommon addition to historical mead recipes. It is used in three of the Wellcome meads in this volume.

Common ground liverwort (Parkinson, 1640, p.1315)

Because liverwort is a broad group of plants identification and acquisition of an appropriate and safe species is difficult. Its use in recipes with numerous ingredients suggests that omitting it may be appropriate.

Maiden Hair (Herb)

Adiantum capillus veneris, or maiden hair fern, is also called Venus heart, Lombardy maiden hair, maidenhair, trichomanes, and polytrichon. Dodoens (1578, p.410) identifies it as dry and between hot and cold. The herb is credited with a number of uses including helping with short breath, helping a hard cough, provoking urine, breaking stone, unstopping the liver, and working against fluxes and moistness of the stomach.

Asplenium trichomanes (maidenhair spleenwort) is another possible identification for this herb, but appears to be much less common.

Maiden hair is somewhat uncommon in historical mead recipes. It is found in two of the Wellcome meads in this volume.

Maiden hair fern is available as a plant and from some sources as a tea.

Ingredients

Marigold (Flower)

Marigolds are almost universally recognized as a brightly colored flowering perennial, often treated as an annual. It is commonly used in modern gardens as an insect repellent. In the language of flowers, marigolds represent the sun. They are associated with the Feast of the Annunciation in Christianity and also honor a variety of gods and religious events in both Aztec and Hindu traditions.

There are two marigolds, similar in appearance and lore, but potentially different in ways that are relevant to mead makers. *Calendula officinalis* (pot marigold, common marigold, ruddles) is native to Europe. *Tagetes erecta* is native to the New World and is therefore unlikely to have displaced its European cousin in the Wellcome recipes. Calendula flowers are edible. Some, but not necessarily all, *Tagetes* flowers are edible.

Marigold flowers are a somewhat rare addition to historical meads. Marigold flower appears in three of the recipes in this volume.

Marjoram (Herb)

Marjoram is one of many herbs added to historical meads which the modern mead maker would more quickly associate with dinner rather than dinner's liquid accompaniment.

Marjoram provides another of the potential confusions of historical mead ingredients, this time with oregano. Oregano (*Origanum vulgare*) is also called wild marjoram. Marjoram (*Origanum majorana*) is also called sweet marjoram or pot marjoram, pot meaning a cultivated herb. As in other cases, there is no guarantee a given historical appearance made this distinction. The flavor of the two is very similar, with oregano having a stronger flavor than marjoram. Substitution is unlikely to provide a major change in the character of the resulting drink, particularly since amounts added are generally uncertain, so the amount added can be easily varied.

Dodoens (1578, p.237) names it marjerom, Majorama vulgaris, and Marum. He stated, "Marjerom is a delicate and tender hearbe, of sweete savour, very well known in this countrie." He characterizes it as hot and dry in the third degree and medicinally good against hydropsie, making urination easier, and taking away bruises.

Marjoram is one of the most common additions to historical meads, and the third most common herb. It is used in proportionally more later recipes than in early ones. It is used in 22 of the Wellcome meads in this volume.

Marsh Mallow (Herb, Flower)

A bag of soft, white, sugary cylinders will not help the mead maker re-create meads with this ingredient, although the two ingredients are related. Marshmallow has a 3000–4000-year history of culinary and medicinal uses. Egyptians combined marshmallow sap with honey and nuts to produce a food reserved for nobility and the gods, although this appears to have been intended to treat a sore throat rather than please the palate. The use of *Althaea officinalis,* the name derived from the Greek "to heal", in dual culinary and medicinal roles continues through the time of the Wellcome manuscript meads.

***Althaea* or marshmallow (Fuchs, 1542, p.15)**

The evolution from root-derived sap and candy to modern sugar-water-gelatin puffs appears to be a result of mallow root's popularity in 18th century France. Candy makers desired a quicker method of making the confection compared to gathering and extracting juice from the root, and the modern marshmallow was born.

Marshmallow is a rare ingredient in historical meads and the leaves and flowers are both used in one of the recipes in this volume.

While marshmallow herb is readily found, the flowers do not appear to be easily available. The plant could be grown to obtain flowers.

Mint (Herb)

The genus *Mentha* includes over a dozen species with similar characteristics and many of these species contain multiple cultivars. Mints are fast growing and can be invasive. Significant members of the genus include: *Mentha piperata* (peppermint), *Mentha spicata* (spearmint), and *Mentha pulegium* (pennyroyal, see below). Dodoens (1578, p.243) recognizes that there are many kinds of mint. In an unusual distinction, he notes that mint while green is hot and dry in the second degree, and once it is dry, it is hot in the third degree.

Mint (Blackwell, 1737, Plate 290)

Based on this, the designation of mint in a mead recipe is notably less definitive than many other herbs. The flavors and odors of different species vary considerably, and the choice of mint variety will affect the character of the resulting mead.

Mint is a relatively common ingredient in historical mead recipes. Its appearance is spread temporally across cataloged mead recipes and it is found in five Wellcome meads in this volume.

Muscovy (Herb)

The first appearance of this mystery herb in mead dates from the mid-17th century. A clue to the identity is given by a description in Digby (1669, pp.65–66), "Take twelve Gallons of water, a handful of Muscovy (which is an herb, that smelleth like Musk), a handful of Sweet-Marjoram, and as much of Sweet-bryar."

The Oxford English Dictionary, defines Muscovy, after the expected references to Moscow, as "A species of Crane's-bill or Geranium, Erodium moschatum." *Erodium moschatum* (musk storksbill) has a history of medicinal use, and is considered the most likely modern identification for Muscovy or Moscow.

Muscovy is a rare addition to cataloged historical mead recipes. It is present in two of the Wellcome meads in this volume.

Neither the plant nor the herb appears to be easily found. Angelica root (p.78) is characterized as having a musk odor, and may be a good substitute.

Oregano (Herb)

As discussed under marjoram, oregano (*Origanum vulgare*) is also called wild marjoram and has a stronger flavor than pot marjoram. Another potential confusion with oregano is pennyroyal, which has alternate names of organie and organy. In general, a vowel after the r indicates oregano and no vowel after the r indicates pennyroyal. However, with variable spelling habits of the time this cannot be used as an absolute rule.

Bailey (1742) instructed, "ORIGANUM or *Wild Origan*, is good against poisons; the leaves are more particularly good against the bitings of venomous creatures. This plant boil'd in wine and applied to the reins [kidneys], removes the difficulty in making water; a decoction of it is good to comfort the nerves, and lax and weak parts."

Oregano is a very uncommon addition to historical meads. It is used in one of the Wellcome meads in this volume.

Parsley (Root)

Parsley (*Petroselinum crispum*) currently has a much more robust reputation as a culinary garnish than as a medicinal herb. The most commonly used part is the leaf, but the root, as called for in the recipes in this volume, was used in both culinary and medicinal applications. Parsley seeds also are used.

Petroselinum, parsley (Brunfels, 1536, p.121)

Culpepper (1725, pp.238–9) stated, "This is so well known, that it needeth no Description."

Ingredients

Parsley root is a somewhat uncommon addition to historical meads from all eras. It is found in five of the meads in this volume.

Pellitory of the Wall (Herb)

Pellitory is another herb where the recipe text helps distinguish between two rather different plants. In the example from the Welcome manuscripts, the recipe tells us to use pellitory of the wall rather than pellitory of Spain.

Pellitory of Spain (*Anacyclus pyrethrum*) looks very much like chamomile. In fact, Spanish chamomile is one of its alternate names. It is in a different family from other plants called pellitory.

The other Pellitory, Pellitory of the wall (*Parietaria officinalis*), is also called lichwort and is named for its tendency to grow in the cracks of walls.

According to Bailey (1742), "PELLITORY *of the Wall*, is of an abstersive, restringent and repercussive quality; being somewhat cold and dry; and when it is quite fresh, half pounded and applied to a new wound, it will cure without applying any thing else."

Pellitory of the Wall is a rare addition to historical meads and is present in only one of the Wellcome recipes in this volume.

Pennyroyal, Organie (Herb)

Pennyroyal (*Mentha pulegium*) is in the Mint family. It is not recommended for culinary use as it is said to be toxic in large amounts. The name is taken from the Latin word flea, pulex, for its reputed ability to repel fleas.

Dodoens (1578, p.232) names it penny royall, podding grass, pulegium, organie, and poley. It is hot and dry in the third degree, of subtle parts and cutting. A very long list of medicinal uses was provided, stating that it brings on menses, cleans the womb, provokes urine, breaks stones, cleans the lungs, stops stomach pains and vomiting, cures venomous bites, and it returns and quickens the senses. It was also used for gout and sciatica.

Pennyroyal is an uncommon addition to historical meads. It is used in one of the Wellcome meads in this volume.

Polypody (Root)

Polypodium is a genus of up to 100 species of ferns with worldwide distribution. The name is from the Greek "poly" for many and "podium" for feet, because the rhizomes (stem-like root) look like feet. It is the rhizome or root of the plant which is used medicinally.

Several species are relatively common in England. The variety of names for polypody in historical mead recipes (polypody, polypody of the wall, polypody of the oak) initially suggests that multiple species may have been intended. But the names all refer to a single species *Polypodium vulgare*, or common polypody. The root is used in cooking for its sweetness and aromatic qualities, and medicinally as a purgative.

Polypody is a rare ingredient in historical mead and has only been cataloged in meads dating from after the mid-17th century. The ingredient is used in one of the Wellcome meads in this volume.

The root is available from specialty sources.

Ribwort (Herb)

Ribwort (*Plantago lanceolate*) is also known as English plantain and lamb's tongue. Bucks Horn Plantain (p.82), is in the same genus.

Ribwort has a long history as a projectile in children's games. The end of the long stem is wrapped around the bottom of the cone-like head and run quickly up the remaining stem length to pop the head off – the distance achieved by the resulting projectile depends on the skill of the practitioner.

Plantain or ribwort, *Plantago* (1774)

Culpepper (1651, p.24) said, "*Plantago*, Plantane. Cold and dry, and herb though common, yet let none despise it, for the decoction of it, prevailes mightily against tormenting pains and excoriations of the guts, bloddy Fluxes, it stops the Terms, and spitting of blood."

Ribwort is an uncommon addition to historical meads, found in one of the Wellcome meads in this volume.

Ingredients

Rosemary (Herb)

Rosemary (*Rosmarinus officinalis*) is perennial in most climates, and is easily recognized by its needle-like leaves which have a piney fragrance. Rosemary has few alternate names.

> The flowers and leaves of rosemary eaten every morning with salt and bread, give ease in the head ache, strengthen the sight and sweeten the breath.
>
> Its flowers in a conserve strengthen the stomach, and are good against melancholy, the falling sickness, convulsions and the palsey.
>
> The seed drank with pepper and white wine, is good against the jaundice, and removes the obstructions of the liver.
>
> A decoction of its leaves in white wine, fortifies oppressed and weak nerves, the head being wash'd with it. (Bailey, 1742)

Rosemary is the most common herb added to historical meads, and one of the few ingredients to rival spices in popularity over time. It is used in 39 of the Wellcome meads in this volume. While a significant number, this is in line with the expected frequency for this herb.

Rue (Herb)

Rue (*Ruta graveolens*), also known commonly as herb of grace, has historically been used for both culinary and medicinal purposes. The common name comes from its use in holy water. The herb is noted for its bitter flavor when used in quantity. Some people have an intolerance for rue and may get stomach irritation from using it.

Culpepper (1725, pp.289–292), identified garden rue as an herb of the sun; the seed and herb were used medicinally. He said, "The Leaves taken either by themselves, or with Figs and Walnuts, is called Mithridates … and causeth all venomous Things to become harmless." He also attributed a great variety of medicinal effects to it.

Rue is a rare addition to historical meads. It is in two of the Wellcome meads and a variant of one of them.

Ingredients

Sage (Herb), Brown Sage (Herb)

Salvia officinalis (garden sage, common sage, culinary sage) has a number of cultivars. These vary significantly in leaf and flower color and pattern, as well as specific taste. One of these versions called for in older books is brown sage. The name itself "salvia" means to save or to heal.

Bailey (1742) wrote:

> This plant is said to be apt to be infected by serpents and toads, with their venemous breaths, and should before it is us'd be wash'd in wine, and to prevent the infection of the said creatures who covet to cover themselves under its shade, some advise that they should be planted together with rue.
>
> This plant is endued with so many and wonderful properties, as that the constant use of it is said to be so salutiferous to mankind, as to render them almost immortal. ...

Sage is a relatively common addition to historical meads. Data suggests that sage is slightly more common in earlier mead recipes than in later. It is used in three of the Wellcome meads in the volume, one of which calls specifically for brown sage. Brown sage does not have a clear association with a specific modern cultivar.

Wild Sage (Herb)

While there are several cultivars of sage that have "wild" as part of their name, "wild sage" appears most likely to be *Teucrium scorodonia*, commonly called wild sage, woodland germander, or sage-leaved germander. Over time the name of wild sage has also been applied to several other non-sage plants including *Lantana Camara* and *Stachys aethiopica*, but both of these have geographical distribution and history that makes them less likely candidates for the Wellcome recipes.

Chomal (1725) said in the entry for sage, "it is very like unto Horehound; except that its Leaves are longer, thicker, harder, more Hairy, whiter, and of a good Smell; that it shoots forth several Branches from its Root, which are also whiter than those of Hore-Hound; that it grows in the Mountains and uncultivated Places, and blooms in *August*; that it is sharp and bitter to the Taste."

106

Wild sage is called for in two of the Wellcome mead recipes in this volume. It is a relatively rare ingredient in historical mead recipes overall.

The dried herb and seed are available from specialty sources.

Sanibell, Sanicle (Herb)

Sanicula europaea (sanicle, sanibell, sanikell, sanicula, poolroot, self-heal) is a woodland herb that grows across Europe. *Astrantia major* (great masterwort, sanicle) and *Prunella vulgaris* (common self-heal) share common names with sanicle, but do not appear to be the sanicle of interest.

Culpepper (1725, pp.300–301) said, "This is one of Venus her Herbs, to cure either Wounds, or what other Mischief Mars inflicteth upon the Body of Man. It is exceeding good to heal all green Wounds speedily, or any Ulcers, Imposthumes, or Bleedings inwardly." An imposthume is an abscess.

Sanicle is a rare addition to historical meads. Its first occurrence in a cataloged recipe was in four recipes and one additional variant recipe in Digby. The one Wellcome recipe in this volume containing this ingredient is very similar to several of the Digby recipes.

Sanicle appears to be most easily obtained as a seed.

Wood sanicle,
***Sanicula europaea* (1778)**

Saxifrage (Herb, Root)

See discussion under Burnet, p.84.

Savory, Winter (Herb)

Summer savory (*Satureja hortensis*) and winter savory (*Satureja montana*) are closely related, with winter savory having a stronger and sharper flavor, and summer savory credited with a sweeter smell. Both are characterized as providing a spicy pepper-like flavor.

Dodoens (1578, p.227, p.230) also differentiated the two. He named common garden savory (summer savory) *Satureia vulgaris*. He said it was much used in meats, and in the same way as thyme, and is hot and dry in the third degree. Winter savory is also called thymbra or cunila. Dodoens stated it was found in France and in gardens in England and was hot and dry like thyme with uses with meats like thyme, summer savory, and hyssop.

Winter savory is a relatively uncommon addition to historical mead recipes. It is used in three of the Wellcome meads in this volume.

Scabious (Herb)

Scabious is a general term for a number of plants in the *Scabiosa* and *Knautia* genera commonly also called pincushion flowers. There is little information to define a specific species. The name scabious comes from historical use as an herb to treat scabies, a rash and severe itching caused by a mite. The disease is also called the "seven-year itch", not because victims will itch for seven years, but because outbreaks historically peaked in a seven-year cycle. It is transmitted by a moderately long period of skin-to-skin contact.

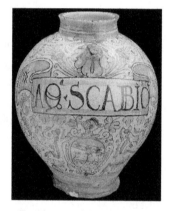

Jar for scabious water, Italy, 1648

Culpepper (1725, pp.307–309) introduced it as, "Scabious, three Sorts", which are identified as common field scabious, field scabious, and corn scabious, the field designation meaning growing in the wild. Their descriptions are very similar and the uses are also similar. Bailey (1742) gave a long list of virtues, longer than for most herbs. He stated: "Great vertues are ascrib'd to this plant, it being of a warming, drying, and cleansing quality."

Scabious is a relatively uncommon addition in historical mead recipes. It is used in two of the Wellcome meads in this volume.

The herb is not generally available, but various species can be grown from seed.

Scammony (Root)

Scammony is *Convolvulus scammonia*, a twining perennial, called a bindweed for its growth habit twining around other plants. It is an uncommon addition to historical meads, and the appearance in Metheglin for Liver & Spleene MS 7391 is the only one after 1600. The recipe does not specify what part of the plant is used, but the root is the most common.

Scammony root does not appear to be generally available; Mexican scammony is a different species.

Sparrow Grass (Root)

See Asparagus p.79.

Spicknell (Root)

Spicknell (spignel, beerwort, baldmoney, *Meum athamanticum*) is the only species within its family. The roots are characterized as carrot-like and have been used as a vegetable and medicinally.

The root is characterized as aromatic, as is the remainder of the plant. The entire plant is said to smell like sweet clover and have a sweet but subtle flavor. That the root is intended for the mead recipe is confirmed by its listing with galingale, which is also a root.

The one Wellcome mead in which it is used employs it in a medicinal manner. Metheglin for Liver & Spleene MS 7391 is also the only historical mead cataloged to date that uses this ingredient.

The root is not readily available, seeds or dried root appear in some specialized catalogs.

Ingredients

Sweet Briar (Herb)

See Eglantine p.91.

Strawberry Leaves (Herb)

It may seem curious that strawberry leaves are a much more common addition to historical meads than the fruits, but this is the case. The leaves contain tannins, and will impart a flavor to mead with elements similar to exposure to wood.

Strawberry leaves are a somewhat uncommon addition to historical mead. They first appear in a cataloged recipe dated about 1634. The ingredient appears in one of the Wellcome meads in this volume.

Thyme (Herb, Flower)

A number of different varieties of thyme appear in historical meads. The genus *Thymus* is part of the mint family and contains about 350 species, many of which are used as culinary herbs. In several cases, a common name is used by more than one species. *Thymus vulgaris* (common thyme, summer thyme, garden thyme), *Thymus citriodorus* (lemon thyme), *Thymus pulegioides* (broad thyme), *Thymus polytrichus* (English wild thyme), *Thymus serpyllum* (wild thyme or creeping thyme), and *Thymus praecox* (wild thyme, mother of thyme) are the species relevant to the Wellcome meads.

Historically, thyme has seen diverse uses for its scent, flavor and medicinal effects. Bailey (1742) said, "A decoction of this in water, and sweetened with hony is good for fevere coughs and shortness of breath; it provokes urine; is good to bring away the after-burden, and dissolves clotted blood in the body. ... The smell of thyme is excellent for those that are subject to the falling sickness."

Varieties of thyme were common additions to historical mead recipes. In total they are the second most common herb addition to meads. The Wellcome meads in this volume call for thyme varieties as follows:

- Thyme: seven recipes
- Broad thyme: three recipes
- Lemon thyme: seven recipes
- Mother of thyme: two recipes
- Thyme flowers: one recipe

Ingredients

Violets (Herb, Flower Syrup)

Violets as either herb or as flower syrup are each included in two of our recipes. The two related appearances of syrup of violets are the only such in the current recipe catalog; violet flowers are one of the more common flowers in mead.

Violets (*Viola odorata*), produce an aromatic flower with a distinctive scent. The extract of the flowers has a history of use in perfumery. The leaves and flowers are edible and often used with food for their color.

Dodoens (1578, p.148) said that syrup of violets is good against inflammation of lungs and breast, pleurisie and cough, and fevers and agues. He noted that it was particularly good for young children. It is cold in the first degree and moist in the second.

Violet leaves were an uncommon addition to historical mead recipes, as were violet flowers.

Walnut Leaves (Herb)

There are 21 species of walnut in the *Juglans* genus. All grow in temperate regions of the New World and Old World. The modern name is derived from an Old English word meaning "the nut from the Roman lands", the origin of the *Juglans regia* tree of historical mead recipes.

Eastern Black walnut (*Juglans nigra*), a native of North America, is also used medicinally, including the leaves. This is unlikely to be the walnut species referred to in our mead recipes.

Culpepper (1725, p.350) said, "The Bark of the Tree doth bind and dry very much, and the Leaves are much of the same Temperature; but the Leaves, when they are older, are heating and drying in the second Degree, and harder of Digestion than when they are fresh, which by reason of their Sweetness, are more pleasing."

Walnut leaves are a rare addition to historical meads. All of the cataloged uses of walnut are after 1674. The leaves are used in one of the Wellcome meads in this volume.

Juglans nigra leaves are available, *Juglans regia* leaves appear to be much more elusive.

Watercress (Herb)

Watercress, or *Nasturtium officinale,* is also called yellowcress. It is known for its sharp flavor and unsurprisingly, is related to radishes and wasabi. It is rich in vitamins and minerals, particularly vitamin K, calcium, magnesium, and potassium.

Watercress is a green herb that grows in waterways, the hollow stems of the plant help it float as it grows. Native to the Mediterranean and Asia Minor, it readily grows in more temperate areas such as England. While it does not appear to have been cultivated in England before about 1800, it is prevalent in the wild.

Culpepper (1651, p.23) characterized watercress as hot and dry.

While most often used fresh, watercress can be obtained as a dried herb.

Watercress was a very uncommon addition to historical meads. It is used in one of the Wellcome meads in this volume.

Wormwood (Herb)

The 1725 edition of Culpepper's *The English Physician Enlarged,* recognized three kinds of wormwood.

1. Sea-wormwood (*Artemesia maritima*), named for its preferred habitat of salty soils, was dismissed as the weakest wormwood.
2. Common wormwood (*Artemesia absinthium*), called absinthe and grand or greater wormwood. It is used to make absinthe and other liquors. This is the most common version.
3. Roman wormwood, which today can mean *Artemesia pontica* or *Ambrosia artemisiifolia. Ambrosia artemisiifolia* is native to North America and is unlikely to be the version in our mead recipes. *Artemeisa pontica*, little absinthe, is used to make both absinthe and vermouth, and is said to be less bitter than common wormwood.

Dodoens in 1578 (p.4) characterized wormwood as hot in the first degree and dry in the third, and "bitter, sharp and adstringent: wherefore it clenseth, purgeth, comforteth, maketh warme and dryeth." The common name, wormwood, derives from longstanding belief that it is a good treatment against worms.

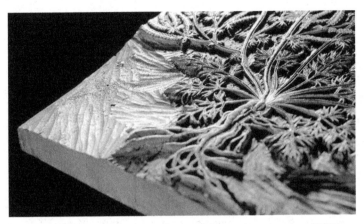

Woodblock: *Ambrosia altera,* **sea wormwood, c. 1560**

Wormwood has a history of use in wine (or mead) as a medicinal drink going back to the early herbal writings of Dioscorides (c. 70 CE). Wormwood water was a common distilled alcoholic water of the 16th–18th centuries. But the most lasting association is with absinthe, a drink that had been alternately celebrated and reviled, sometimes both at the same time. The notoriety is traced to its reputation as the "Fee Verte" (green fairy), muse of intellectuals and renowned hallucinogen (via its thujone content) of the late 19th century. Before the first World War this drink had been banned in many countries. More recent science suggests the psychoactive effects were exaggerated, and the drink is now mostly legal again.

Wormwood was an uncommon addition to historical meads. Two of the meads in this volume use this ingredient.

Miscellaneous Ingredients

Some ingredients in the Wellcome recipes do not fit into the previous categories. They include both brewing ingredients and brewing adjuncts.

Eggs, Egg Shells, and Egg Whites

Use of egg white or egg shells for clarification is a longstanding practice. The mechanism for removal of impurities is slightly different for the two materials.

Egg white, or albumin, captures particles in must by two mechanisms. First the albumin is slightly charged and attaches to charged materials in the must. Secondly, when placed in boiling must, the egg white will coagulate, physically trapping particles. Beating the egg white before addition, a frequent instruction, creates a material that will mix more effectively and capture more particles.

Use of egg whites is well established in the red wine industry, where they are noted for their ability to capture tannins (Best, 1976, p.370). Palladius Rutilius Taurus Aemilianus, commonly known as Palladius, wrote his *Opus Agriculturae* in about AD 460–470. In it, he recommended the use of egg whites to clarify wine (Fitch 2013, p.196).

Egg shells clarify in a different fashion. Some white will stick to the shells, having the same effect as the whites alone. But the major effect is from calcium carbonate in the shells, which is a flocculant (a substance promoting clumping of particles). Finally, the egg shells will form a raft on top of the liquid which physically capture solids in the liquid.

Despite this long history of use in drinks, eggs are not specifically used in cataloged mead recipes until the mid-17th century. Like citrus, despite the late entry of these clarification agents in the history of mead recipes, they quickly became common, appearing in about one-quarter of the recipes in this volume.

Egg whites by themselves were by far the most common addition, but about 20% of the time egg shells were used in conjunction with the egg whites. A small proportion, about 10%, of the recipes using eggs include either the whole egg or egg yolks.

Ingredients

Thirty-seven of the Wellcome recipes in this volume use eggs; all but two use egg whites. Three use egg shells, two in conjunction with the white. The one recipe that uses the shell alone (Mead MS 6812) is the only such recipe cataloged to date. One recipe calls for "eggs", presumably whole.

Isinglass

Isinglass is made from fish swim bladders, an organ that provides buoyancy control. The critical component is collagen which when hydrolyzed, becomes gelatin. Gelatin binds yeast and other particles into a readily removed mass.

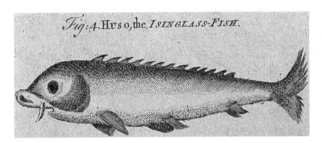

Isinglass fish, engraving T. Jeffreys

Isinglass is used as a fining agent. Many have an aesthetic preference for clear drinks, although removal of material can affect taste and character to some extent. Removal of particles may also extend shelf life. A recent study showed no difference in taste perception or preference among casual drinkers between beer with isinglass finings and without (Barnett, 2017). Its use in white wine is said to improve mouth feel and fruit presence.

The use of Isinglass as an established wine clarifying procedure is attested by its association with Dutch, English, French and Spanish wines in 1669 (Charleton, 1669).

Isinglass appears in one of the recipes in this volume. Overall it is a rare addition to mead and all of the cataloged mentions of it date from the 18th century.

Ingredients

Wheat Flour and Bread Toasts

Wheat flour, as either a direct additive before fermentation or via toasted bread to carry yeast, was a common addition in the Wellcome recipes. Wheat flour is added to the following Wellcome recipes:

- White Mead MS 1026: "if you will have it work soe that it may be riddy to drink presently ... A spoonfull of wheat flower"
- Best Mead Weak MS 4054, Best Mead Strong MS 4054: "new yest, then strew a litle flower upon it ... & so let it worke"
- Meade MS 7721: "a pint of Ale yest with the white of an egge & a little flower and put into it"

Bread toasts were used in about one quarter of the Wellcome recipes, and slightly less frequently in all recipes from the same period. The typical instruction is to toast a piece of bread and coat it on one or both sides with yeast before adding it to the must. When specified, the yeast side is downwards. This technique was first seen in the mid-17th century, and appears to be prevalent in manuscript recipes before appearing in print. Some recipes use malt flour, but wheat flour appears to be much more prevalent.

As discussed in the section on nutrient substitutes (p.39), it seems likely that addition of wheat flour and toasted bread into the must was an experientially based way to add nutrients to the fermentation, and improve yeast performance, even though the scientific basis for using nutrients was not yet understood.

A coarse ground or whole wheat flour is a better match to historical flours than modern white baking flour, which is far more processed than historical flours commonly were. For bread toasts, a whole wheat or brown bread should be used.

Musk and Ambergris

Both ambergris and musk are used in one of the Wellcome recipes, Another White Metheglin MS 3828, and while the ingredients are very different, both have similar stories.

Musk was a rare ingredient in meads. The earliest known appearance of this ingredient in a mead recipe is in the 10th century cookbook of Ibn Saiyar al-Warraq, translated and presented by Nasrallah (2007).

Ingredients

As a general term, musk can refer to a number of aromatic materials used as base notes and fixatives in perfumery. But the term most commonly refers to a material derived from the scent gland of the male musk deer; a small deer species distinguished by growing downward facing tusks instead of antlers. The animal is killed before the gland is removed.

Musk deer

Because the musk deer is endangered due to having been killed for musk for centuries, trade and use of genuine musk is now illegal in many jurisdictions, including the US. A variety of both naturally derived and artificial musk substitutes are used in the perfume industry. The safety of these for culinary use is unknown.

Based on this, genuine musk is not considered available for use. The seed of *Abelmoschus moschatus* (ambrette, musk mallow, musk okra) is used as a musk substitute and has documented culinary and medicinal uses; this might serve as an acceptable substitute for genuine musk.

Ambergris is produced by the sperm whale, also hunted for centuries and currently endangered. Unlike musk, the animal does not need to be killed to recover ambergris, a waxy substance secreted in the intestines. Once excreted by the whale, it floats in the ocean and is typically recovered when it washes up on shore. After ambergris has aged for some time, its character changes from soft and pale white with a fecal odor to hard grey or black with a deep earthy smell. This mature material is highly prized in perfumery as a fixative, and has also been used in foods and medicines.

Ingredients

The legality of ambergris depends on location. In the United States, possession or trade in ambergris is illegal because it is derived from an endangered species. Other countries are less restrictive, and it is fully legal or legal under limited circumstances in many jurisdictions.

There are a number of natural and artificial ambergris substitutes. Because these are not intended for consumption, their safety for food use is not easily determined.

Brandy or Wine

Aside from using brandy or wine casks for fermentation and storage of meads, brandy (or aqua vitae) and wine were occasionally added to mead. These additions were made to stabilize the mead for longer aging times and, in the case of red wine, for coloring the drink. Flavor from the addition is not specifically mentioned in the recipes reviewed, but is probably the reason for using of white wine in those recipes calling for Rhenish wine. Although not seen in the recipes in this volume, red wine was also used in some historical recipes to add color.

Instructions for adding either wine or brandy/aqua vitae do not always provide significant guidance. Diverse wines were available in 17th and 18th century England, and the qualities and derivation of brandies was also very broad.

- Lady Pickering Mead MS 1811 "after it has been in the Vessel six Months, put in half a pint of good Brandy"
- White Mead MS 3009 "putt in a spoonful or 2 Brandy in each Bottle"
- White Metheglin w Spirit of Wine MS 8687 and White Metheglin w Sack MS 8687 "or in Sack or Spirits of Wine, to tincture it if you pleases"
- Mead of Citron MS 1407 "a Qt. of Rhenish Wine"
- Mead MS 3498 "2 quarts of the best Rhenish wine"
- Mead MS 3539 "2 quarts of the best Rhenish Wine"
- White Mead MS 4054 and White Mead w Citron MS 4054 "putt in 2 quartes of Rhenish Wine or good white wine"
- Chumley White Mead MS 8903 "put in 2 quarts of white wine or renish"

These descriptions leave a wide variety of options for interpretation.

Ingredients

White wine: Origin and taste unspecified.

Rhenish wine: Rhine wine from Germany. Historically this would typically be a white wine. Markham (1653, p.117) characterizes it as a white wine.

Sack: A fortified wine, usually white. Modern sherry is the descendant of sack. While most sources indicate that by the 17th and 18th centuries sack was already a fortified drink, others believe that sack was originally a strong white wine and only later was fortified.

Spirits of wine: Distilled multiple times. It is not uncommon for manuscripts to contain recipes for spirit of wine which provide instructions for distilling at home, without barrel aging, with other aging processes, or with additional ingredients added. Because it was distilled multiple times, a spirit of wine could be very high proof if the distillation was well run. Based on this, a straight distilled spirit could be used rather than brandy.

Brandy: When speaking of brandy, the modern person typically pictures a drink distilled from wine and aged in oak barrels. In the 17th and 18th centuries, "brandy" had a much more general meaning and did not necessarily imply wine as the start point, barrel aging, or indeed any aging period at all. Brandy was often distilled locally from the lees or dregs of whatever brewing processes produced local drinks. While it is likely that brandy could be stored in wood, and thus receive some wood character, the modern-day amber spirit with significant wood character is only a subset of what might have been called brandy in the time period of these recipes.

Addition of wine or brandy in the amounts called for in the historic recipes will affect taste. One mead recipe from 1600 used one ounce of brandy in about one-half gallon (64 ounces) of plain mead. I found, using an inexpensive modern brandy as the additive, that there was a distinct change in flavor from the added brandy.

View of a pharmacy in *Dlicht d'apoteker*
(Augustis, 1515, title page)

Selected Recipes

The selected recipes for this volume include 105 named recipes and 29 variants totaling 134 recipes. Over 100 different flavors are added to these meads as detailed in the previous chapter. The possible variants, based on legitimate interpretations of the core recipes is enormous. If the recipes are used for inspiration, the options are innumerable.

Recipe Scaling and Measurements

The source recipes in this book range in batch size from under one gallon to over 30 gallons. Each recipe interpretation has been scaled in the modern instructions to a 1 US gallon batch. Therefore, quantities in the recipe interpretations are not expected to match the original text.

Recipe measurements are presented in US units of pounds, cups, teaspoons, and tablespoons. Those using the worldwide standard metric system should use the following conversions, which are set at two significant digits:

- 1 gallon = 3.8 liters
- 1 quart = 0.95 liters
- 1 cup = 240 ml
- 1 tablespoon = 15 ml
- 1 teaspoon = 4.9 ml

- 1 pound = 450 grams
- 1 ounce = 28 grams

Recipes as a Group

The three figures below illustrate variability of the recipes in this volume. All recipes and variants for which data are available are included in the figures.

Selected Recipes

The number of flavors, sugars, and brewing adjuncts added to individual recipes ranges from none (for plain meads) to over 20 for several of the most complicated metheglin recipes. Figure 1 shows the number of recipes within each range of number of additions.

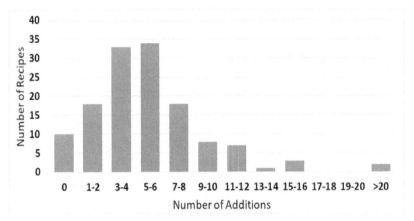

Figure 1: Number of additions to Wellcome meads

Expected OG for the recipes, as shown in Figure 2, ranges from 1.04 to 1.21, with a median expected OG of 1.09. Expected OG can be quite uncertain when issues associated with measurement, boiling evaporation rate, and boiling time are taken into account.

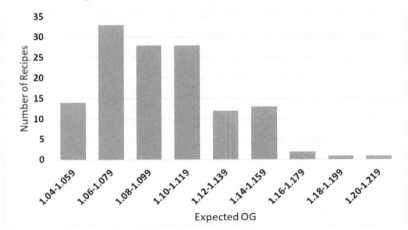

Figure 2: Expected OG of Wellcome meads

Where specified, the batch size ranges from 0.7 US gallons to 31 US gallons, as shown in Figure 3, with an average of 6.2 gallons and median 4.3 gallons. Perhaps not surprisingly, since these manuscripts are for household use, these batch sizes closely mirror typical batch sizes for home mead makers today. Many recipes give only a ratio of honey to water, implying the mead maker would multiply the base volumes to match their equipment and needs.

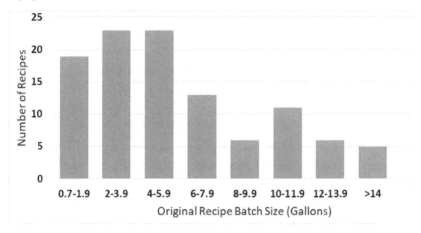

Figure 3: Batch size of Wellcome meads (Gallons)

Recipe Summary by Manuscript

The list below lists the manuscripts and recipes presented in this volume, in order of the Wellcome Library manuscript acquisition number. The following information is presented for each manuscript:

- Wellcome Library manuscript reference.
- Attribution/title for manuscript.
- Dates for manuscript according to the Wellcome Library catalog. Circa is abbreviated c. "?" in catalog date indicates uncertainty.
- Brief description of manuscript, contents, scribes, owners. "Hand" indicates the writing of an individual.
- List of mead recipes from the manuscript in this collection with the name for the recipe (all recipe names are drawn from the manuscripts, including spelling), page where the original recipe and my version are presented, the expected OG, and brief notes on the character of the recipe.

Selected Recipes

MS 144 *Book of receipts* (1650–1739?) contains medical, cooking, and veterinary recipes in several hands. The first recipe from the MS in this volume is in the initial hand for the manuscript, which makes up over half of the volume and is dated to c. 1650. The remaining recipes included are in other hands, and likely are much later as the second main hand has been cataloged with a date range of 1731–1739.

o   Hydromel MS 144, p. 143. Expected OG 1.075. Plain mead.
o   Another Mead MS 144, p.190. Expected OG 1.075. Ginger, bay, and lemon peel.
o   Mead like Sherry MS 144, p.220. Expected OG 1.11. Cinnamon and rosemary.
o   Mead MS 144, p.223. Expected OG 1.08–1.085. Cinnamon, clove, ginger, mace, and nutmeg; caraway seed.
    * Mead w herbs MS 144, p. 223. Expected OG 1.08–1.085. Above ingredients plus balm, bay, marjoram, and rosemary.

MS 184a Catchmay (c. 1625) is a book of varied recipes. The second page noted, "This Booke with the others ... My lady Catchmay lefte with me to be delivered to her sonne ... to lett every one of his Brothers and Sisters to have true Coppyes," attesting to the manuscript's value and generational transmission. The book was written in scribal hands; it was not uncommon for receipt books to be written out by professionals.

o   Metheglan MS 184a, p.228. Expected OG 1.12. Chicory root, fennel root, parsley root, and rosemary.

MS 1026 Ayscough (1692) is a well-organized book with a table at the front detailing the recipes in the first third of the manuscript and the last few pages (which are reversed from the remainder of the text). The initial hand wrote this mead recipe.

o   White Mead MS 1026, p.256. Expected OG 1.08–1.085. Cinnamon, cloves, mace, and nutmeg; bay, eglantine, pennyroyal, rosemary, and thyme, plus option of up to 15 other herbs from list.

MS 1127 Bent (1664–1729) contains two mead recipes; both appear to be in the same hand. The manuscript is primarily cooking recipes.

o   Sack Mead MS 1127, p.153. Expected OG 1.135–1.14. Raisins, fermented in sack barrel.
o   Cleare Mead MS 1127, p.177. Expected OG 1.09. Cloves and ginger; lemon juice and peel.

MS 1321 *Book of Receits* (1675–c. 1725?) contains one mead recipe in the initial hand, which dates the recipe to the c. 1675 initial date. The manuscript includes both cooking and medical recipes.

o   Mead MS 1321, p.216. Expected OG 1.07. Allspice, cloves, and ginger with isinglass for clarification.

MS 1325 *A book of usefull receipts for cookery* (1675–c. 1700) is a moderately long book containing mostly culinary recipes.

o   Mead MS 1325, p.206. Expected OG 1.10. Cloves and mace; cowslip flowers and rosemary; lemon peel.

MS 1343 Branch (1725) is dated by the inscription, "Deborah Branch her book. March 10ᵗʰ 1725." This moderate-length manuscript contains two recipes for mead in a section also containing wine recipes. Both recipes are in the primary hand and are attributed to a Mrs. Pyke.

o   Mrs. Pyke White Mead MS 1343, p.168. Expected OG 1.075–1.08. Refined sugar; lemon juice and lemon peel.

o   Mrs. Pyke Strong Mead MS 1343, p.192. Expected OG 1.15. Cloves, ginger, mace, and nutmeg; lemon peel.

   * Mrs. Pyke Strong Mead w Rosemary MS 1343, p.192. Expected OG 1.15. Above ingredients plus rosemary.

MS 1407 Buckworth (1725–c. 1775?) is given this author attribution not because Mrs. Buckworth is the apparent scribe but because many of the recipes are attributed to her. The manuscript contains seven mead recipes, six of which, including this one, are in the initial hand. The Wellcome catalog notes that this manuscript is associated with MS 3082.

o   Mead of Citron MS 1407, p.194. Expected OG 1.075. Cinnamon, cloves, ginger, and mace; balm and eglantine; white wine and syrup of citron.

MS 1511 Carr (1682) contains 348 numbered culinary recipes and 80 medical recipes in the same hand, followed by 13 medical recipes in a different hand. The mead recipes are in the culinary section.

o   Delicate Metheglin MS 1511, p.178. Expected OG 1.085–1.09. Cinnamon and nutmeg; lemon.

o   White Metheglin MS 1511, p.252. Expected OG 1.14. Cloves, ginger, mace, and nutmeg; marjoram, rosemary, savory, and thyme.

o   Sussex Metheglin MS 1511, p.273. Expected OG 1.12. Cinnamon, coriander, and ginger; nutmeg.

Selected Recipes

MS 1711 Coley (mid 18th c.), contains mostly cooking recipes and a few medical recipes. This mead recipe was on a piece of paper inserted into the book.

o   Small Mead MS 1711, p.167. Expected OG 1.105–1.11. Lemon peel.

MS 1792 *Cookery Book* (late 17th c.) contains a section titled "Meade and Made Wines" with 27 total recipes, including the following:

o   Methegling MS 1792, p.274. Expected OG 1.09. Cinnamon, cloves, ginger, mace, and nutmeg; bay, eglantine, marjoram, thyme, and winter savory.

MS 1794 *Cookery books: 17th–18th century* (1685–c. 1725) contains numbered recipes from 40 to 180 (the front material has been lost), after which bills of fare for each month are given. It contains 2 mead recipes.

o   Meade MS 1794, p.176. Expected OG 1.06–1.065. Cloves and ginger; whole lemon.

o   White Methiglin MS 1794, p.191. Expected OG 1.08. Cinnamon and ginger; rosemary and sage; lemon peel.

MS 1795 *Cookery–book: 17th/18th century* (1685–c. 1725?) is mostly cooking recipes with some medical and veterinary recipes. This recipe is from a section on drinks and is not in the main hand.

o   Small Mead MS 1795, p.222. Expected OG 1.06. Ginger and rosemary.

MS 1796 *Cookery Book: 17th/18th century* (1685–c. 1725?) is in two main hands, and this mead recipe is not the initial hand.

o   Small Mead MS 1796, p.269. Expected OG 1.07. Refined sugar; cloves and ginger; coriander and horseradish; lemon.

MS 1799 *Cookery-books: 18th cent* (1700–1775?) is missing at least the first nine pages. The manuscript contains multiple hands intermixed. This mead recipe is in the cooking section.

o   Lady P. Small Mead MS 1799, p.189. Expected OG 1.06–1.065. Cloves, ginger, and nutmeg; eglantine, lemon balm, and rosemary; lemon peel and juice.

MS 1801 *Cookery-books: 18th cent* (c. 1725) is a short cookbook focusing on fruits and fruit preserves. The single mead recipe is near the end of the book in a group of recipes in one hand.

o   Mead MS 1801, p.150. Expected OG 1.165. Plain mead.

MS 1803 *Cookery-books: 18ᵗʰ cent* (1725?) is written in varied hands that are mixed together throughout the text. It contains mostly culinary recipes.

o   Mead MS 1803, p.175. Expected OG 1.055–1.06. Refined sugar; ginger and cloves; whole lemons.
o   Strong Mead MS 1803, p.204. Expected OG 1.125. Hops.

MS 1806 *Cookery-books: 18ᵗʰ cent* (c. 1750) is almost entirely in a single hand and contains mostly cooking recipes.

o   Meath Lemons MS 1806, p.262. Expected OG 1.065. Lemon juice and zest, large amount of ale barm.
    * Meath Oranges MS 1806, p.262. Expected OG 1.065. Orange juice and zest, large amount of ale barm.

MS 1808 *Cookery-books: 18ᵗʰ cent* (1750?) is a short work that is believed to have become separated from a larger manuscript. The text is mostly written on one side of each page; occasional additions in other hands are on the other sides.

o   Maide MS 1808, p.181. Expected OG 1.10–1.105. Cinnamon, cloves, ginger, and mace; coriander; lemon peel.

MS 1810 *Cookery-books: 18ᵗʰ cent* (1750?) is primarily cooking recipes, with some household and medical recipes. The first two-thirds of the text is mostly in one hand, including this mead recipe.

o   White Mead MS 1810, p.168. Expected OG 1.075–1.08. Refined sugar; lemon juice and lemon peel.

MS 1811 *Cookery-books: 18ᵗʰ cent* (1750?) is a collection of recipes in perhaps half a dozen hands. This mead recipe appears to be in the hand that dominates the first half of the manuscript.

o   Lady Pickering Mead MS 1811, p.205. Expected OG 1.16. Refined sugar, hops.

The feminin' monarchi'
(Butler, 1639, frontspiece)

Selected Recipes

MS 2323 Eyton (1691–1738) is inscribed to Amy Eyton, with a list of the contents of her closet, dated 1691. Other hands follow hers, and one later recipe is dated 1738. This recipe appears to be in Amy Eyton's hand.

o   Small Meth MS 2323, p.234. Expected OG 1.06–1.065. Ginger; bay and rosemary.

MS 2477 Garside (c. 1655) has been damaged; the first 38 numbered pages and any prefatory material is lost. The edges of the manuscript are also damaged. It appears to be written mostly in a single hand.

o   Meath for Stomach & Liver MS 2477, p.240. Expected OG 1.11. Cinnamon, ginger, and nutmeg; agrimony and pellitory.

MS 2535 Godfrey (1686) is a short book containing medical and cooking recipes.

o   Mrs. Heath's Mead MS 2535, p.154. Expected OG 1.065–1.07. Medicinal mead with raisins and currants; china root, coriander, eringo root, licorice root, and rosemary.

MS 2954 Hudson (1678) is dated by an inscription and written in a single hand.

o   Another Braggat MS 2954, p.265. Expected OG 1.08. Cinnamon, cloves, ginger, mace, and nutmeg.

o   Braggat MS 2954, p.266. Expected OG 1.07. Cloves, nutmeg, and pepper; anise and licorice.

MS 3008 Jackson (1743) contains 330 pages, of which approximately 100 are blank. The majority of the recipes are culinary. The mead recipes are included in a section covering mead, wines, and brandies and all appear to be in the same hand, which is the dominant hand in the manuscript.

o   Mrs. Parkins Small Mead MS 3008, p.142. Expected OG 1.06. Plain mead.

o   Mead MS 3008, p.242. Expected OG 1.21. Cinnamon, cloves, mace, and nutmeg; marjoram and rue.
   * Newer Mead MS 3008, p.242. Expected OG 1.18. Same ingredients as above.

Selected Recipes

MS 3009 Jacob (1654–c. 1685), includes both medical and cookery recipes with many mead recipes in at least half a dozen different hands.

o   White Meade MS 3009, p.159. Expected OG 1.08. Apple, nutmeg, and bay.
     * White Meade w Brandy MS 3009, p. 159. Expected OG 1.08. Above, with brandy added at bottling.

o   Lady Parkhurst Mead MS 3009, p.172. Expected OG 1.095. Nutmeg and whole lemon.
     * Lady Parkhurst Quick Mead MS 3009, p.172. Expected OG 1.095 Nutmeg and whole lemon.

o   Mead II MS 3009, p.211. Expected OG 1.075 or 1.09–1.095. Nutmeg.
     * Mead II w Lemon MS 3009, p.211. Expected OG 1.075 or 1.09– 1.095. Nutmeg and lemon juice.

o   Mead MS 3009, p.213. Expected OG 1.11. Cloves, ginger, and mace.
     * Mead from Combs MS 3009, p.213. Expected OG 1.11. Cloves, ginger, and mace.
     * Mead Stronger Flavor MS 3009, p. 213. Expected OG 1.11. Cloves, ginger, mace, and nutmeg.
     * Mead from Combs Stronger Flavor MS 3009, p. 213. Expected OG 1.11. Cloves, ginger, mace, and nutmeg.

o   Metheglin MS 3009, p.250. Expected OG 1.125. Cloves, mace, and nutmeg; agrimony, anise seeds, balm, betony, caraway seeds, fennel seeds, marjoram, rosemary, sage, saxifrage, and thyme.

MS 3082 Johnson (1694–1831) is a collection of mostly cooking recipes attributed to Elizabeth Philipps (1694) as the original compiler with other hands dated as late as 1831. The mead recipes are in different hands.

o   Mead MS 3082, p.221. Expected OG 1.095–1.10. Cloves, ginger, mace, and nutmeg; rosemary.

o   Neece Green's Mead MS 3082, p.233. Expected OG 1.08–1.085. Ginger and mace; marjoram, rosemary, and lemon thyme.

MS 3087 Johnstone (1725?) was written by Charlotte Val Lore Johnstone, Dowager Marchioness of Annandale (1700–1762). The manuscript includes medical recipes with a single recipe for mead

o   Meade MS 3087, p.209. Expected OG 1.10–1.105. Maker's choice of spices.

Selected Recipes

MS 3098 K. (1735?) is a brief manuscript densely packed with medical and culinary recipes. Numbered medical recipes are entered from the front of the book, and numbered culinary recipes from the back. The majority of the text is in a single hand, with others interspersed and between the two text sections. The mead recipes are included with the culinary recipes.

o   White Mead MS 3098, p.168. Expected OG 1.075–1.08. Refined sugar, lemon juice and lemon peel.

o   Strong Mead MS 3098, p.192. Expected OG 1.15. Cloves, ginger, mace, and nutmeg; lemon peel.
     * Strong Mead w Rosemary MS 3098, p.192. Expected OG 1.15. Above ingredients plus rosemary.

MS 3498 Matthey (1750–1900?) begins with a series of culinary recipes including the mead recipe. The manuscript contains a number of hands, as well as recipes inserted on slips of paper.

o   Mead MS 3498, p.194. Expected OG 1.08–1.085. Cinnamon, cloves, ginger, and mace; balm, eglantine, marjoram, and mint; white wine, lemon syrup, and syrup of violets.

MS 3500 Meade (1688–1727) contains medical, cookery, and veterinary recipes with some pages missing. The manuscript is two volumes later bound together. The mead recipe is in the second section, which contains dates of 1717 and 1727.

o   Very Good Meed MS 3500, p.171. Expected OG 1.095. Rosemary; whole lemon and lemon peel.

MS 3539 Michel (mid 18th c.) contains about 100 pages of recipes, mostly in a single hand, but the mead recipe is in another hand.

o   Mead MS 3539, p.194. Expected OG 1.08–1.085. Cinnamon, cloves, ginger, and mace; balm, eglantine, marjoram, and mint; white wine, lemon syrup, and syrup of violets.

MS 3547 Miller (1660) inscribed, "Mrs Mary Miller her Booke of Receipts 1660" is mostly cooking recipes, and includes some later recipes.

o   Mead MS 3547, p.244. Expected OG 1.125. Cloves, ginger, mace, and nutmeg; anise seed and licorice root.

Selected Recipes

MS 3582 *Miscellany receipts* (1725?) contains three recipes for meads, all in the primary hand for the manuscript. The manuscript includes medical and cookery recipes.

o   Meade MS 3582, p.145. Expected OG 1.095. Plain mead.
o   Small Meade MS 3582, p.227. Expected OG 1.045. Bay, betony, and rosemary.
    * Bottled Small Meade MS 3582, p.227. Expected OG 1.045. Above ingredients plus cloves.
o   Mrs. Salendines Metheglin MS 3582, p.246. Expected OG 1.08–1.085. Cloves, ginger, and nutmeg; eglantine, marjoram, muscovy, and thyme.

MS 3768 Parker (1663) includes both medical and cookery recipes.

o   Sir John Ioland's Mead MS 3768, p.154. Expected OG 1.06. Medicinal mead with raisins and currants; china root, coltsfoot, coriander, eringo root, licorice root, and rosemary.
o   Sir George Holand's Mead MS 3768, p.154. Expected OG 1.06. Medicinal mead with raisins and currants; china root, coltsfoot, coriander, eringo root, licorice root, and rosemary.

MS 3769 Parker (1651) was inscribed, "Mrs. Jane Parker her Boock Anno 1651," and contains a single mead recipe. This is in the main hand for the manuscript and is located in the cooking section.

o   Methegling MS 3769, p.218. Expected OG 1.08–1.085, or 1.035–1.04 for lower gravity version. Cinnamon, cloves, mace, and nutmeg.

MS 3828 Percivall (mid 18th c.) *Collection of cookery recipes*, contains about 75 pages of mostly cooking recipes with some medical. An inscription "Mrs. Mary Percivall" is on the last page of the book in very small script.

o   White Metheglin MS 3828, p.215. Expected OG 1.10–1.105. Large amounts of ginger, plus cinnamon and nutmeg.
o   Another White Metheglin MS 3828, p.270. Expected OG 1.115–1.12. Cinnamon, cloves, ginger, mace, and nutmeg; asparagus root, bay, borage, bugloss, chicory root, fennel root, parsley root, and rosemary; musk and ambergris.

MS 4047 *Receipt book* (1669) contains groups of earlier records from 1638–1642, and later recipes. This recipe is in the main hand.

o   Mead MS 4047; p.248. Expected OG 1.085. Cloves, ginger, and nutmeg; agrimony, marjoram, muscovy, rosemary, and lemon thyme.

Selected Recipes

MS 4050 *Receipt book* (1675?) is organized into sections including one on wines. These two mead recipes are in different hands.

o Best Mead MS 4050, p.141. Expected OG 1.05–1.055. Plain mead.

o Mr. Hame Strong Mead MS 4050, p.148. Expected OG 1.13. Plain mead fermented in a sack barrel.

MS 4054 *Receipt-book* (1690–1710?) is well organized with an index at front. The recipes are broken into sections: preserving, stilling, household and personal care, surgery & physick, wine and other liquors, syrups, and cookery. It is mostly written in a single hand, with additions at the end of sections in other hands. The mead recipes are all in the primary hand.

o White Mead MS 4054, p.194. Expected OG 1.07. Cinnamon, cloves, ginger, and mace; balm, burnet, eglantine, marjoram, and mint; white wine and lemon.

   * White Mead w. Citron MS 4054, p.194. Expected OG 1.075. Above plus lemon syrup.

o Braggat MS 4054, p.266. Expected OG 1.07. Cloves, nutmeg, and pepper; anise seed and licorice root.

o Best Mead Strong MS 4054, p.255. Expected OG 1.13. Anise seed, coriander seed, and fennel seed.

   * Best Mead Weak MS 4054, p.255. Expected OG 1.075. Anise seed, coriander seed, and fennel seed.

MS 4683 Springatt (1686–1824) was inscribed Frances Springatt (later Ayshford) 1686, with the dates 1688/9 as well. These two recipes from near the middle of the text are in two different hands.

o White Mead MS 4683, p.241. Expected OG 1.10–1.105. Ginger, mace, and nutmeg; eglantine, marjoram, and thyme.

o Methegling MS 4683, p.245. Expected OG 1.14–1.145. Cloves, ginger, mace, and nutmeg; marjoram, rosemary, and thyme.

MS 4759 Tallamy (1735–1806) begins with a printed book on distillation (French, 1651) into which notes on herbs and recipes were added in blank spaces. After the printed text, recipe continue in about 140 added pages in several hands. The title inscription is 1735; several recipes are annotated "Re 1738" others 1806. The mead recipes are in two hands.

o Very Good White Mead MS 4759, p.168. Expected OG 1.075–1.08. Refined sugar and lemon peel.

o Mead any Time MS 4759, p.183. Expected OG 1.055–1.06. Cloves, and ginger; rosemary; whole lemons.

o   Strong Mead MS 4759, p.192. Expected OG 1.15. Cloves, ginger, mace, and nutmeg; lemon peel.
   * Strong Mead w Rosemary MS 4759, p.192. Expected OG 1.15. Above ingredients plus rosemary.
o   Artificial Malmsey MS 4759, p.207. Expected OG 1.10–1.105. Makers choice of spices in boil or ferment.
o   White Mead MS 4759, p.241. Expected OG 1.10–1.105. Ginger, mace, and nutmeg; eglantine, marjoram, and thyme.
o   Metheglin MS 4759, p.258. Expected OG 1.145–1.15. Maker's choice of agrimony, angelica, balm, burnet, eglantine, hyssop, lemon thyme, or others.
   * Metheglin w Spice Boiled MS 4759, p. 258. Expected OG 1.145–1.15. Herbs as above plus cinnamon, cloves, and ginger in boil.
   * Metheglin w Spice Ferment MS 4759, p. 258. Expected OG 1.145–1.15. Herbs as above plus cinnamon, cloves, and ginger in ferment.

MS 5431 *English recipe book* (c. 1700) is a relatively short manuscript with culinary and medical recipes, mostly in a single hand. Page numbering suggests a number of initial pages are missing.

o   Metheglin MS 5431, p.274. Expected OG 1.09. Cinnamon, cloves, ginger, mace, and nutmeg; bay, eglantine, marjoram, thyme, and winter savory.

MS 6812 *English medical notebook* (1575–1663). The catalog entry dates the start of this manuscript to 1650. The majority of the manuscript is in a single neat hand; this mead recipe is in a different hand.

o   Mead MS 6812, p.249. Expected OG 1.10–1.105. Cloves, mace, and nutmeg; maker's choice of herbs (liverwort, maiden hair, strawberry leaves, and violet leaves.)

MS 7102 *Recipe book* (18th c.) contains 706 medical and culinary recipes almost all in one hand.

o   Mead MS 7102, p.174. Expected OG 1.055. Cloves and lemon peel.
   * Superfine Mead MS 7102, p. 174. Expected OG 1.095. Cloves and lemon peel.

MS 7391 *English recipe book* (mid-17th–early 19th c.) is written almost entirely in a single difficult hand, with additions in a few other hands in the last few pages. The recipes are all medicinal in nature.

o   Metheglin for Liver & Spleene MS 7391, p.230. Expected OG 1.15–1.12. Maker's choice from long list of herbs, roots, and spices.

MS 7721 *English recipe book* (1675–1800?) is tightly written and additional recipes have been added in available blank space (e.g. in the front index) with a few being dated as late as 1789.

o   Aunt L. Mead MS 7721, p.183. Expected OG 1.055–1.06. Cloves and ginger; rosemary; whole lemons.
o   Mead MS 7721, p.210. Expected OG 1.05–1.055. Nutmeg.
o   Meade MS 7721, p.253. Expected OG 1.085. Ginger; agrimony, eglantine, marjoram, rosemary, and walnut tree leaves.
   * Meade from Scum MS 7721, p.253. Expected OG variable. No flavors added.

MS 7787 Peacock (late 17th c.) is a compilation of manuscript pieces and fragments. One piece has two or three hands and an end-title page, "Mary Peacock her Book 1699"; and includes the mead recipe.

o   Small Meade MS 7787, p.187. Expected OG 1.065. Cinnamon, cloves, and ginger; rosemary; whole lemon.

MS 7788 Repp (1703), in its 172 leaves, contains cooking, medical, household, and veterinary recipes. The ownership inscription is to "Dorothea Repp's 1703."

o   Sir Holland's Small Mead MS 7788, p.154. Expected OG 1.055–1.06. Medicinal mead with raisins; china root, coltsfoot, coriander, eringo root, and rosemary.
o   Strong Mead MS 7788, p.212. Expected OG 1.10–1.105. Mace.

MS 7849 *English recipe book* (late 17th c.) is a collection of both medical and cooking recipes, mostly in one hand.

o   Welsh Wine MS 7849, p.160. Expected OG 1.11. Hawthorn berries and sloes.

MS 7850 Thompson (1749) is a relatively short volume inscribed "Eliz. Thompson's Book December 14, 1749." Medical recipes were written from the front, and culinary from the back.

o   Mead MS 7850, p.178. Expected OG 1.08. Maker's choice "bag of spice"; coriander; lemon peel.

MS 7851 *English recipe book* (late 17th–early 19th c.) includes cookery recipes from the front and medical recipes from the back. The earliest owner's inscription is "Elizabeth Browne 1697" and the latest "Mary Dawes Jan 18 1791."

o   Sir Petast Small Meade MS 7851, p.154. Expected OG 1.06. Medicinal mead with raisins and currants; china root, coltsfoot, coriander, eringo root, licorice root, and rosemary.

MS 7892 *Cookery and medical recipe book* (late 17th–18th c.) contains seven titled recipes for mead in a section of the manuscript containing varied wine, mead, and drink recipes. The mead recipes are in at least four different hands; the selected recipes here represent three of those hands.

o   Evelyn Birch Wine MS 7892, p.161. Expected OG 1.105. Birch sap; cloves; lemon peel.
    * Worlidge Birch Wine MS 7892, p.161. Expected OG 1.10. Birch sap; cinnamon and mace.
o   Mrs. W Mead MS 7892, p.183. Expected OG 1.055–1.06. Cloves and ginger; rosemary; whole lemons.
o   Mrs. W Mead II MS 7892, p.148. Expected OG 1.13. Plain mead, fermented in sack barrel.
o   Mrs. Wig Mead MS 7892, p.183. Expected OG 1.055–1.06. Cloves and ginger; rosemary; whole lemons.
    * Mrs. Wig Mead w Herbs MS 7892, p.236. Expected OG 1.055–1.06. Cloves and ginger; balm, rosemary, and lemon thyme.
o   Spanish Methegline MS 7892, p.259. Expected OG 1.115. Agrimony, angelica, balm, bugloss, burnet, fennel root, marigold flowers, marjoram, parsley root, rosemary, sage, and thyme.
    * Spiced Spanish Methegline MS 7982, p.259. Expected OG 1.115. Above herbs plus cloves, ginger, and nutmeg.

MS 7976 Palmer (1700–1739) *A collection of ye best receipts* is a moderately long recipe book covering cooking, preserving, housewifery, physick, and chirurgery, "Carefully selected from the best hands and the most choice & authentick Manuscripts." This inscription dates the manuscript to 1700 by Mrs. Palmer, who wrote, "Note, there is room left for a Supplement, to this book of what shall come in after the compiling of it." All the mead recipes are in the main hand.

o   Mead MS 7976, p.226. Expected OG 1.055. Refined sugar and lemon thyme.

Selected Recipes

MS 7979 *Recipe book* (18th c.) includes mostly culinary with some medical recipes.

o   Small Mead MS 7979, p.188. Expected OG 1.06. Cloves and ginger; eglantine; whole lemons.

MS 7997 Heppington (late 17th–early 19th c.) is primarily written in two hands. "1723" is written on one page and a recipe dated 1816 was inserted in the volume.

o   Meade Egg MS 7997, p.144. Expected OG 1.085. Plain mead.
   * Meade Volume MS 7997, p.144. Expected OG 1.145. Plain mead.

MS 8002 *Loose receipts* (1663–1740) is as the title indicates. Varied hands have written the mead recipes. The group is connected to MS 7997.

o   October Strong Mead MS 8002, p.147. Expected OG 1.125. Plain mead.
   * October Strong Mead Lemon MS 8002, p.147. Expected OG 1.125. Lemon and peel added in bottling.
   * October Strong Mead Saffron MS 8002, p.147. Expected OG 1.125. Saffron added for color

o   Strong Mead MS 8002, p.235. Expected OG 1.115–1.12. Cinnamon, ginger, and saffron; balm, marigold flowers, and marjoram.

MS 8097 *English recipe book* (17th–18th c.) has medical recipes from the front of the book and many more culinary recipes from the back. The mead recipes are clustered with other drinks in the culinary recipes.

o   Smale Mead MS 8097, p.180. Expected OG 1.04. Raisins; cloves, mace, and nutmeg; lemon peel.

o   Metheglin MS 8097, p.224. Expected OG 1.08–1.085. Cloves, galingale, and ginger; angelica root.

o   Another Mead MS 8097, p.233. Expected OG 1.06–1.065. Ginger; angelica and eglantine.
   * Another Mead w Rosemary MS 8097, p.233. Expected OG 1.06–1.065. Ginger; angelica root, eglantine, and rosemary.

o   Braggot MS 8097, p.264. Expected OG equivalent of 1.02 of honey added to finished ale. Allspice and ginger; anise seed, bay berries, caraway, seed, docus seed, and juniper berries.

MS 8450 *English culinary and medical recipe book* (1680–c. 1740?) is attributed to the Blackett family of Northumberland. The manuscript is divided into "Receits in Cookery", "Sweetmeats, syrrups, jelly, conserves, preserves, candys, creams, distilled, and other waters, pickles, made wines, and other liquors", and "Receits in physick and surgery." The mead recipes are with the sweetmeats group and are all in the same hand.

o   White Metheglin MS 8450, p.215. Expected OG 1.10–1105 Large amount of ginger, with cinnamon and nutmeg.

MS 8687 Tully (1732–?) has an inscription noting ownership by Sarah Tully, Lady Hoare. Sarah Tully married Sir Richard Hoare, a London banker (and later Lord Mayor of London) in 1732 and died in 1737. The manuscript is in several hands and includes medical, culinary, household, and veterinary recipes.

o   White Metheglin MS 8687, p.238. Expected OG 1.11. Maker's choice of spices; coriander, eglantine, and eringo roots.
   * White Metheglin with Gilliflowers MS 8687, p.238. Expected OG 1.11. Clove gilliflowers added to above for color.
   * White Metheglin with Sack MS 8687, p. 238. Expected OG 1.11. Clove gillyflower tincture in wine added to above for color.
   * White Metheglin with Spirit of Wine MS 8687, p. 238. Expected OG 1.11. Clove gilliflowers in brandy added to above for color.

MS 8903 Carteret (1662–mid 18th c.) has an ownership inscription to Grace Carteret, 1st Countess Granville. The catalog notes this manuscript contains what may be the earliest known recipe for ice cream.

o   Mrs. Michaels Mead MS 8903, p.183. Expected OG 1.055–1.06. Cloves and ginger; rosemary; whole lemons.
o   Chumley White Mead MS 8903, p.194. Expected OG 1.07. Cloves, ginger, and mace; balm, eglantine, marjoram, and mint; white wine, lemon syrup, and lemon peel.
o   Chosin's Malt Drink MS 8903, p.266. Expected OG 1.07. Cloves, nutmeg, and pepper; anise seed and licorice root.

**A physician and a surgeon pointing to herbs
(engraving, 1671)**

Plain Meads

Overall, just under 15% of cataloged historical mead recipes are for plain mead, also called traditional or show mead, in which honey and water are the sole ingredients. In the Wellcome manuscripts plain meads are less common, representing about seven percent of the total recipes, a proportion in line with 17th and 18th century recipes as a whole. This lower frequency may represent a preference in that time period for meads with additional flavors, or it could simply reflect that basic mead-making was an assumed skill and recipes were not written down.

A recipe for plain mead might be thought to add little depth to the discussion of historical recipes. After all, honey plus water is the basis of mead making. But these recipes illuminate overarching topics by stripping away the complexities of additional ingredients.

The plain mead recipes selected for this volume were chosen in part to show the range of honey content in the Wellcome recipes as a whole. These recipes, their grouping in the sections below, and expected original gravities are as follows:

- Best Mead MS 4050, Small Mead, OG 1.05–1.055
- Mrs. Parkins Small Mead MS 3008, Small Mead, OG 1.06
- Hydromel MS 144, Middling Strength, OG 1.075
- Meade MS 7997, Middling Strength, OG 1.085 (or OG 1.145)
- Meade MS 3582, Middling Strength, OG 1.095
- October Strong Mead MS 8002, Strong Mead, OG 1.125
- Mr. Hame Strong Mead MS 4050, Mrs. W Mead II MS 7892, Strong Mead, OG 1.13
- Mead MS 1801, Strong Mead, OG 1.165

The potential ending alcohol content for the meads in this sample ranges from about 6.5% to over 20%. This corresponds to a bit over one and one half pounds per gallon honey to well over four. The recipes instruct that the meads be drunk between ten days and "many years" after making.

In addition to the meads in this chapter, Mead from Combs MS 3009 (p.213) gives alternate instructions for making the recipe with water used to rinse honeycombs once the majority of the honey was drained, rather than by simply adding honey to water. I have interpreted this as an alternate method to prepare the must while using the same spice additions as the core recipe. However, this could also be interpreted as a completely separate recipe for a plain mead. Using water to rinse valuable honey from the combs while cleaning the equally valuable wax is historically common, and using that honey water for mead is an obvious step. Recipes making mead from the whole honeycomb were also relatively common historically; this mead was often called apomel.

Photograph of cemetery marker, Winchester

Small Meads – Modern 'Hydromel'

The term "small mead" is almost certainly derived from small ale/beer, which is a drink made from the second (or even third) extraction of sugars from malt, producing a weaker or smaller brew. These meads are typically low in initial sugar and therefore ferment quickly, producing a mead with low alcohol and few or no residual sugars. They are also generally intended to be drunk quickly, often within one or two weeks. It is probable that some were drunk before fermentation was complete. This class of drink was often viewed as inferior, and many references refer to them as drinks for servants or hired hands.

These lower alcohol drinks are now often called session meads because you can drink a number in one session. They can also be called quick or short meads, a variant on the small terminology. In modern competition guidelines these are called hydromels with a typical OG of 1.035–1.080 and final ABV of 3.5–7.5%. Here I use the term small mead, the most common term used in the manuscripts.

It is important to note that the term small mead, like other terms, is not used consistently within manuscripts. The title is used for some recipes that do not fit the description of lower initial honey and final alcohol. The modern designation of hydromel for these meads also presents a disconnect with historical terminology. The Latin term hydromel translates to English as "honey water" and was historically a general term for mead.

Best Mead MS 4050

MS 4050 *Receipt book* (1675?) on folio 36v of the manuscript instructed in the initial hand:

> To make mead the best
>
> Take 2 quartes of the best honey, and put to it 24 quartes of springe water set it on a slow fire and skime it very cleane, let it boile till it comes to 18 quartes then put it into an Earthen pott that hath a spigott and fassett, and when it is lukewarmes, or a little more, have a tost of household bread toasted very hard and yeist put upon both sides and put that into it, and beat it very well, soe set it a working, and doe soe every day for three or foure daies, and be sure you keep it close covered, then let it stand at least 8 or 10 daies in the earthen vessell close covered after it has done workeing, and then draw it into bottles, and in a fortnight or less it will it will be ready to drinke, this mead being soe shorte will not keep good above two moneths.

Notes for interpretation and choices:

- The yeast and bread appear to be beaten into the liquid during the daily beating period. This is unusual.
- The total fermentation and aging period is three to four weeks, suggesting that it will most likely ferment to completion at under ten percent alcohol.
- Fermentation in earthen vessel and bottling after gives few opportunities for flavor introduction from containers.
- Using modern bottles and specified timing risks bottle bombs.

Instructions for Best Mead MS 4050:

1. Add 1.4 pounds (1 scant pint) of honey to 6 quarts of water.
2. Boil down to 1 gallon, skimming, let cool.
   [Mix water with 1.4 pounds (1 scant pint) of honey to make 1 gallon.]
3. Place in neutral fermentation container (earthenware, glass, stainless, or plastic). Expected OG 1.05–1.055.
4. Toast a piece of coarse bread until it is hard, spread yeast barm on both sides, add to fermenter.
5. Mix thoroughly once per day for 3–4 days.
6. Let stand and ferment 8–10 days more.
7. Decant into containers which can continue to let out fermentation gases. Let age up to 14 days before drinking.
8. Consume within 2 months.

Mrs. Parkins Small Mead MS 3008

MS 3008 Jackson (1743) on page 204 of the manuscript instructed:

> Small mead Mrs. Parkins
>
> Take 30 quarts of water, & 8 pound of honny, boyle it 3 hours, which will bring it to 20 quarts. Let it stand till cold, then put it into your Vessel, & do not work it. Bottle it off.

Notes for interpretation and choices:

- Both boiling time (three hours) and total liquid loss are given.
- "Do not work it" probably refers to intentionally not adding yeast. A wild yeast approach could be used, or the mead maker

could assume yeast is supplied from residual in the fermentation vessel (modeled by adding yeast).

- The "vessel" for fermentation is unspecified, wood or earthenware are most likely.
- Timing is not defined. Since the drink is bottled, it implies at least a short aging period.

Instructions for Mrs. Parkins Small Mead MS 3008:

1. Add 1.6 pounds (2 generous cups) honey to 6 quarts water.
2. Boil down to 1 gallon.
   [Mix 1.6 pounds (2 generous cups) honey with water to make 1 gallon.]
3. When cool, place in fermenter. Expected OG 1.06.
4. Rely on wild yeast, or add yeast of choice.
5. Follow preferred fermentation, aging, and bottling protocols.

Ambiguities in the recipe provide opportunities to explore historically plausible choices to influence the character of the mead. Using boiling time only would vary liquid loss and OG. Timing of fermentation and aging can be varied. Yeast choice is open. A wooden fermentation container with varying previous contents would affect flavor.

Hydromel MS 144

MS 144 *Book of receipts* (1650–1739?) on p.33 instructed in the initial hand for the manuscript (approximately 1650):

To make hydromel

Take eight quartes of spring water & put to it 4 pownd of english hony & stirr it till it bee all dissolved then boyle it till it wast 3 pints scume it when the froth begineth to looke a litle darke put it into a kooler to coole when it is almost cold make a browne toast & spread it all over with neew yeast then put it into the kooler & cover itt very close the next day when itt is wrought up with a cap put it into a vessell when it have done working stope itt up & when itt is cleare botle it upp & with in tenn days drinke itt

---

Notes for interpretation and choices:

- A cooler is a broad, shallow open container providing rapid cooling for beer/ale wort. This arrangement allowed exposure to wild yeasts or contaminants.
- Fermentation timing is unclear. "Done working" would refer to visible signs of fermentation, which is typically much sooner than actual end of fermentation. Not bottling until clear typically would take some time. Drinking within ten days of bottling implies a very short overall cycle.

Instructions for Hydromel MS 144:

1. Add 2 pounds (3 scant cups) honey, to 1 gallon water, mix.
2. Boil down to 1 gallon, skimming.
   [Add 2 pounds (3 scant cups) honey to water to make 1 gallon.]
3. When almost cold, spread working yeast over toasted wheat bread and place yeast down on must. Expected OG 1.075.
4. The next day place in a fermenter (it should show a yeast 'cap").
5. Follow preferred fermentation protocols.
6. When it has cleared, bottle it.
7. Drink within 10 days.

Meads of Middling Strength

The following two mead recipes have a moderate OG and represent the class known in modern terms as "standard meads" (OG of 1.080–1.12 and ABV 7.5–14.0%).

Meade MS 7997

MS 7997 Heppington (late 17th–early 19th c.), briefly detailed on p.145 of the manuscript:

> To make meade
>
> To every gallon of water 3 pints of the best hony & make it beare an egg (before it is boyll'd) & let it stand A day & A night & then boylle it an houre & A quarter, keep it well scumed & when it is cold, tun, it

Notes for interpretation and choices:

- There are no fermentation or aging specifics provided.
- The specified honey and water amounts do not align with the egg floating instruction. Three pints honey to one gallon of water is a gravity of about 1.12, not the 1.07 of an egg just floating (which would require three cups honey in one gallon). Both options are equally plausible, both are presented below.

The lower gravity option for Meade MS 7997:

1. Add 2.2 pounds (3 cups) honey to 1 gallon of water.
2. Boil down to 1 gallon, skimming.
   [Add water to 2.2 pounds (3 cups) honey to make 1 gallon.]
3. When cool, place in fermenter, add yeast. Expected OG 1.085.
4. Use preferred fermentation, aging, and bottling protocols.

The higher gravity option for Meade MS 7997:

5. Add 4 pounds (5 ⅓ cups) honey to 14 cups of water.
6. Boil down to 1 gallon, skimming.
   [Add water to 4 pounds (5 ⅓ cups) honey to make 1 gallon.]
7. When cool, place in fermenter, add yeast. Expected OG 1.145.
8. Use preferred fermentation, aging, and bottling protocols.

It is worth noting that because a constant percent total liquid is lost in the boiling step, doubling the honey does not double the OG.

Meade MS 3582

MS 3582 *Miscellany Receipts* (1725?) on p.12 instructed:

To make meade

Take 4 quarts of Water 1 of honey, Mingle the Water & honey well together in some kettle; and set it over the fire to Boyle, when you have well skimed it, which you will perceive by no more Riseing Take it off the fire, and pour it into an Earthen, and Wooden Vessel And let it stand soe till it be blood Warm. Then have ready att the fire a Brown Tost spread with yeast, and putt it to the Liquor, And so lett it work some houres When you think it hath Wrought Enough Take out the Tost, and put your mead into a Vessell, and lett it work there a Day or Two before it is stopped up, you may Drink it sooner or later as the Weather is hotter or colder

---

Notes for interpretation and choices:

- "Earthen and Wooden Vessel" is ambiguous. This could be an error in original of "and" for "or."
- "Wrought enough" seems to imply having finished obvious active fermentation, but the phrase immediately following is 'some hours' which could imply a period of 12–24 hours. Decanting into another container after 1–2 days is a common instruction.
- Overall timing is ambiguous.
- Recognition of changes in fermentation time with ambient heat is not unusual.

Instructions for Meade MS 3582:

1. Add 2.6 pounds (3 ½ cups) honey to 14 cups water.
2. Boil and skim until volume returns to 1 gallon.
3. Pour into earthen or wooden container.
   [Mix 2.6 pounds (3 ½ cups) honey with water to make 1 gallon.]
4. When lukewarm, place a toasted piece of brown bread spread with yeast in the vessel. Expected OG 1.095.
5. After 1 day, remove bread and decant into fermenter.
6. Follow preferred fermentation, aging, and bottling protocols.

Strong Meads – Modern 'Sack'

Sack, at the time of the Wellcome recipes, referred to sweet and sometimes fortified wines imported to England from Spain and the Canary Islands. They were widely drunk in England, notably by Shakespeare's Sir John Falstaff, the aging drunkard companion to Prince Hal (later Henry V), who expounded (Henry IV Part 2 Act 4, Scene 3):

> A good sherris sack hath a two–fold
> operation in it. It ascends me into the brain;
> dries me there all the foolish and dull and curdy
> vapours which environ it; makes it apprehensive,
> quick, forgetive, full of nimble fiery and
> delectable shapes, which, delivered o'er to the
> voice, the tongue, which is the birth, becomes
> excellent wit. The second property of your
> excellent sherris is, the warming of the blood;

> which, before cold and settled, left the liver
> white and pale, which is the badge of pusillanimity
> and cowardice; but the sherris warms it and makes
> it course from the inwards to the parts extreme.

The recipes below offer the potential to achieve the strength and sweetness of sack wine, and also meet the definition of modern sack mead, having an OG of 1.12–1.17 and ABV of 14.0–18.0%.

October Strong Mead MS 8002 and Variants

Catalog item 108 in MS 8002 *Loose receipts* (1663–1740), was written with notably poor spelling:

> mead the bes to mak any strong in october Boyle your wate let it stand all night to setle put 4 L of huny to a galon boyle it and whil any scum will Rise Let it stan un till it be cold than tun it in to the Barill it will kee half a year or year in the Baril & 2 yea in the Botle you may put Lem pill & Lemon no spice you may put saforon if you hav mind to hav it a sack culer

Notes for interpretation and choices:

- The instruction to make in October may influence honey choice.
- The indicator for honey amount ("L") is somewhat ambiguous. It has been interpreted as pound.
- Variant recipes are presented below but discussed on p.167 (lemon) and p.212 (saffron). The two variants could be combined for a lemon/saffron mead.

Instructions for October Strong Mead MS 8002 and lemon and saffron variants:

1. Add 3.4 pounds (4 ½ cups) honey and to 13 ½ cups water.
2. {Saffron variant: Add 1 gram saffron.}
3. {Lemon variant: Add the juice of one lemon.}
4. Boil down to 1 gallon, skimming (about 45 minutes). [Add water to 3.4 pounds (4 ½ cups) honey to make 1 gallon.]
5. {Lemon variant: Add peel of one lemon when taking off heat.}
6. When cool place in fermenter. Expected OG 1.125. {Add oak if desired.}
7. Follow preferred fermentation, aging, and bottling protocols, bottling once fined.

Mr. Hame Strong Mead MS 4050; Mrs. W Mead II MS 7892

These two recipes use almost identical phrasing, indicating a common source. They also offer slightly differing details on the mead making process.

MS 4050 *Receipt book* (1675?) on f.37v instructed:

To make strong Mead Mr. L Hame

Take a quarte of honey, and 3 good quartes of faire water, when the honey is melted set it over the fire, when it begins to boile scume it all the while till an houre be expired, then put it into a cleane sweet vessell bigg enough to work it in, and when it is but lukewarme set about a quarter of a pinte of good Ale barme on it and worke it beating it in 2 or 3 times a day, and when you think it fitt tun it into a sweet caske, one that hath had sack in it is best, when it hath done workeing in the vessell stop it close up, and let it stand 6 moneths then draw it into bottles, and if it be possible keep it as longe againe before you drinke it

---

This recipe was written in MS 7892 *Cookery and medical recipe book* (late 17th–18th c.) on f.53r in one of the multiple hands in the manuscript; the notation "Mrs W" was added in a different hand:

To make Mead Mrs W.

Take to 1 quart of Hony, 3 quarts of fair Water, & when the Hony is melted, set it over the fire & when it boyls, skim it all the while, till an hour is expired, then put it into the Vessel, big enough to work it, & when it is but luke warm. put on it, a spoonfull of yest, & so let it work beating it in, 3, or 4 times in a day, when it hath wrought enough, tunn it into a cask, one that hath had sack in it, stop it close up, & let it be 6 months in the Vessel, & 6 months in the bottles before you drink it, March & September are the best months to make it in.

Plain Meads

Notes for interpretation and choices:

- The mead maker can follow one recipe with its ambiguities or build a combined recipe that is more explicit.
- The choice between 1 spoonful of yeast of unspecified source versus 4 ounces of ale barm will make a distinct difference in final taste due to the total batch volume being under 1 gallon.
- See p.27 for information on modeling use of a sack cask. In modern terms sack could be port, sherry, or a sweet Spanish wine.
- The second recipe tells us to brew in March or September, suggesting options for honey choice.

Instructions for Mrs. W Mead II MS 7892 and Mr. Hame Strong Mead MS 4050:

1. Add 3.6 pounds (5 scant cups) honey to 14 ½ cups water.
2. Boil and skim for one hour, reducing volume to 1 gallon.
   [Add 3.6 pounds (5 scant cups) honey to water to make 1 gallon.]
3. When cool, add yeast. OG should be about 1.13.
   {Add 4 ounces barm from actively fermenting ale.}
4. Rack into fermenter, with port–soaked oak to model sack cask.
5. Let ferment, stirring three times a day for 3–4 days.
6. Follow preferred fermentation protocols.
7. Bottle after 6 months.
8. Age for 6 months before drinking.

Again, this simple recipe offers multiple choices for manipulation of the process and expected flavors. The yeast choice and choice of how to model the sack cask are key elements.

Mead MS 1801

The strongest of the plain meads presented here was written in MS 1801 *Cookery books: 18th cent* (c. 1725) on image 74:

To make mead

To a gallon of water put six pound of hony stir it till it is all dissolved, then boyle it an hour very gently (when it begin's to boyle put the white of eggs in to clear it and scum it very clean when it is cold make a brown bread toast an spread it on both sid's with barm put it into your mead and let it work two day's then tun it and let it stand a year in the vessel then draw it of the lee's and put into another vessell of the same size and fill it up with new made mead and let it stand another year then Draw it of into bottle's it will be very fine and keep many year's.

Notes for interpretation and choices:

- The proportion of honey here is significantly higher than typical, either historically or in the modern day. After one hour of boiling, the must will contain well over four lb/gal honey.
- Recognition of liquid loss during fermentation occurs in a number of recipes. Making up lost liquid with fresh must is the usual response.

Instructions for Mead MS 1801:

1. Add 4.5 pounds (6 cups) honey to 12 cups of water.
2. As it begins to boil add one slightly beaten egg white.
3. Boil gently about 1 hour, skimming, until down to 1 gallon. [Add 4.5 pounds (6 cups) honey to water to make 1 gallon.]
4. When cool, place in fermenter with a toasted piece of wheat bread covered with active yeast barm. Expected OG 1.165.
5. After 2 days rack.
6. Follow preferred fermentation, aging, and bottling protocols.
7. Bottle after 2 years.

The mead maker may decide to replace the called for schedule of racking and bottling with their own preferred schedule. They should keep in mind the specified bulk aging and bottle aging periods. The one year of aging sur lie will introduce complex flavors.

Meads with Added Sugars

Sugars added to meads can be divided into three groups: fruit sugars, refined sugar, and sap sugars. The use of each of these in fermented drinks in general and mead in particular shifted significantly across the 17th century.

Meads with fruits added are called melomels in the modern day. Their modern popularity is mirrored historically. About 30% of historical mead recipes from before 1600 included fruit sugars. The prevalence of these meads then saw a sharp reduction, about 20% of the recipes from the first two-thirds of the 17th century contain such sugars, and between 1670 and 1750 only 10% of the recipes contain such sugars.

At the same time, we see a rise in the use of refined sugar in mead recipes. Before 1600, refined sugar was not seen as an ingredient in mead recipes. Refined sugar then appears sporadically through the first two-thirds of the 17th century, and in the period between 1670 and 1750 almost 15% of mead recipes used refined sugar.

The obvious conclusion from these broad statistics, that refined sugar replaced fruits in mead recipes as the 17th century progressed, is not the case. The more accurate generalization is that refined sugar replaced honey, in a series of shifts reflecting a number of simultaneous trends:

1. Refined sugar became both dramatically cheaper and much more widely available as the 17th century progressed.
2. Additional fermentable sugars for fruit wines which had historically been provided by honey came to be almost invariably provided by refined sugar, turning melomels into fruit wines, which are then no longer classified as meads.

3. Refined sugar was used as a replacement for some, and occasionally all, of the honey in mead recipes that also contain other herbs and spice flavors.

4. Agricultural and trading trends increased the supply of raisins and currants to England. With this, raisins and currants appeared more often as ingredients in meads, presumably partly as a cheaper fruit sugar source, but also providing flavor and color, and also further displaced the use of honey in fruit wines.

5. A single recipe for mead using birch sap was copied and adapted, appearing multiple times in varied English language recipe sources as discussed starting on p.161. These recipes muddy the data for mead recipes containing non-honey sugars.

The primary driver for these shifts was almost certainly economic, as the timing closely matches the price drop of table sugar and increased trade in raisins/currants. A number of secondary elements are also likely, among them the trendiness of using novel ingredients.

This is bad news relative to this collection of recipes and for fans of melomels, who will need to look to earlier recipes to find more containing fruits. Alternatively, they could turn some of the varied fruit wine recipes in the Wellcome manuscripts into meads by replacing refined sugar with honey. Recipes that explicitly allow substitution of honey for sugar are frequent enough to make such a substitution historically plausible.

The 17th century also saw an explosion in the use of citrus in meads, which is covered in the next chapter. Although use of citrus will add some sugar, it was typically added in quantities which would not add a significant amount of sugar. In addition, citrus peel was often the sole portion used. Based on this, citrus meads are presented separately and citrus use is considered much more an issue of flavor than of sugar addition.

This chapter presents a selection of the Wellcome mead recipes using fruit sugars and sap sugars. Recipes containing refined sugar are included in the chapters corresponding to the other flavors added, because those flavor additions are expected to be more significant in determining the final character of the mead than the use of refined sugar.

Raisins and Currants

Raisins and their close kin currants were a relatively common source of sugar in meads from the era of the Wellcome manuscripts. The recipes presented here provide some options that explore the use of these fruits.

Sack Mead MS 1127 – Raisins

This recipe was written in MS 1127 Bent (1664–1729) on p.92:

Sack Mead

To twenty 4 quarts of watter take 5 quarts of honney and 6 pound of raisons of the sun cleane picked when it begins to boyle scum it clean and when the raisons are soft take them up and beat them in a bowle then put them in againe and let the mead boyle to 20 quarts then take it of the fire and set it to coole when it is something coole straine out the raisons so tun it up into a sack vessel let it be blood warm lett it stand six months then bottle itt up for your use take care that your raison be new or it will spoile it

---

Notes for interpretation and choices:

- Raisins contain about 15% water. After being rehydrated then squeezed out they may contain 30–50% liquid, including water and honey from the must. Based on this liquid balance, less honey is added when honey is not boiled to allow for the honey left with the raisins upon removal.

- The recipe calls for use of a sack barrel. Modeling use of a sack cask can be done in various ways (see p.27). In modern terms sack could be port, sherry, or a sweet Spanish wine.

Grape vine (*Vitis vinifera*), after Polydore

Instructions for Sack Mead MS 1127:

1. Add 3.7 pounds (5 cups) honey and 1.2 pounds (about 4 cups) raisins to 6 quarts of water.
2. Boil and skim approximately ½ hour until raisins are plump.
3. Remove raisins and crush, return to liquid
4. Boil down to about 5 quarts total volume. Let cool.
5. Remove raisins and squeeze liquid from raisins back into the must. Place must in fermenter. Expected OG 1.135–1.14.
6. [Follow steps 1–4 omitting honey, add 3 pounds (4 cups) honey to liquid to make 1 gallon.]
7. Add port-soaked oak to model use of a sack barrel.
8. Ferment, age, and bottle using preferred protocols.
9. Bottle after 6 months.

Holland's Mead

Four of the Wellcome manuscripts contain 5 closely related recipes. These are mirrored by recipes in 5 other manuscripts to date, but the recipe has not yet been seen in a printed book. Dates for the manuscripts containing these recipes range from the 1660's to about 1725. The versions in the Wellcome manuscripts, each with their approximate date and a letter identifier used in discussion, are:

A. After 1663 Sir John Ioland's Mead MS 3768
B. After 1663 Sir George Holand's Mead MS 3768
C. 1686 Mrs. Heath's Mead MS 2535
D. 1700 Sir Petast Small Mead MS 7851
E. 1703 Sir John Holland's Mead MS 7788

A number of the appearances note that the recipe is used medicinally against consumption. Consumption is an old term for tuberculosis, or TB, which at this time was also called the King's Evil or scrofula, and has been recognized as a wasting sickness for over 2500 years. One version of the recipe stated, "this cured Sr John Holland of a consumption at 66 who was alive in ye year 1675" (Folger 247, p.54).

The John Holland referenced seems likely to be Sir John Holland (1603–1701), 1st Baronet of Quidenham in Norfolk (northeast of London and Cambridge). He would have been 66 in 1669, and by 1675 would have had a notable survival time.

Meads with Added Sugars

This recipe highlights the difficulties of dating manuscripts and specific recipes. The 1675 date in the Folger manuscript above suggests that the earliest appearance of this recipe connected to Holland's name should be 1669, even if the core recipe appeared earlier. Yet the earliest three appearances are in manuscripts whose earliest dates predate 1669. The mead maker could inadvertently give these recipes a date earlier than that which is justified based on more in-depth analysis. Additional research, most specifically connecting the names on the recipes and manuscripts, would almost certainly prove interesting.

The recipe also highlights the variability almost always seen in multiple versions of a recipe. Of the five recipes, none agree in all particulars, although the two versions in the same manuscript are almost identical, suggesting that perhaps both were copied from the same source. Some variations appear to be intentional, while others could either be transcription error or intentional. The text for each of the versions is presented below.

Recipe version A was written in MS 3768 Parker (1663) f.15v:

The mead Drink of Sr John Iolands

Take five galons of water a pound of reasons sliced half a pound of corrants bruised an ounce of liquorish 3 ounces of Ekinjoe roots uncandied a quarter of an ounce of corader seeds an ounce of china 2 handfulls of colts foot 2 sprigs of rosmary three pints of honey and half boyle this to four galons & when it is cold work it up & when it is a week old bottle it up.

Recipe version B was also written in MS 3768 Parker (1663) f.70r, in a different hand, near the back of the manuscript:

Sr Go Holands mead drink for a cough of the lungs & a consumption

Take 5 galons of water a pound of Rasons stoned half a pound of corants an onnce of liqurish 3 ounces of oringoe roots in candied a quarter of an ounce of coliander seeds on ounce of china 2 handfuls of coltsfoot 2 sprigs of Rosmary 3 pints & half of hony boyle that to 4 galons & when it is cold work it up in & a week you may botle it up drinck noe other drink

---

Meads with Added Sugars

Recipe version C was written in MS 2535 Godfrey (1686) p.117:

Mrs. Heaths mead good for a consumption

Take 5 gallons of watter 4 pints of honny one pound of stoned raysons halfe a pound of Currants well washed & picked three ounces of ringer root not candyed one ounce of Licorish and one ounce of china 2 sprigs of rosemary a quarter of an ounce of Coriander seeds boyle all these together in watter till it comes to 4 ~~quarts~~ gallions then strayne it and when its cold work it with yeast like ale is worked at 7 dayes old draw it into bottles and when its ripe drink of it when you please

---

Recipe version D was written in MS 7851 *English recipe book* (late 17th–early 19th c.) on f.58r:

S John Petast

To Make small Meade

Take of china roots on ounce and halfe of ringo roots un canded 3 ounces of liquorish one ounce of coles foot dryed 2 handfulls 2 sprigs of Rosmarey of Reasons of the son stond and cut one pound of coriander seed a quarter of an ounce of Blew corants halfe a pound of honney 3 pints & a halfe boyle all these in 5 gallons of water and keep it & scuming boyle it till it comes to 4 gallons then strain it and let it stand till it be allmost cold then work it up with yest and tune it into a vesell and when it is 4 days old draw it out into botells puting in a litle syrope of lemons into each botle

---

Finally, recipe version E was written in MS 7788 Repp (1703) on f.16r:

Sir John Hollands small Mead

Take of China an Ounce & a halfe, of Eringo Roots not canded 3 Ounces Colts foot dried 2 handfulls, 2 spriggs of Rosemary, of Raisons sliced a pound, of Corriander seed a quarter of a pound of hony 3 pintes and a halfe Boyle all these in 5 gallons of Water, skim it, to 4 gallons put the Liquor from it and work it with yeast and Tun it and after it be 7 or 8 Days old you may Drink it

---

Notes for interpretation and choices (letters refer to recipe version):

- The use of currants with raisins and their treatment makes it clear that the currants are dried grapes rather than currant berries.
- The amount and treatment of the raisins and currants in the recipes varies. Recipes B, C, and D remove the "stones" or seeds from the raisins. Recipe E omits currants, which in recipe C are well washed and picked. Recipe D uses "blue currants."
- The amount of honey is 3 ½ pints, except for recipe C which uses 4 pints.
- It is recommended that coltsfoot not be ingested due to the presence of toxic alkaloids. Coltsfoot has therefore been omitted from my recipe. Coltsfoot is omitted from recipe C, and in recipes D and E it is dried.
- Eringo root in recipe D is written "ringer", without knowledge of the other recipes this could be read as ginger. Using ginger would change that taste.
- Recipes A and B do not specify straining out the must before fermentation, the instruction to "work it up" in these recipes typically means to add yeast. Recipe C strains the must then uses ale yeast. Recipes D and E strain then add unspecified yeast.
- Other appearances of this recipe vary in other ways, providing additional basis for comparison.

This table provides a comparison of key elements of each recipe.

Recipe	A	B	C	D	E
Water (gal)	5	5	5	5	5
Honey (cups)	7	7	8	7	7
Raisins (lb)	1	1	1	1	1
Currants (lb)	½	½	½	½	
Boil to Gallons	4	4	4	4	4
Expected OG	1.06	1.06	1.065–1.07	1.06	1.055–1.06
China (ounces)	1	1	1	1 ½	1 ½
Licorice (ounces)	1	1	1	1	
Coltsfoot (handfuls)	2	2		2	2
Strain			Yes	Yes	Yes
Lemon Syrup				Yes	
Coriander (ounces)	¼	¼	¼	¼	4
Eringo (ounces)	3	3	3	3	3
Rosemary (sprigs)	2	2	2	2	2

Meads with Added Sugars

The mead maker can choose a specific recipe as written or a create a composite. This recipe interpretation for Holland's Mead combines the versions:

1. Add 1.4 pounds (2 scant cups) honey to 5 quarts water.
2. Add 5 ounces raisins and 2 ½ ounces currants (raisins), sliced open.
3. Add: ¾ ounce eringo root, ¼ ounce of china root, ¼ ounce licorice root, 1 teaspoon coriander seeds, and ½ sprig rosemary.
4. Boil until volume is 1 gallon plus 2–3 cups.
5. Let cool, strain, removing herbs/spices and squeezing liquid out of the raisins and currants before discarding the solids.
   [add 1.4 pounds (2 scant cups) honey to water treated as above to make 1 gallon.]
6. Place in fermenter and add ale yeast. Expected OG 1.06.
7. Follow preferred fermentation protocols.
8. After 7 days rack and consume.

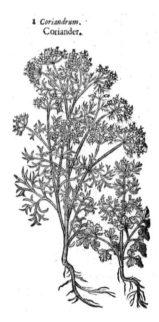

Coriander
(Gerard, 1633, p.1012)

Possible modifications, based on specific recipes:

- Using more honey.
- Adding 1 ½ ounces china root rather than 1 ounce.
- Following recipe E: omit licorice and use 4 ounces coriander (it seems likely this is a transcription error). A less extreme version would omit the licorice and keep the coriander at ¼ ounce.
- Omit currants.
- Follow recipes A and B to leave raisins/currants and roots/seeds in during fermentation.
- Add lemon syrup at bottling. The amount is unspecified, I recommend about 1 teaspoon per 12–ounce bottle.
- Substitute ginger for eringo root.

Other Fruits

The Wellcome meads include relatively few made with fruits. The two below made with apples and with sloes/hawthorn berries are examples.

The vast majority of historical mead recipes containing fruits use juice rather than whole fruit. There is a subset of recipes, many of which are attributed to Moscovian or Russian sources, that extract fruit flavor by soaking fruit in water prior to using that water to make mead. Both of these recipes use this methodology, although there is no indication that either has been influenced by recipes from these regions.

White Meade MS 3009, White Mead w Brandy MS 3009 (Pippins)

The recipe written in MS 3009 Jacob (1654–c. 1685) on p.341 (from the rear) uses apples, spice, and herb to flavor the mead and also provides the intriguing option to add brandy when it is bottled:

To make White Meade

Take one Gallon of Honey: 6 gallons of water in which water you must steep all night 20 or 30 Pippins being pared & sliced thinn & when you Boyle it up straine out your Pippins, & put in your Honey with the whites of 10 eggs being well beaten which is to Clarify the Honey then sett it over a clear fire & keep it sterring till it be ready to boyle, and when you have taken of the scum clean. Add to it 6 nuttmeggs sliced & one Dozen of Bay Leaves & keep it boyleing one hour & then take it off, when cold worke it up with Ale yeast as you doe other Drinke, only spread your yeast on a Toast. If you pleas you may putt in a spoonful or 2 Brandy in each Bottle.

Notes for interpretation and choices:
- Pippins are characterized as tart and flavorful, with spicy tones. They can be hard to find; apple varieties more readily available may include Granny Smith or MacIntosh.
- The size and number of apples selected will affect flavor.
- Recipe wording is ambiguous whether apples are removed before or after the initial boiling, I have chosen before.
- Specifics of fermentation and bottling conditions are ambiguous.
- The mead maker must choose whether or not to add brandy at bottling and how much. This addition will add a notable flavor.

Meads with Added Sugars

Instructions for White Meade MS 3009 and White Mead w Brandy MS 3009:

1. Take 1 pound of tart, flavorful apples, peel, core and slice thin.
2. Place apples in 1 gallon of water and let soak overnight.
3. Strain out apples and add 2 pounds (2 ½ generous cups) honey.
4. Add the whites of 2 eggs, beaten.
5. Bring to a boil and remove the first scum that rises.
6. Add 1 crushed nutmeg and 2 bay leaves.
7. Boil 1 hour, returning to 1 gallon.
8. Allow to cool. Expected OG about 1.08.
   [Add 2 pounds (2 ½ generous cups) honey to apple water boiled with nutmeg and bay to make 1 gallon.]
9. Toast a small piece of bread, spread with active ale yeast, place yeast down in fermenter.
10. Follow preferred fermentation, aging, and bottling protocols.
11. {At bottling, if desired, add 2–4 ounces of brandy per gallon.}

Welsh Wine MS 7849 (Sloes, Hawthorn Berries)

This brief recipe was scribed in MS 7849 *English recipe book* (Late 17th c.) on f.2v:

> To make Welsh wine
>
> Take a quantity of slowes, and the like quantity of Whit thorne Berries lay them in steep in water. till itt come to the colour you would have itt on, then draw itt from the Leays and putt honey to itt – to take of the sharpeness and soe keepe itt for your use.

Notes for interpretation and choices:

- The relative amounts of berries, water, and honey are not specified.
- Both sloes (blackthorn) and whitehorn (hawthorn) berries are uncommon fresh and can be obtained more readily dried.
- Historically, both berries are typically used medicinally and as flavoring agents rather than as a sugar source. This implies smaller amounts may be used in this recipe.
- The recipe language suggests the berries are used for coloring.
- Fermentation conditions are not specified.

Instructions for Welsh Wine MS 7849:

1. Take 1 ½ ounce each of dried hawthorn berries and sloe berries (equivalent to about ½ pound fresh).
2. Soak berries in 4 quarts water for several days, stirring occasionally, until the berries have colored and flavored the water.
3. Strain the berries from the water and press out the juice.
4. Allow liquid to settle, then take 3 quarts clear liquid off the top.
5. Add 3 pounds (1 quart) honey, mix. OG should be about 1.11.
6. Ferment, age, and bottle using desired protocols.

This recipe provides almost unlimited freedom for the mead maker to choose both the overall amount of berries used and the concentration of honey in the must. Those choices will have a profound effect on the finished mead. One of the few concrete instructions is to use the same amount of both berries. I have chosen a middle of the road approach. The flavor extracted from the berries can be easily assessed when the extraction is finished and additional berries can be added or additional water used to adjust the flavor.

Two Birch Wines MS 7892

Birch sap is substituted for water in a few core recipes with several dozen appearances in both manuscript and printed sources. These recipes more often bolster the fermentable sugars from the birch sap with refined sugar, but some versions use honey, like the recipe presented here.

The first appearance of this recipe is in the writings of John Evelyn (1620–1706). Evelyn was one of the founders of the Royal Society, formally "The President, Council, and Fellows of the Royal Society of London for Improving Natural Knowledge." He wrote extensively and was also a prodigious correspondent and compiler of information. Evelyn's 1664 *Sylva, or a discourse of forest-trees and the propagation of timber in his majesty's dominions* is credited as one of the most influential books ever printed on forestry, and includes the birch wine recipe.

The British Library possesses hundreds of volumes of the Evelyn family archives. A number of these manuscripts are large volumes (about 11 x 17 inches), each with hundreds of pages, in the original red leather bindings and stamped with the Evelyn gryphon in gold. Two of these volumes contain recipes for birch wine, dating from as early as the 1650's, and mark the first known appearance of the use of birch sap in a written mead recipe (Evelyn, 1651–18th c., and Evelyn, 1655–early 18th c.).

The majority of birch wine recipes cataloged to date clearly derive from the Evelyn recipe. John Worlidge in his 1678 *Vinetum Britanicum*, presents a similar, but not obviously related recipe.

Both the Evelyn and Worlidge recipes were written in MS 7892 *Cookery and medical recipe book* (late 17th–18th c.) on f.42r. without specifically attributing either of the authors:

To make Birch Wine.

To every gallon of Birch water, put a quart of honey, then boyle it almost an houre with a few cloves and a little limon peell keepeing it weell scummed, when it is sufficiently boyled & become cold adde to it 3 or 4: spoonfull of good ale yest to make it worke, which it will doe like new ale, & when the yest begins to settle bottle it up as you doe other winy liquors the wine may be made as successfully with sugar in stead of honey, one pound to each gall of water, or you may dulafie it with Rasons & compose a Rason wine of it, the quantity of the sweet ingredients something might be somewhat leseened, & the operation improved others boyles it but a quarter or halfe an houre then seting it to coole, & a very little yest to ferment & purg it, & soe barrell it with a small proportion of cinamon & mace bruised a bout halfe & ounce of both, to ten gallons closse stoped & to be bottled a month after, care most be taken to set the bottles in a very coole place, to preserve them from flying & the wine is rather for present drinking then of long duration, unless the refrigeratory be extraordinary cold.

Notes for interpretation and choices:

- It is not clear from the text if this is intended as two recipes or the second is an option adding cinnamon and mace to the first. The mead maker could choose to make this as a combination of the two recipes based on the ambiguity in this text, or they could choose one of the two recipes. Based on knowledge of the sources, it seems likely these are separate recipes.
- The amount of spice used may overwhelm the birch sap flavor.

Because the history of the recipes indicates two separate recipes, I have chosen to present two recipes, one for each version.

Instructions for Evelyn Birch Wine:

1. Add 2 ¾ pounds (3 ¾ cups) honey to 15 cups birch sap.
2. Add 3 cloves and the peel of ½ lemon.
3. Boil about 1 hour until down to 1 gallon. [Add 2 ¾ pounds (3 ¾ cups) honey to birch sap boiled with cloves and lemon to make 1 gallon.]

Birch (*Betula* species)

4. When cool, strain into fermenter and add ale yeast. Expected OG about 1.105.
5. Use preferred fermentation, aging and bottling protocols.

Instructions for Worlidge Birch Wine:

1. Take 14 cups birch sap, add 2.6 pounds (3 ½ cups) honey.
2. Boil about ½ hour until down to 1 gallon. [Add 2.6 pounds (3 ½ cups) honey to boiled birch sap to make 1 gallon.]
3. Add ½ stick cinnamon and 3 blades of mace to ferment, tied in a bag to help removal.
4. Add yeast. OG about 1.10.
5. Use preferred fermentation, aging, and bottling protocol.

The longer boiling period of the first recipe leads to a slightly higher OG. The first version also adds cloves and lemon in the boiling. These flavors are more typically added during fermentation.

Woodcut of kitchen from *Kuchenmeisterey*, 1507

Citrus Meads

Citrus has been used in European foods from at least Roman times, but citrus in mead has a much shorter documented history. Citrus is not used in any of the hundreds of cataloged mead recipes dating from before 1600, after this date, citrus quickly became a standard ingredient in mead, appearing in about 10% of the meads from the first two-thirds of the 17th century and in close to 25% of the meads between 1670 and 1750. The citrus used is almost always lemon, although citron and orange are also specified in some recipes.

One third of the cataloged recipes from the Wellcome manuscripts contain some form of citrus. Lemon peel and/or lemon juice are by far the most frequent. Other than containing citrus, these recipes are quite varied.

I treat citrus as a separate type of flavor addition, rather than as a fruit or alternate sugar source, for two main reasons. First, although addition of citrus juice will add some sugars, the use of citrus seems to focus on its flavor, as suggested by frequent use of peel alone. Secondly, citrus is often added in ways and at times during the brewing and fermentation process that differ from how other sugar sources are treated.

Citrus is also used differently than other flavor additions. Historically, other than spices, additions to meads are most commonly added during boiling. Spices are more often added during fermentation, but can also be added during boiling. Citrus is most commonly added during fermentation, and is not often added during boiling. More significantly, citrus is frequently added during cooling after boiling, which is a very uncommon treatment for other additions. Citrus is also one of the few ingredients sometimes added as part of the bottling process. Each of these addition methods can be expected to provide a different flavor profile, and each is used below in at least one recipe.

In the recipes where lemon juice is added, that addition will also affect acidity of the must and thus potentially affect fermentation. It is not currently clear whether or not historical mead makers were actively aware that this acid addition could affect the fermentation process.

Because citrus is treated in a notably different manner in the recipes, the recipes using citrus are grouped together. The group of citrus recipes presented here have been divided into five groups:

- Recipes for which the only flavor addition is citrus
- Lemon-rosemary, which includes one recipe with citrus and herbs but no spices
- Citrus and spice, using ingredients in these two classes but no herbs
- Citrus, herb, and spice including ingredients from all three classes
- Rhenish Wine and Citrus Syrup, a group of relatively complex recipes marked by their use of these two ingredients

Citrus Only

Citrus as the only addition to a mead recipe is relatively uncommon. Because these recipes use different forms of citrus and add combinations of peel and fruit using different methods, the resulting drinks are expected to display different flavors.

Meath with Lemons MS 1806 and Meath with Oranges MS 1806

Meath with Lemons MS 1806 and Meath with Oranges MS 1806 are presented with the braggots on p.262 because they use a relatively large addition of ale barm, adding significant grain flavor. The lemons or oranges are added as fruit and peel and are the only flavor additions.

October Strong Mead Lemon MS 8002

The October Strong Mead recipe presented on p.147 with the plain meads includes an option for addition of lemon and lemon peel. The original text and recipe for the citrus option are presented with the main recipe. Additional notes for choices specific to the lemon option are:

- The recipe calls for "Lem pill & Lemon." The form of the lemon could be whole or juice only. Given that peel is also specified, I chose juice as more likely.
- The instructions for how lemon and lemon peel are added and the amounts of each are not specified.
- The timing for citrus addition is not specified. The selected option is a common scenario, adding lemon juice in the boil and peel of half of the lemons during cooling and left in for the fermentation. Often when both lemon and peel are used peel is only added from a portion of the lemons used.
- The mead maker could choose to adjust the amount or addition timing/method for the lemon and peel to highlight different flavors.

Small Mead MS 1711

On a slip of paper inserted between p.38 and p.39 of MS 1711 Coley (mid 18th c.) a recipe was written as follows:

Small Mead

To every gallon of cold Water add three Pounds of Honey and one white of Egg well beat = boil it gently till it looks clear constantly skiming of the dross as it rises when clear, pour if hot over as many Peels of Lemons as you have gallons of Liquor when cool put in a spoonful of yeast and let it work in this open vessel two or three Days, then put it into your Barrel and let it stand a month before you drink it

N B it is very good if drank out of the vessel but when it grows flatt Bottle it

---

This recipe provides no specific concerns beyond the general issues of choosing fermentation and aging conditions and deciding on whether/how to model barrel use. It is worth noting that the expected OG at 1.105 does not meet typical definitions of a small mead.

Instructions for Small Mead MS 1711:

1. Add 3 scant pounds (4 scant cups) honey to 15 cups of water.
2. Add one beaten egg white.
3. Boil and skim for about 1 hour.
4. Take off heat and add the zest of one lemon.

   [Add lemon zest to 13 cups water just as it begins to boil. Take off heat immediately. When somewhat cool, add enough liquid to 3 scant pounds (4 scant cups) honey to make 1 gallon.]
5. When cool, place in fermenter and add yeast. Expected OG 1.105–1.11.
6. Follow preferred fermentation, aging, and bottling protocols.
7. Drink after 1 month.

The recipe is interesting and rare in that it specifically recognizes the eventual loss of carbonation as the drink sits in the barrel.

White Mead with Sugar

A series of four Wellcome recipes, all dating to the second quarter of the 18th century, give almost identical versions of a recipe using honey, sugar, and lemons. This recipe is repeated in other manuscripts and printed sources from the same time. These recipes show a high degree of consistency, but also appear to cover a relatively short time period of about 25 years, which might explain why so little change is seen. All the appearances in the Wellcome manuscripts are called white mead.

A version attributed to Mrs. Pyke was written in MS 1343 Branch (1725) on p.72:

White Mead (Mrs. Pyke)

To every gallon of water, put a pint of honey, and half a pound of loaf suger, stir in the whites of eggs beat to a frothe and boile it as longe as aney scum will a rise when cold worket with yeast, to every gallon put the Juce and peall of a large lemon, when it had done working stop it up and bottle it of in ten days

---

Citrus Meads

This "very good" version was written in MS 3098 K. (1735?) as culinary recipe number 25 (from the rear):

> ### White Mead, very good 25
>
> To every gallon of Water put a pint of Honey and half a pound of loafe Sugar; stir in the whites of Eggs beat to a froth, and boil it as long as any scum rises, when tis cold work it with yeast, and to every gallon put the juice and peel of a large lemon. Stop it up when it has done working, and bottle it in ten days.

The version written in MS 4759 Tallamy (1735–1806) on f.133v was also "very good" but omitted the lemon juice:

> ### Whitte Mead Very Good
>
> To every Gallon of watter put a pint of Honey & half a pound of Loave sugar stir in the whittes of Eggs beat to a froth & boyle it as long as any scum arises when tis cold work it with yeast & to every gallon put the Peel of a large Lemon stop it up when it has don working & bottle it in ten days

Finally, MS 1810 *Cookery books: 18th cent.* (1750?) on f.24r of later numbering gave a recipe written in the initial hand for the manuscript. The first line of the recipe has an unusual symbol for the amount of loaf sugar, which based on context has been transcribed as ½, which if ½ pint, or one cup, would be roughly equivalent to the half-pound of sugar in the other versions.

> ### To Make White Mead (No. 45)
>
> To every Gallon of water put a pint of Honey & ½ of Loaf sugar, stir in the whites of Eggs. Beat to a froth, & boil it as long as any scum arises, when its cold work it with yeast & to every Gallon put the Juice & peel of a large Lemmon, stop it up when it has done working & Bottle it in 10 days

Notes for interpretation and choices:

- MS 1810 does not give a measuring unit for sugar, if it is interpreted as ½ pint it changes ratios slightly.
- The mead maker can decide to use sugar or convert sugar to its equivalent in honey, as I have done in this case. If using sugar, use 1.5 pounds (2 cups) honey and ½ pound (1 cup) raw sugar.
- MS 4759 uses only lemon peel; all other versions use juice and peel.

Instructions for White Mead with Sugar:

1. Add 2.1 pounds (2 ¾ cups) honey to 1 gallon water.
2. Add 1 egg white beaten until frothy.
3. Boil down to 1 gallon (about 1 hour) skimming.
   [Add 2.1 pounds (2 ¾ cups) honey to water to make 1 gallon.]
4. Let cool, strain into fermenter, add yeast. Expected OG 1.075–1.08.
5. Add the juice and zest of one lemon.
6. Follow preferred fermentation, aging, and bottling protocols.

Woodcut of a chef from *Koch und Kellerei* (1549?, title page)

Lemon and Rosemary

The combination of lemon and rosemary in this recipe is a classic flavor combination in cooking and works wonderfully in mead, particularly when there is enough residual sugar to balance the acid of the lemons and pine of the rosemary with honey flavor and sweetness. In my opinion this flavor combination works particularly well when carbonated and chilled.

This recipe was written in MS 3500 Meade (1688–1727) on page 82 (f.103v) of the second set of manuscript pagination:

To make Meed a very good way

Take Twelve Gallons of spring water to which put in 12 quarts or better of very good Honey the whites of Ten Eggs well beaten which put into your Kettle of water and Honey stiring it while the honey is pretty well disolved then set over the fire and stir it some times when it boyles all over the take of the scumme as it rises as long as any rises there must be your peeles of 4 Lemons boyled in and two branches of Rosemary when it is boyled well and no scumm rises – run it through A hare sive into the Tub you intend to worke it in and slice in 8 Lemons then afore it is quite cold beat near a quart of good ale yest and set it aworking when it hath worked a while tunn it up in A vessell just to hold it when done working stop it close you may bottle it in A forthnight

Notes for interpretation and choices:
- Timing for boiling is unclear.

Instructions for Very Good Meed MS 3500:
1. Take 7 pints of water and add 3 ½ cups (2.6 pounds) honey.
2. Bring to a boil and add 1 beaten egg white.
3. Add peel of ⅓ of a lemon and 1 teaspoon rosemary leaves.
4. Boil back to 1 gallon, skimming.
5. Strain into fermenter, add ⅔ of a lemon sliced.
   [Add 3 ½ cups (2.6 pounds) honey to water boiled with lemon and rosemary to make 1 gallon.]
6. Add 3 ounces ale barm. OG about 1.095.
7. Follow preferred fermentation, aging, and bottling protocols.

Citrus and Spice

The Wellcome citrus meads include a number where only mead spices are added. Compared to the single recipe that includes only herbs, this suggests that spices were seen as a more natural complement to citrus.

The nine recipes in this group vary by OG, specific spices added, form of citrus used, and when the citrus and spice are added. The bullets below provide a ready reference for differences:

- Lady Parkhurst Mead MS 3009. OG 1.095. Whole lemon in boil, optional lemon juice in ferment. Nutmeg in boil. No yeast specified. Lemon form unclear.
- Mead MS 7102, Superfine Mead MS 7102. OG 1.055 / 1.095. Lemon peel in ferment. Cloves in ferment. Barm for yeast.
- Mead MS 1803. OG 1.055–1.06. Whole lemon in ferment. Ginger and cloves in boil. Refined sugar added. "New yeast" used.
- Mead MS 1794. OG 1.06–1.065. Whole lemon in last quarter of boil. Ginger and cloves in boil. Refined sugar added. Yeast on toasted bread.
- Cleare Mead MS 1127. OG 1.09. Lemon juice and peel after boil. Ginger and clove in ferment. Refined sugar added. Barm on toasted bread.
- Delicate Metheglin MS 1511. OG 1.085–1.09. Lemon peel in boil. Nutmeg and cinnamon in boil. Yeast.
- Mead MS 7850. OG 1.08. Lemon peel in boil. Coriander and "spice" in boil. Yeast on toasted bread.
- Smale Mead MS8097. OG 1.04. Lemon peel in bottle. Cloves, nutmeg, and mace in boil. Ale yeast.
- Maide MS 1808. OG 1.095. Lemon peel in ferment. Ginger, cloves, cinnamon, mace, and coriander in boil and ferment. Ale yeast.

Lady Parkhurst Mead MS 3009

Lady Parkhurst Mead MS 3009, and its variant, Lady Parkhurst Quick Mead MS 3009, combine lemon and nutmeg. The quick mead variant adds lemon juice to speed readiness to drink. This instruction is repeated in the variant recipe for Mead II MS 3009 (p.211), which also adds only nutmeg. Despite these similarities, the word choices and proportions of the two recipes do not suggest they are directly related.

Citrus Meads

Lady Parkhurst Mead was written in MS 3009 Jacob (1654–c. 1685) p. 208 from the rear. The recipe is in a different hand from the attribution to Lady Parkhurst. This recipe has been roughly crossed out.

To make Mead the Lady Parkhurst

The proportion is 5 quarts & a pint of water to one quart of honey. To every gallon of liquor one lemon & a quarter of an ounce of nuttmegs it must rise till the scums rise black. If you would have it ready quickly to drink squeese in a lemon when you tunn it up: you must let it be cold before you tuned it up

---

Notes for interpretation and choices:

- A quarter of an ounce is one medium sized nutmeg.
- The initial ratio of honey to water is very specific but the boiling time is uncertain, which will affect the OG.
- I have interpreted the recipe as adding whole lemon (sliced) for boiling and lemon juice optionally at bottling. Other forms could be assumed.
- No yeast addition is mentioned.

Instructions for Lady Parkhurst Mead MS 3009:

1. Add 2.6 pounds (3 cups) honey to 1 gallon water.
2. Add 1 lemon sliced, and one nutmeg crushed.
3. Boil, skimming, about 1 hour, until it returns to 1 gallon.
4. Strain into fermenter
   [Add 2.6 pounds (3 cups) honey to water boiled with lemon and nutmeg to make 1 gallon.]
   {Add juice of second lemon if desired.}
5. Add selected yeast. Expected OG 1.095.
6. Follow preferred fermentation, aging, and bottling protocols.

Citrus Meads

Mead MS 7102, Superfine Mead MS 7102

Recipe 512 in was written in p.80 of MS 7102 *Recipe book* (18th c.):

Mead

to 2 galons of water put a quart of hony, boyl and scum wel when ~~cold~~ cool barm it work 24 hours then take of the barm botle it in every botle put a clove a litle lemon peel in 5 days it wil be fit to drink if you would have it stronger double the quantity of hony and it wil make superfine

---

Notes for interpretation and choices:

- Two distinctly different versions are offered, one with twice the honey of the other. The version with lower honey is truly a quick mead, with instructions to drink five days after making.
- The fermentation for this recipe takes place in the bottles, which is not safe with effective bottle closures.
- The quantity of cloves is adjusted to account for the size of 18th century bottles, which were typically 1 quart or larger.
- The mead appears to be meant to be drunk almost immediately which will leave it still fermenting and cloudy.
- The instructions to drink after five days may not be appropriate if you double the initial honey, as greater fermentation time will probably be needed.

Instructions for Mead MS 7102 and Superfine Mead MS 7102:

1. Add 1.5 pounds (1 pint) honey to 1 gallon of water.
   {Add 2.6 pounds (3 ½ cups) honey to 14 cups water.}
2. Boil down to 1 gallon skimming.
   [Add 1.5 pounds (1 pint) honey to water to make 1 gallon.]
   {[Add 2.6 pounds (3 ½ cups) honey to water to make 1 gallon.]}
3. Let cool, add yeast. Expected OG 1.055
   {Expected OG 1.095.}
4. After 24 hours working, add 3 cloves and the peel of ¼ lemon.
5. Serve after 5–7 days.
   {Follow preferred fermentation, aging, and bottling protocol.}

Mead MS 1803

This brief recipe was written in MS 1803 *Cookery-books: 18ᵗʰ cent* (1725?) on p.100:

> To make Mead
>
> Take 12 quarts of water, 1 quart of Honey, 3 Races of ginger, 20 cloves, & 1 pound of loaf sugar, boyl them together till no scum arise, when it is allmost cold put in 2 or 3 Lemons, first squeeze in the juyce, then put in the skins & 3 spoonfulls of new yest, work it well 3 days & cork it close, set the bottles on the side to prevent them breaking.

Notes for interpretation and choices:
- The sugar could be replaced with a half-pound of honey.
- Removal of spice is not specified; it could remain in the ferment.

Instructions for Mead MS 1803:
1. Add 1.1 pounds (1 ½ cups) honey and ¾ cup (6 ounces) raw sugar to 1 gallon water.
2. Add a 1 inch piece of ginger root, sliced, and 7 cloves.
3. Bring to a boil and boil for about 30 minutes, skimming.
4. Take off heat, and when cool, strain into fermenter.
   [Add 1.1 pound (1 ½ cups) honey to enough water boiled with sugar, ginger, and clove to make 1 gallon.]
5. Slice a lemon. Squeeze in the juice; add the residual.
6. Add yeast. Expected OG 1.055–1.06.
7. Follow preferred fermentation, aging, and bottling protocols.

**Cloves
(Acosta, 1578, p.30)**

Meade MS 1794

Recipe 161 for meade was written in MS 1794 *Cookery books: 17th–18th century* (1685–c. 1725):

To make Meade 161

Take 20 quarts of Water 6 pounds of honey 2 pound of Loaf Sugar and some ginger and cloves as much as you think fitt but let your Water boyle first then putt all these things together letting itt boil 3 quarters of an hour after then scum itt well squeese in the juice of 6 Lemons and putt in Rhines and all then lett it boil a quarter of an hour take itt of and lett itt cool then putt itt into a vessell and putt a Toast of white bread spread itt over with yest lett itt stand six dayes then bottle itt

---

Notes for interpretation and choices:
- Amounts for ginger and clove are not specified.
- The sugar could be replaced with a half-pound of honey.

Instructions for Meade MS 1794:
1. Add 1.2 pounds (1 ½ generous cups) honey and 6.5 ounces (3/4 cup) raw sugar to 1 gallon of water.
2. Once boiling add ½ inch piece of ginger root sliced and 2 cloves.
3. Boil 45 minutes skimming.
4. Squeeze in the juice of one large lemon then add the residue.
5. Boil another 15 minutes.
6. Take off heat. Allow to cool. Strain into fermenter. Expected OG 1.06–1.065.
   [Add 1.2 pounds (1 ½ generous cups) honey to water boiled as above with sugar, spices, and lemon to make 1 gallon.]
7. Add white bread toasted and covered with active yeast.
8. Follow preferred fermentation protocol, racking off after 6 days.
9. Follow preferred aging and bottling protocols.

Cleare Mead MS 1127

This recipe is similar to the preceding but has a somewhat higher OG. It was written in MS 1127 Bent (1664–1729) on p.147 of the manuscript:

To Make Cleare Meade

Take 4 Gallons of spring watter set it on the fire when it is redy to boyle put in 2 quartes of honey 3 pound of suger scim it as long as any scum rises then take it of the fire and squese in the juce of 6 lemons and put the pills into and let it stand till cold then straine it put 40 cloves full one f ounce of ginger sliced then tun it up then put in a hot toast with 4 spoonfull of east upon it stop it in a day time let it stand one month and bottle it

---

Notes for interpretation and choices:
- The mead maker may choose to replace sugar with one pound honey.
- 40 cloves in the must for a month is likely to give very strong clove flavor.
- The amount of ginger could be six ounces; the character transcribed as "f" and assumed to be scribal error, is similar to this writer's "6."

Instructions for Cleare Mead MS 1127:
1. Add 1.5 pounds (1 pint) honey and ¾ pound (1 ½ cups) raw sugar to 1 gallon water.
2. Boil, skimming for about 1 hour, reducing to 1 gallon.
3. Take it off heat and immediately add juice and zest of 1 ½ lemons.
   [Add 1.5 pounds (1 pint) honey to water to which lemons have been added after boiling, making 1 gallon.]
4. When cold strain into fermenter then add 10 cloves and 1 inch section of ginger sliced. Expected OG 1.09.
5. Add a small piece of toasted bread with barm spread on it.
6. Follow preferred fermentation, aging and bottling protocols.

Delicate Metheglinn MS 1511

Recipe number 317 for "metheglinn a very delicate way" with cinnamon and nutmeg was written in MS 1511 Carr (1682):

> Take a quart of pure honey to 5 quarts of water & nuttmegg with a quarter of an ounce of cinamon boyle it with the rinde of a Lemon shred in boyle it well together neer upon an hour skim it clean then sett it a cooleing & when it is as cold as you use to set beer a working putt yest to it & let it worke & tunn it as you doe beer or ale when it is clear bottle it & drinke it when you please.

Instructions for Delicate Metheglinn MS 1511:

1. Add 2.4 pounds (3 ¼ scant cups) honey to 1 gallon water.
2. Add 1 nutmeg crushed, 2 small cinnamon sticks, and the peel of 1 lemon.
3. Boil 1 hour, skimming down to 1 gallon.
4. When cool, strain into fermenter and add yeast. Expected OG 1.085–1.09.
   [Add 2.4 pounds (3 ¼ scant cups) honey to water boiled with spices and lemon to make 1 gallon.]
5. Follow preferred fermentation, aging, and bottling protocol.

Mead MS 7850

This recipe is identical in honey content to the previous, but the mix of spices is left to the mead maker's discretion. It was written in MS 7850 Thompson (1749) on f.32v:

> Mead
>
> Take 5 Quarts of Water to one Quart of Honey, brew these 3 Hours with a Bowl in a Large Tub continually. Then boil it '2 an Hour with a little Bag of Spice some Lemon peel & Coriander seed. Then take 10 whites of Eggs well beaten put to it & when it boils up strain it thro a sieve & afterwards thro a strainer that it may be clear, when it is blood warm put to it 2 Toasts spread well with Yeast. Let it work about 12 Hours then put it in a Vessel, let it stand three Weeks then Bottle it Note 3 pound of Honey is a Quart.

Notes for interpretation and choices:

- The boiling instructions include an ambiguous letter or symbol. The best match to the hand appears to be a numeral "2", which I have placed in the transcription. I have interpreted it as "½" for a half hour boiling time.
- The phrase "brew these 3 Hours with a Bowl" is ambiguous. It could mean mixing alone. It is also possible that "brew" means boil and 'Bowl" is a mis-spelling of boil. I have chosen the former, the latter would lead to an approximate 1.13 OG.
- The lemon and coriander could be the "bag of spice" or the bag of spice could be in addition to the specified ingredients. If the spice is additional the specific spices and amounts need to be chosen. I have used only coriander in my recipe.
- The number of egg whites called for can probably be reduced without significant effect.

Instructions for Mead MS 7850:

1. To 4 quarts of water add 2.2 pounds (3 scant cups) honey, mix thoroughly.
2. Add the peel of ½ lemon and 1 teaspoon coriander seed. {Add additional spice(s) as desired.}
3. Boil ½ hour down to 1 gallon.
4. Mix in the beaten whites of 7 eggs, boil about 2 minutes.
5. Take off heat, strain immediately, and let cool. [Add 3.5 pounds (4 ¾ cups) honey to water boiled with lemon and spice to make 1 gallon.]
6. When blood warm place in fermenter. Expected OG 1.08.
7. Add toasted piece of bread covered with working yeast.
8. Follow preferred fermentation, aging, and bottling protocol.

Smale Mead MS 8097

This mead with several spices was written on p.78 of the culinary section (from the rear of the manuscript) of MS 8097 *English recipe book* (17th–18th c.):

A Smale Mead.

Take one quart of honey, 12 quarts of water, 4 or 5 cloves, one nutmege, 2 blades of mase, boyle this near an hour & scum it well, when it is coole put a little alle yest to it & stir it, then put it in a vessell fitt for it, & when it hath done working, stop it close after 9 days bottle it, & put in each bottle 2 or 3 raisons & a little lemon peile, it should be tyed down fast, this will not keep long. This is made soon & drank the soon of any.

Notes for interpretation and choices:
- The raisins probably serve the function of a bottling sugar and provide a little carbonation in the bottle.
- It is clear that this mead is intended to be drunk quickly after making.

Instructions for Smale Mead MS 8097:
1. Add 1.1 pounds (1 ½ cups) honey to 17 cups water.
2. Add 2 cloves, ⅓ nutmeg, 3 blades mace.
3. Boil gently, skimming, for about 50 minutes.
   [Add 1.1 pounds (1 ½ cups) honey to water boiled with spices and lemon to make 1 gallon.]
4. Let cool and strain into fermenter. Expected OG 1.04.
5. Add ale/beer yeast and let ferment, using preferred protocols.
6. After 9 days rack, adding 8 raisins and the peel of ¼ lemon.
7. Follow preferred bottling protocol.

Maide MS 1808

This recipe with unusually detailed instruction was written on image 62 of MS 1808 *Cookery books: 18th c.* (1750?) with a unique spelling for the word mead and an ambiguous attribution to "D."

To Make Maide D}

Take 12 quarts of Honey and Twelve gallons water and the whites of Eighteen or twenty Eggs very well beaten & stirr your Honey, water & Eggs all together & when your hony is a little melted sett it ore the fire not tuching or stiring of it till it boyle then scum it very well & put in some Cold water some times to raise the Scum & be sure put in as much as you boyle away before make enough to fill your Vessell let it boyle away a ~~let it bo~~ bout one Gallon & let it boyle one houre then take a quarter of an ounce of Ginger & as much Cloves mace simanon - bruse them a little & put them into a bagg with ane ounce an half of Correander seeds brused & let it boyle a little before put in noe hearbs that ~~it~~ will quite spoile youre maide & make it turne sower Take the peels of three Lemons & put into your bag With the spice & put into your Tub, You must not boyle your Lemon peele that will make it Bitter but pour your Liquor scalding hott on it Then straine in your Liquor on it & sett it a Cooleing as you Doe wort then take a quarter of a pint of good ~~ale~~ Ale yeast & When your Liquor is cold sett it a working as you Doe Ale then put it all together & when you have put in your yeast cover it close & sett it a working in the Tubb – the next day tunn it & put in your bagg of spice & Lemon peele & when it has Don working stop it up close And in ten days or a fortnight bottle it & in ten Days or a fortnight it will be fitt to Drink

Notes for interpretation and choices:
- This recipe notes that boiling lemon peel in the must will add bitterness.
- The small amount of ginger called for could imply the use of dried ginger.
- This recipe uses coriander as a mead spice, even though it is usually included with herbs when used in historical recipes.

Instructions for Maide MS 1808:

1. Add 2.8 pounds (3 ¾ cups) honey and to 15 cups water.
2. Add one well beaten egg white.
3. Boil for one hour, skimming, adding ¼ cup cold water twice to raise more scum. Remove that scum.
4. Add in a bag 1 slice dried ginger, 1 clove, 2 blades mace, ¼ stick cinnamon, and 2 teaspoons (¼ ounce) coriander seed. Boil about 10 minutes more.
5. Remove from heat. Remove the bag of spice, but save it. [Add 2.8 pounds (3 ¾ cup) honey to water boiled with spices to make 1 gallon.]
6. Add the peel of ¼ lemon. Expected OG 1.10–1.105.
7. When cool, transfer to fermenter and add ale yeast.
8. The next day, add the bag of spice back to fermentation.
9. Follow preferred fermentation, aging and bottling protocol, ensuring you rack off lemon and spices after 10 days.

Citrus, Herbs, and Spices

The next group of citrus meads expands the universe of flavors by adding one or more herbs to the citrus and spices. Cloves and ginger remain the most common spices in these recipes, with nutmeg, cinnamon, and mace making less frequent appearances.

The core elements of these recipes are as follows:

- Five recipes for Small Mead with Clove, Ginger, and Rosemary. OG 1.055–1.06. Whole lemon added while cooling. Ginger, cloves, and rosemary added to boil or while cooling. Refined sugar added. Varied yeast sources.
- Small Meade MS 7787. OG 1.065. Whole lemons in ferment. Ginger, cloves, cinnamon, and rosemary added while cooling. Refined sugar added. Yeast.
- Small Mead MS 7979. OG 1.06. Whole lemons in ferment. Ginger, Cloves, and eglantine in ferment. Refined sugar added. Ale yeast.
- Lady P Small Mead MS 1799. OG 1.06–1.065. Lemon juice and peel in ferment. Ginger, cloves, nutmeg, rosemary, lemon thyme, and eglantine in boil. No yeast addition specified.

- Another Mead MS 144. OG 1.075. Lemon peel in ferment. Bay and ginger in boil. Yeast on toasted bread.
- White Metheglin MS 1794. OG 1.08. Lemon peel in ferment. Rosemary and sage in boil. Ginger and lemon in ferment. Yeast.
- Strong Mead, Strong Mead with rosemary. OG 1.15. Lemon peel in ferment. Optional rosemary in boil. Ginger, cloves, nutmeg, and mace in ferment. Yeast on toasted bread.

Small Mead with Clove, Ginger, Rosemary

The five recipes here are quite similar, and appear to be closely related to each other and to recipes in other manuscript sources. As is typical, each recipe is unique and would produce a drink of slightly different character.

Version A was written on p.28 of MS 7721 *English recipe book* (1675–1800?):

Aunt L   Mead

Take 10 quarts of water 1 quart of hony 1 pound of suger. boyle these and scum them while any scum riseth. Cut 4 lemons with there peele into a stand sume rosmary ginger and cloves. Pour the liquor hot on them, when it is coole enough put in a brown bread tost spread with yest after 3 or 4 days working bottle it, in 10 dayes it will be fit to drink and will keep about 6 weekes

---

Version B was written in MS 7892 *Cookery and medical recipe book* (late 17th–18th c.) on ff.52r–52v with the notation "Mrs W" in a different hand:

To make Mead   Mrs W.

Take 10 Quarts of water, & let it be hot then take 1 Quart of Hony, & a pound of Loaf sugar, beaten, & let it boyl, till no schim arise, which will be about ¼ of an hour, ~~hower~~ then pour it forth into a Pot, that hath a Tap, & squeeze in the Juice of 4 Lemmons rinde, & all, in, when it is a litle cold, put in 20 cloves, 2 Rases of ginger, 2, or 3 sprigs of Rosemary let it then stand, till it be just cold, then take 2, or 3 spoonfulls of Good Yest, being spread upon tosts of Bread, put them in warm, & so let it stand 4, or 5 days, & bottle it, it will be fit for drinking in a week.

Citrus Meads

Version C was also written in MS 7892 *Cookery and medical recipe book* (late 17th–18th c.) on ff.56v–57r. It appears to be in the same hand as the previous recipe, although other hands were used for intervening recipes. The note "Mrs Wig" was added in a different hand from the main recipe.

How to make Mead Mrs Wig

Take 10 Quarts of Water, let it be hot, then take 1 Quart of Hony & 1 pound of sugar, let it boil till no scumm arise, then pour it into a pot, or Tub, that hath a Tap, & squeeze in the Juice of 4 Lemmons rinds & all in, when it is a little cool, put in a sprig of Rosemary, 20 Cloves, 2 Rases of ginger let it stand, till it is just cold, then take 2, or 3 spoonfulls of good Yest, spread your Toasts of bread, put them in warm, so let it stand, 4, or 5 days, then bottle it, it is fit to drink in 1 weeks time instead of Lemmons I put in Balm, & Lemmon Time which doth very well.

Version D was written in MS 4759 Tallamy (1735–1806) on scan f.133r:

To Make Mead at any time of the year

Take watter 10 quarts Honey one quart suger 1 pound cloves .30. a race or .2. of ginger brused 2 or 3 sprigs of Rosemary when the watter is near boyling put in the Honey suger & spice let it boyle ½ quarter of an hour (skim it often) take it off the fire & squeeze into it four Lemmons break their Rinds & put them in allso when its allmost cold cover it in the vessell or steenpot with tosts of Wheaten bread covered with Barme or yeast & layed on the Lickor & when it has wrought (: like new Alle): 4 or 5 dayes & runes clare put it in Bottles & stop them close keep it in a coole place tis a pleasant drink in sumer in hot weather.

Version E was written in MS 8903 Carteret (1662–mid 18th c.) on f.102r:

To make mead Mrs Michels way

Take 20 quarts of spring water: 2 quarts of Honey & 2 pound of Double refined sugar: Boyle it half an houer skiming all the while then put ino it 4 sprigs of Rosemary 4 Races of ginger sliced; 40 cloves: then boyle it A litle more after they are in, then straine it & put to it whilst it is hot the Juce of 8 Lemons & all the peels of them: let it stand to cool & when it is about new milk warm put to it about 4 or 5 spoonfulls of ale yeast; Let it work A day & a night: then stop it up and lett it stand A week then bottle it & it will bee fit to drink in A fortnights time

---

The five recipes are summarized in the following table:

Recipe	A	B	C	D	E
Water (Quarts)	10	10	10	10	20
Honey (Quarts)	1	1	1	1	2
Sugar (Pounds)	1	1	1	1	2
Boil (Hours)	Scum	¼	Scum	½	½
Cloves	Some	20	20	30	40
Ginger (Sliced Races)	Some	2	2	1–2	4
Rosemary (Sprigs)	Some	2–3	1	2–3	4
Boil After Added	No	No	No	Yes	Yes
Lemons	4	4	4	4	8
Type of Yeast	Yeast	Good	Good	Barm / Yeast	Ale
Spoonfuls of Yeast		2–3	2–3		4–5
Tost of Bread	Yes	Yes	Yes	Yes	No
Bottle after days	3–4	4–5	4–5	4–5	8
Fit to drink after Days	10	7	7		14
Keep Weeks	6				
Substitute for Lemons	No	No	Yes	No	No

There are a number of considerations in deriving a recipe:

- The mead maker can use one specific recipe, or combine several.
- The amount of individual herbs and spices to add is variable.
- The mead maker can choose to replace sugar with honey or not.
- Herbs/spices can be boiled in must or added after boiling.
- Specifications for the yeast vary.

Recipe B appears to be representative of the group, and has been chosen as the core recipe here. Instructions for Mrs. W Mead MS 7892:

1. Add 1.1 pounds (1 ½ cups) honey and 6 ounces (¾ cup) raw sugar to 15 cups warm water and mix.
2. Boil for about 15 minutes.
3. Take off heat and add 1 ½ lemons, squeezing out the juice. [Add lemons and sugar to 14 ½ cups of warm water, then add 1.1 pounds (1 ½ cups) honey.]
4. When cool, place in fermenter and add 7 cloves, 1 sprig rosemary, and about ¾ inch ginger root sliced.
5. Add yeast spread on a slice of toasted bread. Expected OG 1.06.
6. Follow preferred fermentation, aging, and bottling protocols.

Alternative versions could follow the specifics of another recipe or a preferred combination. The recipe C variant substituting lemon balm and lemon thyme for the lemons (Mrs. Wig Mead w Herbs MS 7892) is presented on p.236.

De viribus herbarum carmen
(Macer, between 1500-1599?, title page)

Small Meade MS 7787

This recipe mirrors many aspects of the previous with the addition of cinnamon, increasing the spice character. It also has a slightly longer boiling time and thus a higher OG. It was written in MS 7787 Peacock (late 17th c.) on the third scan of the manuscript. Square brackets mark extrapolations for letters lost by damage to the manuscript:

> To Make small meade:
>
> Take 20 quarts of watter & 2 quarts of honey & 2 pound of fine suger boyle them halfe an hour in the watter & scum it well & than pour it on a little ginger rosmary 20 cloves & a litle cinnamon whan its cold clear it of the sediment of the bottom than put in 3 lamons & set on a litle yest & let it sta[nd] 5 days & than if clear bottle it & it will be fitt to drink in a fort[night] or 3 weeks you must not stir in the yest after its set on:

Notes for interpretation and choices:
- Decide if replacing sugar with additional honey.
- Decide amount of herbs and spices to add.
- The recipe specifies taking clear liquid off of the sediment after boiling but does not say whether rosemary and spices are also removed, I have assumed they are.

Instructions for Small Meade MS 7787:
1. Add 1.3 pounds (1 ⅔ cups) honey and 7 ounces (1 scant cup) raw sugar to 17 cups warm water.
2. Boil for about 30 minutes, skimming.
3. Take off heat, immediately add 7 cloves, ¼ stick cinnamon, ½ inch piece of ginger root sliced, and 1 small sprig rosemary.
4. When cool, take 1 gallon of clear liquid off, excluding herbs and spices.
   [Add 1.2 pounds (1 ½ cups) honey to 14 ½ cups water that has been boiled with sugar and had spices added during cooling.]
5. Add 1 lemon sliced and squeezed.
6. Add yeast. Expected OG 1.065.
7. Rack after 5 days.
8. Follow preferred fermentation, aging, and bottling protocols.

Small Mead MS 7979

This recipe again follows the recipes above, substituting sweet briar for rosemary and adding more lemons. It was written in MS 7979 *Recipe book* (18th c.), on f25r:

To make small Mead

Take 10 quarts of water & let it be hot then put in one quart of hony, & a pound of loaf sugar, & let it boil till no scum rises, which will be a quarter of an hour, then let it stand till almost cold, & put in the juice of 6 lemons & cut in the rinds, & put in 10 cloves, & 2 races of ginger, a handful or 2 of sweet bryer, 3 spoonefuls of good Ale yest, spread on a toast of bread, let it stand 4 or 5 days then strain it for your use. Mrs. Plitheron

---

Notes for interpretation and choices:
- The sugar can be replaced with additional honey.
- Sweet briar is eglantine.
- Intended time to drinking is less than a week.

Instructions for Small Mead MS 7979:
1. Warm 15 cups water.
2. Add 1.1 pounds (1 ½ cups) honey and 6 ounces (¾ cup) raw sugar.
3. Boil for about 30 minutes, skimming.
4. Take off heat, allow to cool.
   [Add 1.1 pounds (1 ½ cups) honey to water to make 1 gallon.]
5. Add 2 large lemons sliced and squeezed.
6. Add 3 cloves, 1 small handful eglantine, and about ¾ inch sliced ginger root.
7. Add yeast spread on a slice of toasted bread. Expected OG 1.06.
8. Follow preferred fermentation, aging, and bottling protocols, racking off herbs/spice after 5 days.

Lady P Small Mead MS 1799

This mead uses a common herb grouping of rosemary, lemon balm, and eglantine. Combined with lemon, and with uncertain amounts of nutmeg and cloves, this recipe provides a lot of room for experimentation. It was recorded in MS 1799 *Cookery books: 18th cent* (1700–1775?) on f.36v:

> A Receipt to make small Mead – By Lady P
>
> To a quart of Honey, put 7 quarts of water a sprig of Rosemary a sprig of Baulm a little sweet Bryar a little ginger and Nutmeg a few Cloves bruised very well & tied in a cloth Let all these boil in it very well & let it boil till no scim rises, then put it in a stand till Coole and squease in the juice of 4 Lemmons to half an Anchor, then put it in the Barrel being very Coole with the peel of one Lemmon stop it very Close, and att the 10 dayes end it must be bottled this Mead will keep a year you may drink it 10 dayes after it is bottled.

Notes for interpretation and choices:
- An Anchor (the Dutch Anker) was a measure used for wine or brandy, equivalent to 10 gallons.
- Sweet briar is eglantine.
- Amounts for each ingredient are not defined.

Instructions for Lady P Small Mead MS 1799:
1. Add 1.7 pounds (2 ¼ cups) honey to 1 gallon water.
2. Add, tied together in a cloth: 1 sprig rosemary, 1 sprig lemon balm (1 Tablespoon dried), 2 teaspoon eglantine (dried), 3 slices fresh ginger, ½ nutmeg crushed, and 2 cloves.
3. Boil, skimming for 40 minutes.
4. Take off heat and let cool. Remove herbs. Expected OG 1.06–1.065.
   [Add 1.7 pounds (2 ¼ cups) honey to water boiled with herbs/spices to make 1 gallon.]
5. Add juice of 1 lemon and zest of ¼ lemon.
6. Use preferred yeast.
7. Follow preferred fermentation, aging, and bottling protocols, ensuring racking after 10 days to remove lemon peel.

Another Mead MS 144

The recipe written in MS 144 *Book of receipts* (1650–1739?) on f.93v of the scans is slightly less complex than the previous:

Another To Make Mead

Take 2 pound of honey to one gallon of water Boyle it very well one houre, Boyle in it on ounce of sliced ginger and a few bay leaves, when its boyled, let it stand and settle then clear it ofe the lees, the next day worke it up with a wheat Bread toast with east spread upon it, when it has stood two or three dayes, tun it up, and put in it the pills of two fresh Lemmons, and with in 8 or 10 dayes you May Bottle it ofe

---

Instructions for Another Mead MS 144:
1. Add 2.3 pounds honey (3 cups) to 18 cups of water.
2. Add 2 slices of ginger root and 2 bay leaves.
3. Boil about one hour, skimming to a bit over 1 gallon.
4. Let stand to cool.
5. Rack 1 gallon of clear must off the settled material.
   [Add 2 pounds (2 ⅓ cups) honey to water boiled with herbs/spices to make 1 gallon.]
6. Add yeast on a piece of toasted bread. Expected OG 1.075.
7. Rack after 3 days, adding zest of 2 lemons.
8. Rack again after 8–10 days.
9. Follow preferred fermentation, aging, and bottling protocols.

White Methiglin MS 1794

This metheglin recipe was written as recipe 53 in MS 1794 *Cookery books: 17th–18th century* (1685–c. 1725). Words cut off at the edge of the page are filled in as noted within [ ].

To make white methiglin

Take five quarts of water & a handfull of Rosemary & a handfull of sage boyle them well togather & then t[ake] out the herbes & put in A quart of huney lett itt boy[l] A little and scum itt as itt boyles then take itt of a[nd] strane itt & lett itt stand till itt be Almost cold then [put] your yest to itt and lett itt worke as youer beare doth then tun itt up & when you stop itt put sume sinom[on] and ginger and leamon peele in A Bagg and sett itt hang in the vesell.

Instructions for White Methiglin MS 1794:

1. Add 2 sprigs each of fresh rosemary and sage to 14 cups of water.
2. Boil approximately 20 minutes, Take off heat
3. Remove herbs and add 2.2 pounds (3 cups) honey.
4. Boil approximately 20 minutes, skimming. Take off heat. [Add 2.2 pounds (3 cups) honey to water boiled with herbs to make 1 gallon.]
5. Place in fermenter and add yeast. Expected OG 1.08.
6. Use preferred fermentation protocol.
7. Upon first racking (about 1 week), add a bag containing ½ a small stick of cinnamon, 3–4 slices of ginger root, and the zest of ½ lemon.
8. Remove bag of spices before using preferred bottling protocol.

Strong Mead, Strong Mead with Rosemary

This recipe for strong mead with a variant adding rosemary was repeated in three of the Wellcome manuscripts. It has also been cataloged in at least one other manuscript of the period and several printed books.

The initial source for this recipe could be Noel Chomal's 1725 *Dictionaire oeconomique: or, the family dictionary* published in London (Chomal, 1725, entry for Mead). All manuscript appearances also contain Chomal's recipe for White Mead, but none contain either metheglin recipe from later in the same book. The brief time frame for the five appearances of this recipe is from about 1725 to 1740. In all cases, it is called Strong Mead.

The first version was written in MS 1343 Branch (1725) on p.71:

Strong Mead   (Mrs. Pyke)

Take 4 gallons of water, put 18 pound of honey beat the whites of 4 Eggs, stir them in with the honey, till it be all melted. Scum it well, as long as aney a riseis when it boile, it must boile one hour and half. If you like the tast you may put in a sprig of rosmary in the boiling. When it is cold Worke it with a tost spred with yeast, and when you put it into the vesselle hang in one large nutmeg. The wheight of that in mace, the same quantetey in cloves, 4 rasies of ginger, put them in a bite of musling. The spice must be beaten and puting the peals of 2 lemons when it has done working, stop it up and let it stand 6 monthes be for you bottell it

---

Culinary recipe 29 in MS 3098 K. (1735?) detailed the following:

To make strong Mead.

To four Gallons of Water put eighteen pound of honey, beat the whites of four Eggs, stir them in with the honey till all be melted; scum it well as long as it boils, and be sure it boils an hour and half if you like the taste you may put a sprig of Rosemary in the boiling: when tis cold, work it with a toast spread with yeast; and when you put it into the Vessel, hang therein one nutmeg, the weight of it in mace, & the same quantity in cloves, with four races of ginger in a bit of muslin, the spice must be beaten, put in the peel of 2 limons. When it has done working, stop it up and let it stand

---

Citrus Meads

This version was written on f.133v of MS 4759 Tallamy (1735–1806):

To Make Strong Mead

To four gallons of Watter put Eighteen pound of honey beat the whites of 4 egs stir them in with the honey till it be all melted scum it well as long as it boyles & be sure it boyle an hour & half if you like the tast you may put a sprig of Rosemary in the boyling when it is Cold work it with a tost spread with yest & when you put it into the Vessell hang therein 1 nutmeg mace & cloves & 4 Races of ginger in a bit of muslin the spice must be beaten put in the peil of two Lemons when it has don working stop it up & lett it stand six months before you bottle it

---

Notes for interpretation and choices:

- All versions are very close in wording. The one potential variation is MS 4759, which has no specific amount for mace and cloves.
- The spice load is relatively heavy. Keeping in mind that historical recipes often place "done working" at five to ten days, it is recommended to monitor flavor and remove spices when desired.

Instructions for Strong Mead and Strong Mead with Rosemary.

1. Add 4.2 pounds (5 ½ cups) of honey to 1 gallon of water.
2. Add 1 egg white beaten, and ¼ sprig of rosemary.
   {Omit rosemary for variant recipe.}
3. Boil for 1 ½ hours, skimming.
4. Let cool, transfer to fermenter, straining out rosemary. Expected OG 1.15.
   [Add 4.2 pounds (5 ½ cups) honey to water boiled with egg white and rosemary to make 1 gallon.]
5. Add a piece of bread well toasted and spread with active yeast.
6. Hang in fermenter, in a bag, 1 ½ nutmeg crushed, 10 cloves, 3 blades of mace, 1 inch of ginger root sliced, and peel of ½ lemon.
7. Use preferred fermentation protocol, racking off of spices and lemon after primary fermentation.
8. Use preferred aging and bottling protocol, with 6 months bulk aging.

Rhenish Wine and Citron Syrup

Five of the Wellcome manuscripts contain versions of a relatively complex recipe incorporating herbs, spices, wine, and citrus syrup. The earliest version dates as early as 1662 and the latest about 1750. Versions of this recipe are also found in other manuscripts, but the recipe has not yet been cataloged in a printed book. The Wellcome appearances include:

A. Chumley White Mead MS 8903 (c. 1662–19th c.)
B. White Mead MS 4054 (c. 1690–1710);
   White Mead w Citron MS 4054 (c. 1690–1710)
C. Mead MS 3539 Michel (mid–18th c.)
D. Mead MS 3498 (c. 1750–1900?)
E. Mead of Citron MS 1407 (1725–c. 1775?)

Four modern recipes are presented below for the five historical recipes. MS 3539 (C) and MS 3498 (D) are presented together as they are almost identical.

The table below shows the combination of ingredients in each recipe

Recipe	A	B	C	D	E
Cloves	X	X	X	X	X
Mace	X	X	X	X	X
Ginger	X	X	X	X	X
Cinnamon		X	X	X	X
Balm	X	X	X	X	X
Eglantine	X	X	X	X	X
Marjoram	X	X	X	X	
Mint	X	X	X	X	
Burnet		X			
Rhenish Wine	X	X	X	X	X
White Wine (Alternate)	X	X			
Lemon Syrup	X				
Lemon Peel	X				
Lemon		X			
Citron Syrup		X	X	X	X
Violet Syrup			X	X	
Egg White	X	X	X	X	X
Toasted Bread	X	X	X	X	
Ale Yeast	X	X	X		X
Yeast				X	

Notes for interpretation and choices:

- Each recipe varies in proportions, timing, and the specific herbs and spices added.
- Three recipes produce an OG of about 1.07, one of about 1.075, and the other two of about 1.08–1.085.
- All mention Rhenish wine, from the modern Rheinhessen region. Two recipes allow substitution of white wine.
- All recipes use balm and eglantine (sweet briar), four add marjoram and mint, one also adds burnet.
- All use cloves, ginger and mace; all but also add cinnamon.
- Initial fermentation volume in the modern recipes is slightly under one gallon to allow for later additions. Addition of wine is expected to have little effect on final ABV.
- It is unclear if measure for spices is cumulative or individual. I have used cumulative. Relative amounts are also generally unclear.
- All recipes use egg whites to clarify.
- Four of the five recipes use toasted bread to hold the yeast.

Citron (*Citrus medica*)
Colored etching by J. Pass c.1800

The sole version (A) without cinnamon, using lemon syrup (and cut lemon and peel) rather than citron syrup, and leaving the spices in the fermentation was written in MS 8903 Carteret (1662–mid 18th c.) on p.122:

Sa: Chumley The White Mead

Take a Gallon of water 2 lb of the best honney. In a quantitie of 10 Gallons allow one Gallon over; set it over a Cleare wood fire; & when ye honney is disolv'd with stirring; put in 2 or 3 Whites of Eggs beat very well with a Rod, Stir them In with a quick fire, make it boyle when you see it begin to break & the scum rise up; put in some of the old Gallon of water, so keep putting it in by a pint at a time & keep stirring so long as you see any scum Rise; boyle it an hour a pace, after the first scuming put in Cloves Mace Ginger of all an ounce one handfull of sweet Margorum & balme, a little Sweet Brier & a few topps of Mint & when it hath boyld an hour straine it out into a vessell to coole & put the spices in againe but not the herbs, & when it is cold put it into a deepe vessell to work in & have as many Toasts of Bread as will cover the vessel take them hot from the fire & spread one side with good Ale yeast Lay that side downwards & so cover that side with a Cloath, & 2 dayes after put in 2 quarts of white wine or renish & a faire Leamon sirrup of some of the outside & pill and cut it round as you do for a glasse of wine then in 5 or 6 dayes you may tun it up; in hot wether sooner; straine all the things out, & let it standinge Caske a month then Bottle it

---

Citrus Meads

Chumley's White Mead MS 8903:

1. Add 1.9 pounds (2 ½ cups) honey to 15 cups of water.
2. Bring to a boil, adding a small quantity of beaten egg white.
3. As the scum begins to rise, 10–30 minutes after boiling starts, remove it.
4. Add 3 cloves, 2 blades of mace, and 3 slices dried ginger tied together in a bag.
5. Add also 1 ½ teaspoon whole marjoram, 1 ½ teaspoon balm, 1 teaspoon eglantine, and ½ teaspoon mint.
6. Add, about 2 ounces at a time, 1 ½ cups of cold water. Keep skimming.
7. Boil for 1 hour total (½ hour after herbs and spices added).
8. Take off heat. Remove spice bag, strain out herbs.
9. After it has cooled, add spice bag back in. Volume should be about 15 cups to allow for later additions.
   [Add 1.9 pounds (2 ½ cups) honey to water boiled with herbs and spices as above, making 15 cups total.]
10. Place in fermenter. Add toasted bread spread with active ale yeast on bottom side. OG approximately 1.07.
11. Follow preferred fermentation protocol.
12. After 2 days, add 6 ounces German white wine, 1 ½ ounces lemon syrup, and zest of ¼ lemon.
13. After 5-6 days, rack off spices and lemon.
14. Bulk age for 1 month.
15. Follow preferred bottling protocol.

Citrus Meads

The only version (B) to use burnet was written in MS 4054 *Receipt book* (1690–1710?) on p.185:

To make white Mead.

Take two pounds of the best and whitest Honey to one Gallon of water, and to about thirteene Gallons of water putt in one gallon over & above for fear it be to strong & high coloured – then sett it over a clear wood fire, and whe the Honey is dissolved take 2 or 3 whites of eggs, and with a wiske or burchen rod whisk them very well in the liquor, that it may rise the scum, & keep – a pretty quick fire under it, and when the scum riseth putt in some of the gallons of water you were bid to add to the other, so as the scum riseth putt in the water a pint at a time; so when it has a good thick scume scum it very well so as long as any wil rise, then take some mace, cloves and ginger of all these about three quarter of an ounce, one ounce of cinamon, and a small handfull – of these hearbs sweet Marjoran sweet bryer Burnatt Balme, and the tops of mint, Boyle it one houre, then straine it, and when it is almost cold, sett it a worke with some Ale Yest upon a brown toast, in a Narrow Tubb that the toast may cover it, when it hath – stood 2 days putt in 2 quartes of Rhenish Wine or good White wine you must putt it in by the side of the tub that you break not – the yest, putt in also a Lemon cutt as you doe for a glass of wine so lett it stand 3 or 4 days more, then straine it & tunn it up and keep it close stoped a Month, then botle it up, 3 weekes – end it will be fitt to drink

a pint of syrrup of sitterne to that quantity.

Citrus Meads

White Mead MS 4054, White Mead w Citron MS 4054:

1. Add 1.9 pounds (2 ½ cups) honey to 15 cups of water.
2. Bring to a boil, adding a small quantity of beaten egg white.
3. As the scum begins to rise, after about 30 minutes, remove it.
4. Add 3 cloves, 1 blade of mace, 2 slices dried ginger, and 1 small stick cinnamon tied together in a bag.
5. Add also 1 teaspoon whole marjoram, 1 teaspoon balm, 1 teaspoon eglantine, 1 teaspoon burnet, and 1 teaspoon mint.
6. Add, about 2 ounces at a time, 1 ½ cups of cold water. Keep skimming.
7. Boil for 1 hour total (1/2 hour after herbs and spices added).
8. Take off heat. Strain out herbs and spices.
   [Add 1.9 pounds (2 ½ cups) honey to water boiled with herbs and spices as above, making 15 cups total.]
9. Place in fermenter, add toasted bread spread with active ale yeast on bottom side. OG approximately 1.07. Total volume about 15 cups.
10. Follow preferred fermentation protocol.
11. After 2 days, add 6 ounces German white wine and a lemon slice.
    {Option add 1 ½ ounces citron syrup.}
12. After primary fermentation ends, strain and age for 1 month.
13. Follow preferred bottling protocol.

Citrus Meads

This version (C) was written in MS 3539 Michel (mid–18th c.) ff.58r–58v:

> -Mead-
>
> Take the best honey, and to every two pounds put a gallon of faire spring water, and in the quantity of 10 or 11 gallons you may exceed one gallon of water, else it will be of the strongest. Put the honey into the water, then set it over a pretty quick fire in a kettle, when the honey is disolved take the whites of 2 eggs well beaten and put into it, then take a birch rodd, and whip it very well in the water, and if the fire be quick the scum will sooner rise, the which scum off continually till its cleane. Then put into it of cloves, mace, ginger and cinnamon, into the quantity of about 14 gallons one ounce, then of marjoram and balme each a litle handfull, of sweet brier & mint half so much, let these boyle well together about 2 houres, then take it off the fire and straine it, and when it is cold put it into a vessell where in you use to work Ale, then taking as many Toasts of wheaten bread as will cover it, and when they are throly hard and well toasted, spread one side of them thin over with the best Ale yeast and lay that side downewards upon the mead, cover it close over with a cloth. The next day put into this quantity whilest it works 2 quarts of the best Rhenish Wine, 3 or 4 ounces of the syrrup of Citterns and 2 of Violets. When you see this hath wrought Yeast betwixt and about the Toasts, which it will do in 4 or 5 dayes, then take out the Toasts and straine the mead, and so tun it up into a sweet Vessell and bung it up close, so let it stand six weeks or 2 moneths, and then bottle it out. Drink it not till 3 moneths after. The longer you keep it the better it will be. In scumming it when it is boyling put in the od gallon of water by Pints at a time cold, it will make the scum rise the faster.

An almost identical version (D) was written in MS 3498 Matthey (1750–1900?) on f.16r of the manuscript. It varies from the above only in specifying "yeast" rather than "ale yeast":

> To make Mead
>
> Take the best Honey, & to every 2 pound, put a Gallon of fair Water from the spring, & in the quantity, of 10, or 11 Gallons you may exceed a Gallon of water or else it will be of the strongest put the Honey into the Water then set it over a pretty good Fire in a kettle & when the Honey is

disolved take the whites of 2 Eggs well beaten & put to't. then take a birch rod, & whip it well in the water, & if the fire be quick the scumm will sooner rise, which must be scumm'd of continually & when its clean off, put into it of Cloves, Mace, Ginger & Cinnamon, into the quantity of about 14 Gallons one ounce of all theses together, then take Margorum & Balm, of each a little handfull, of sweet Brier, & Mint half as much let these boyle well together in all about 2 hours. Then take it off the fire & strain, it & when it's cold put it into the Vessel you used to work'd Ale in then take as many Toasts of wheat bread as will cover it, & when they are throughly hard, & well toasted, spread one side of them with yest, & lay that side downwards on the mead, cover it close over, the next day putt into this quart, whilst it works, 2 quarts of the best Rhenish Wine & 3 or 4 ounces of Cittron Sirrup & 2 of Violets.

Mead MS 3539 Mead MS 3498:

1. Add 2.2 pounds (3 cups) honey to 20 cups of water.
2. Bring to a boil, adding a small quantity of beaten egg white.
3. As the scum begins to rise, remove it, until no more rises (about 45 minutes).
4. Add 3 cloves, 2 blades of mace, 1 slice dried ginger, and ¼ stick cinnamon tied together in a bag.
5. Add 1 teaspoon whole marjoram, 1 teaspoon balm, ½ teaspoon eglantine, and ½ teaspoon mint.
6. Add, about 2 ounces at a time, 1 ½ cups of cold water. Keep skimming.
7. Boil for a total of 2 hours (1 hour 15 minutes hour after herbs and spices added). Ending volume slightly under 1 gallon.
8. Take off heat, remove spice bag, strain out herbs.
   [Add 2.2 pounds (3 cups) honey to water boiled with herbs and spices as above, making 15 cups total.]
9. Place in fermenter, add toasted wheat bread spread with active yeast on bottom side. OG approximately 1.08–1.085.
10. Follow preferred fermentation protocol.
11. The next day, add 6 ounces German white wine, ½ ounce citron syrup, and ¼ ounce syrup of violets.
12. Follow preferred aging and bottling protocol.

Citrus Meads

The final version (E) was written in MS 1407 Buckworth (1725–c. 1775?), which lacks pagination:

Mead of Citron.

To 6 Gallons of Water 12 Pound of Virgins honey, beat in the Water the whites of 4 Eggs boil it an hour, as the skim rises take it off clean, Eglentine or sweet brier & balm 6 small sprigs of each, mace 6 drams, 2 of Cloves, a race of Ginger, ½ an Ounce of Cinnams boil it in the Liquor in a Muslin bag, & when ½ boil'd an hour take it off, & set it in the Tub you work it in to cool, take 2 spoonfuls of Ale Yest, 4 ounce of Sirrup of Citron beat 'em well together & strain it, put a Quart of Rhenish Wine, be sure fill your vessel that it work over, let it stand 6 days before you bottle it.

Mead of Citron MS 1407:
1. Add 2 pounds (2 ⅔ cups) honey to 15 cups of water.
2. Bring to a boil, adding a small quantity of beaten egg white.
3. As the scum begins to rise, after about 30 minutes, remove it.
4. Add 3 cloves, 2 blades of mace, 2 slices dried ginger, and ½ small stick cinnamon tied together in a bag.
5. Add 1 teaspoon whole marjoram, 1 teaspoon balm, ½ teaspoon eglantine, and ½ teaspoon mint.
6. Add, about 2 ounces at a time, 1 ½ cups of cold water. Keep skimming.
7. Boil for 1 hour total (1/2 hour after herbs and spices added).
8. Take off heat, remove spice bag, strain out herbs. Volume should be about 15 cups to allow for later additions.
   [Add 2 pounds (2 ⅔ cups) honey to water boiled with herbs and spices as above, making 15 cups total.]
9. Place in fermenter, add toasted bread spread with active ale yeast on bottom side. OG approximately 1.075.
10. Follow preferred fermentation protocol.
11. After 2 days, add 6 ounces German white wine and 1 ounce citron syrup.
12. After primary fermentation ends, strain and age for 1 month.
13. Follow preferred bottling protocol.

Flower Forward Meads

Flowers are a consistent ingredient in mead recipes across the historical record. In the period of the Wellcome recipes, hops, violets, and cowslips are the most common flowers used; in earlier recipes hops, elderflowers, and roses were dominant. Roses were favored in recipes from Classical era authors such as Dioscorides and feature in fewer later recipes. Cowslips and violets may be more common in the Wellcome recipes because of their strong history as English country flowers; English Violet is a common name for violets.

In the Wellcome recipes, flowers are used medicinally, for flavor, and as a colorant. Metheglin for Liver & Spleene MS 7391 (p.230) uses flowers for their expected medicinal properties. The two hopped meads below use them for flavor, and Mead MS 1325 uses cowslip for flavor, although they will also add some color. White Metheglin MS 8687 (p.238) has three variants using clove gilliflowers for red color. Strong Mead MS 8002 (p.235), and Spanish Metheglin MS 7892 and Spiced Spanish Metheglin MS 7892 (p.259) all use marigold flowers for yellow coloring. Saffron, which is included with the spices, is used as a yellow/orange coloring.

Hops

Hops are the most prevalent flower in historical meads. They appear in about one-third of the recipes containing flowers. While other recipes often add hops in both the boil and the ferment, these two both add hops only for the boil. Both of these hopped meads have a high gravity and are given a very long aging time. Hopped historical meads tend towards higher gravities, but there are also lower gravity instances.

Strong Mead MS 1803

This recipe for strong mead was written in MS 1803 *Cookery—books: 18th cent* (1725?) on pp.149–150:

For Strong Mead

To twelve Gallons of Water put four Gallons of Honey, set it on a Clear Fire & put in three ounce of Hops, whilst the Liquor is but just warm, let boil an Hour scuming it very well as the scim rises, when it has boiled an Hour pour it into a clean Vessell, & when near cold set on five Pints of new yeast, work it in a warm Room & cover it with a Wollen Cloath, it is hard to get it to work well, so whenever you see it is well risen in the Guilefat, it must be well done in, you may know when its Leaded & wrought enough by the shilling of the drink like Ale. April or September is the best time to make it in when its done working in the cask bung it close up & let it stand 3 Months before you Bottle it. It will keep 7 years.

Notes for interpretation and choices:
- The recipe does not specify if/when the hops are removed from the must.
- Yeast is added at about five percent of total volume, which may affect final flavor with carried liquid.

Instructions for Strong Mead MS 1803:
1. Add 3.4 pounds (4 ½ cups) honey to 14 cups water.
2. Add 0.2 ounces dried noble hops.
3. Boil 1 hour, skimming.
4. Strain and let cool.
   [Boil hops in water for 1 hour, strain and cool then add that water to 3.4 pounds (4 ½ cups) honey to make 1 gallon.]
5. When cool, add 5 ounces yeast. Expected OG 1.125.
6. Follow preferred fermentation protocols.
7. Allow to bulk age 3 months before bottling, using preferred protocol.

Lady Pickering Mead MS 1811

MS 1811 *Cookery—books: 18th cent* (1750?) on page 12 instructed:

> To Make Mead Lady Pickering
>
> To a gallon of Water take 3 pound of Honey, & two pound of good sugar, boyle and scum them, then have redy the whites of 3 Eggs wisked up to a froath, with a pint of fair Water, put that in also, and scum it as long as any scum will rise, and just as you take it off the fire, shake in half an ounce, of good hops, let them boyle a little, then strain of your Liquor, & work it as you do Beer, so tun it up, and after it has been in the Vessel six Months, put in half a pint of good Brandy and lett it stand the whole year or longer if you pleas
>
> NB this Mead will keep as long as you will but not fit to drink under 7 years.

Notes for interpretation and choices:
- The mead maker can use sugar or substitute an additional 1.9 lb/gal (2 ½ cups) honey.

Instructions for Lady Pickering Mead MS 1811:
1. Add 2.4 lb honey (3 ¼ cups) to 12 cups water and 1 ½ pounds (3 cups) raw sugar.
2. Bring to a boil, boil for about 15 minutes, skimming.
3. Add the beaten whites of 3 eggs mixed with 1 ½ cups water.
4. Boil another 30 minutes, skimming.
5. Take off heat, add 0.4 ounces hops.
6. Boil another 15 minutes.
7. Take off heat and strain. Expected OG 1.16.
   [Add 2.4 pounds (3 ¼ cups) honey to water boiled with hops as above to make 1 gallon.]
8. Let cool, place in fermenter, add desired yeast.
9. Follow preferred fermentation protocol.
10. After 6 months aging, add 6 ounces brandy.
11. Follow preferred bottling protocol. Drink after 7 years, unless you cannot wait.

Mead MS 1325 with Cowslips

Cowslips are one of the more common flowers in historical mead recipes. This ingredient that marks its entry into the mead landscape with the advent of the 17th century.

This recipe was written in *A book of usefull receipts for cookery* (1675–c. 1700) on pp.203–4 of the manuscript:

To make Mead

Take twelve gallons of spring water to every gallon a pound and half of Honey put your honey & water one together and when it boyles scum it very well then putt in lemon pills two spriggs of Roemary a litle cloves and mace and to every gallon one ounce of cowslips and soe lett it boyle half gallons away and when you have soe done sett it to coole, when it is cold putt it into a vessell that you doe intend to draw it off in and soe work it up with Ale yest as you doe beer and soe lett it stand a week before you bottle it up.

Notes for interpretation and choices:
- It is not stated whether cowslip flowers are dried or fresh. Fresh is assumed, so the two ounces per gallon of fresh cowslip is estimated at under an ounce of dried flowers.

Instructions for Mead MS 1325:
1. Add 2.7 pounds (3 ½ cups) honey to water to make 2 gallons.
2. Boil and remove scum until scum stops rising, about 1 hour.
3. Add 1 teaspoon lemon peel, 1/3 sprig rosemary, 1 clove, and 2 blades mace.
4. Add ⅔ ounces dried cowslip flowers.
5. Continue to boil until 1 gallon remains.
6. When cool, strain into fermenter. Expected OG 1.10.
   [Add 2.7 pounds (3 ½ cups) honey to water boiled with herbs, spices, and flowers to make 1 gallon.]
7. Add ale yeast.
8. Follow preferred fermentation, aging, and bottling protocol.

Spice Focused Meads

Spices were a very popular addition for historical mead recipes and are used in almost three quarters of the Wellcome recipes. The recipes in this chapter are ones for which the spice character is expected to dominate.

As discussed in the Ingredients chapter, for purposes of historical mead making, spices are defined as additions which the recipes themselves identify as spices. A number of ingredients that are technically spices (i.e. roots, seeds, fruits, or barks) are included with herbs.

Mead Maker's Choice of Spices

Many recipes simply instruct the mead maker to add "spices" or the spices they choose. These two representative recipes provide mead makers the opportunity to work freely within the group of spices used in the time period of the Wellcome manuscripts. The table showing spice usage starting on p.65 can be used as a guide to identify typical combinations. Grains of paradise, cardamom, and cubeb are spices which appear in meads of this period but which do not appear in recipes in this volume. Care must be taken in balancing the amounts of individual and total spice.

Artificial Malmsey MS 4759

Rebecca Tallamy's recipe book (MS 4759) is unusual in that it includes a printed book (the first edition, 1651, of John French's *Art of Distillation*) to which additional pages have been added, more than doubling the length. Recipes were written in the blank spaces and margins of the original book and continue into the new pages in a number of hands.

The manuscript portions of the book are dated by the Wellcome Library to 1735–1738 with a few later recipes, the latest date being 1807. The choice to use this 1651 book as a core for Rebecca's cookbook more than 80 years later is unexplained.

French's book contained a recipe for mead (French, 1651 p.122):

An artificial Malmsey.

Take two gallons of English Honey, put it into eight gallons of the best spring-water, set these in a vessell over a gentle fire, when they have boyled gently an houre, take them off, and when they be cold, put them into a small barrell or runlet, hanging in the vessell a bag of spices and set it in the cellar, and in halfe a year you may drinke thereof.

It is unexpected that the manuscript repeated this recipe, with no suggestion that the scribe was aware of its presence a few hundred pages before (MS 4759 Tallamy, 1735–1806, f.174v):

To Make Artificial Malmsey

Take two Gallons of English Honey put into it Eight gallons of spring watter set these in a vessell over a gentle fire, when thy have boyld gently an houre take them off & when thy be cold put them into a small Barrell hanging in the vessell a bag of spice or you may boyle it in it, set it in a celler & in half a year you may drink it

This second recipe is almost identical to the original, but adds the instruction that the spices may either be boiled in or added during fermentation. The original calls for them being added in fermentation.

Notes for interpretation and choices:

- Malmsey was historically a strong, sweet white wine from Greece or the eastern Mediterranean.
- The mead maker must choose whether to boil spices in, add them to the fermentation, or boil them and then transfer to fermentation as well.
- The mead maker must also choose spices and amounts.

Instructions for Artificial Malmsey MS 4759:

1. Add 2.8 pounds (3 ¾ cups) honey to 15 cups water.
2. Add a bag of selected spices.
3. Bring to a boil and boil, skimming, for about 1 hour.
4. Take off heat and let cool. Expected OG 1.10–1.105.
   [Add 2.8 pounds (3 ¾ cups) honey to water boiled with spices to make one gallon. {If spices added to fermentation, add plain water.}]
5. When lukewarm, add toasted bread covered with working yeast.
6. {Add a bag of selected spices to fermentation rather than to boil, OR place bag of spices from boil into ferment.}
7. Ferment, age, and bottle using preferred protocols.

Meade MS 3087

In MS 3087 Johnstone (1725?) a recipe was written on page 17:

For Meade

A Gallon of water & a quart of hony & spice boyle it untill all scum be of let it stand untill it is near cold take a white toast & when it is hott spread it with barme & put it into the meade the next morning tun it up & stop it.

Notes for interpretation and choices:

- Specific spices and the amounts added must be chosen.
- Timing for addition and removal of spices is not clear.

Instructions for Meade MS 3087:

1. Add 2.8 pounds (3 ¾ cups) honey to 15 cups water.
2. Add a bag containing selected spices, bruised.
3. Bring to a boil and boil, skimming, for about 1 hour.
4. Take off heat and let cool. Expected OG 1.10–1.105.
   [Add 2.8 pounds (3 ¾ cups) honey to water boiled with spices to make 1 gallon.]
5. When lukewarm, add toasted bread covered with working yeast.
6. After 1 day, take off bread, and place in fermenter.
7. Follow preferred fermentation, aging, and bottling protocols.

One Spice

Addition of a single spice to a mead is common. About ⅓ of the cataloged recipes containing spices use only a single spice, although most of these recipes also add other flavors such as herbs, flowers, or citrus. Ginger, nutmeg, and cloves are the most common sole spices. The initial two recipes here are for low OG and higher OG nutmeg meads. The other recipes feature two of the less common spices.

Mead MS 7721

This recipe using nutmeg was written in MS 7721 *English recipe book* (1675–1800?) p.44:

To make mead

Take 3 quarts of water, a pound of hony mix them together till the honey be well desolved, set it upon the fire Let it boyle an houre take the scum of as it rises then put in a nutmeg when it is as cool as new milk put yest to it, let it stand covered 28 hours beating it over in fore or 5 hours as thay do Ale, then tun it & draw it into bottles, in the summer at a fortnight in the winter at 3 weeks

---

Notes for interpretation and choices:
- The mead maker must choose when to remove the nutmeg.
- The choice of yeast is not specified.

Instructions for Mead MS 7721:
1. Add 1.4 pounds (2 scant cups) honey to 17 cups water.
2. Boil for one hour, skimming.
3. Take off fire and add 1 crushed nutmeg.
   [Bring 14 cups of water to a boil, take off heat, add 1 crushed nutmeg. Add 1.4 pounds (2 scant cups) honey and mix.]
4. When warm, add yeast. Expected OG 1.05–1.055.
5. Follow preferred fermentation protocols, racking off nutmeg at 2–3 weeks.
6. Follow preferred aging and bottling protocol.

Mead II MS 3009

Another recipe with nutmeg, this one with an option to add lemon, was written in MS 3009 Jacob (1654–c. 1685) on p.38 of the culinary portion (from the rear). The recipe has been roughly crossed out, suggesting one of the owners of the manuscript found it lacking.

> How To make Mead: Take a Eleven pints of water, two pints of honey, mixt it with a littel nuttmeg boyle it and scum it two, ore three whits of Eggs to clearifie it and then Boyle it a lettell while and when it be cold spread a stost with yest and putt into it, lett it stand in a close corner twill next day, then bottell it with a nob: of suger it will keep a mounth: in three dayes you may drinck of it; if you keepe it longer putt in more honey, it will be ripe soner if you squies a pece of leamond

Notes for interpretation and choices:

- The time for boiling is not clear.
- More honey is suggested for a longer aging mead. See note after the recipe for details on one choice for this option.
- Use of lemon is optional.
- The use of sugar in bottling would typically be as a priming sugar. If it is bottled after one day as the recipe requires, the bottles will almost certainly explode.

Instructions for Mead II MS 3009:

1. Add 2 pounds (2 ⅔ cups) honey to 14 ⅔ cups water.
2. Add ½ crushed nutmeg, bring to a boil.
3. Add 3 egg whites after 15 minutes boiling.
4. Boil another 15 minutes.
5. Take off heat and let cool. Expected OG 1.075.
   [Add 2 pounds (2 ⅔ cups) honey to water boiled with nutmeg.]
6. {If desired, add juice of ½ lemon.}
7. Add active yeast spread on a toasted piece of bread.
8. Follow preferred fermentation, aging, and bottling protocols, using priming sugar if desired. Note that the called for bottling timing will lead to exploding bottles.

To make with 2.5 pounds honey (3 ⅓ cups) per gallon, start with 14 cups water. OG will be 1.09–1.095.

October Strong Mead Saffron MS 8002

The recipe for plain mead from this recipe is given on p.147. This variant adds saffron to provide color. The instructions for this variant are with the main recipe. Notes for interpretation and choices:

- The amount of saffron to add is undefined.
- Saffron could be added to the boil or the ferment.
- The recipe states that saffron is used to color the mead. Saffron will also add a somewhat earthy flavor.

Strong Mead MS 7788

A recipe attributed to Mr. Rishars was presented in MS 7788 Repp (1703) f.84r:

Strong Mead

Take such a Quantity of Water as you desire to use and boyle it two hours, scumm it, & settle it, and to every Gallon put three pound of Honey, boyle it a full hour & scumm it well. lett there also be put into every 4 Gallons an Ounce of Mace, in a bag to boyle with it. When it is Cold put it into a vessel with the mace, and it ought to stand on the vessel nine months or near a year before you bottle it.

Mr John Rishars

Notes for interpretation and choices:
- Mace is very lightweight. 1 ounce is a significant volume.
- The amount of mace may provide a very strong flavor.
- The recipe is clear that the mace is in both the boil and ferment.

Instructions for Strong Mead MS 7788:
1. Add 2.8 pounds (3 ¾ cups) honey to 15 cups water.
2. Add 7 blades of mace.
3. Bring to a boil and boil, skimming, for about 1 hour.
4. Take off heat and let cool. Expected OG 1.10–1.105.
   [Add 2.8 pounds (3 ¾ cups) honey to water boiled with mace to make 1 gallon.]
5. When lukewarm, add toasted bread covered with working yeast.
6. Follow preferred fermentation, aging, and bottling protocols, leaving mace in for 9–12 months.

Three or More Spices

As the number of different additions in a mead increases, considerations for balancing flavors get more complex. The choice of flavor balance is as much personal as it is technical.

Mead MS 3009, Mead from Combs MS 3009 Mead Stronger Flavor MS 3009, Mead from Combs Stronger Flavor MS 3009

This recipe includes two strengths and two spicing options leading to four recipe variants. The recipe specifies that the choice to add the 4th spice is made at the time the mead is moved to bulk aging, which allows the mead maker to adjust flavor at that point if they desire. It was written on p.106 of the culinary section (from the rear of the manuscript) of MS 3009 Jacob (1654–c. 1685) p.106:

To make Mead

Take to every gallon of honey, 4 gallons of water, mix them well together and let them boile, takeing of the scume, then put in of cloves, and mace, and ginger, slict, the other whole, and soe let them continue boiling till it will beare an Egge, then take it of. and strain, and strain it through a sive, then let it stand till it be almost cold, and then put in some Ale yeast, and let it stand, ~~till it be almost~~ some 4 houre, being cover'd, let it work like beare, then put it into a vessell, and when it hath done working, stop it up close, if you doe perceive that it be not strong enough of the spice, then you may when you stop it up, put in some Nutmegg cutt in quarters, and a few cloves, you may if you please bottle it when it is 2 or 3 Months old. this will keep a yeare if it lye in a good seller. When you doe take beese, lay the Combes in Water. After you have drain'd the honey, all from them, and soe let the combes lye in the Water q 8 or 9 houres, and then stire them in the Water, soe that all the honey may be out, then strain the Water, through a sive, and of the Water, you may make mead as before, but be sure you boile it Enough, till it beare and Egge halfe Above the Liquor.

Notes for interpretation and choices:

- The wording implies that gravity readings with the egg are taken while boiling. The gravity when the must is cool will be higher.
- Spice amounts are not defined.
- The mead from honeycombs is considered a separate recipe because residual materials in the comb will affect flavor.
- Mead from combs could be interpreted as not including spices.
- For the honeycombs version, the instructions say to make it as before, which results in an OG of about 1.11. The clarifying instruction immediately following then says it should bear an egg half exposed above the liquid. This last instruction would result in an extremely high OG, and is probably an error.

Instructions for Mead MS 3009 and Mead Stronger Flavor MS 3009:

1. Add 3 pounds (1 quart) honey to 1 gallon water.
2. Bring to a boil.
3. Add: 3 cloves, 8 blades of mace (about 2 grams), and 4 slices of fresh ginger root.
4. Boil, skimming, for about 1 ½ hours total.
5. Take off heat, strain, and let cool. Expected OG 1.11.
   [Add 3 pounds (1 quart) honey to water boiled with spices to make 1 gallon.]
6. Add actively working ale yeast.
7. Follow preferred fermentation protocols.
8. {After primary fermentation, if more spice flavor is desired, add 2 cloves and ½ crushed nutmeg in a bag for bulk aging.}
9. Follow preferred aging and bottling protocols ensuring spice is removed after 2–3 months.

The option for making the mead from combs requires slightly more attention to the gravity. Use a hydrometer to achieve an OG of about 1.11, or accept the variance that would have historically occurred. This option is not practical without boiling to concentrate the must.

White Metheglin MS 8450, White Metheglin MS 3828

This recipe, using copious amounts of ginger, cinnamon, and nutmeg, was copied into two of the Wellcome manuscripts, and has been cataloged as early as Digby's *Closet* in 1669.

MS 8450 *English culinary and medical recipe book* (1680–c. 1740?) instructed on p.32 of the manuscript in recipe 139:

> To make white methiglin
>
> Set on the fire, boyl & scum clean 5 gallons of water, & one gallon of white honey then set it by & take 6 ounces of ginger, 2 ounces of cinamon, & an ounce of nutmegs, which bruise grossly & put into the hot Liquor, & cover it close, so let it stand till cold, the put to it as much Ale-yeast as will make it work, & keep it in as warm a place as you do Ale, & when it has wrought well, tun it as Ale or Beer, & when a week old, drink it, but the older, the better.

With some variations, MS 3828 Percivall (mid 18th c.) pp. 24–25 recipe 68 instructed:

> To make white Metheglin
>
> Take 5 Gallons of Water, and put to it one Gallon of Honey then set it on the Fire, and boil it very well, and scum it clean & then take it off the Fire, and put into it 6 Ounces of Ginger 2 of Cinamon, and one of Nutmegs, bruise them grossly, and put them in hott, cover it close and let it stand till it is cold then put in as much Ale Barm as will make it work, spread the Barm on a Toast, keep it in a warm place as you do Ale, and when it has workt well tun it as you do ale you may drink it at a Week old but the older the Better.

Notes for interpretation and choices:

- Choose whether to use a bread toast or not.
- The amount of spice may overwhelm if left in for a long fermentation.

Instructions for White Metheglin MS 8450 and White Metheglin MS 3828:

1. Add 2.8 pounds (3 ¾ cups) honey to 15 cups water.
2. Boil for about 1 hour, skimming.
3. Take it off the heat an immediately add 1.4 ounces sliced ginger, 3 sticks cinnamon, and 1 small nutmeg, all bruised. Expected OG 1.10–1.105.
   [Add spices to 13 cups boiling water then add 2.4 pounds (3 ¾ cups) honey.]
4. Add active ale yeast {spread on a piece of toasted bread}.
5. After 1 week, strain.
6. Use preferred fermentation, aging, and bottling protocols.

Mead MS 1321

There are a number of uncertainties in the recipe written on p.6 of MS 1321, *Book of receits* (1675–c. 1725?):

To make Mead

Take 30 quarts of water, and boyle it tell a 5th part be wasted keeping it well scumed all the while it boyleth then take it off the fire and put so much of the hott water into a gallon of Hony as will dissolve it, the hardest hony is the best then mix it with the remainder of the water and sett it over the fire againe and lett it boyle a little time takeing of the scum as it riseth and put into it of sliced ginger of Cloves and jemaca pepper mixed to gather a good handfull, then take it off the fire and sett it a cooling in wood or stone and when it is of a due heat as usually they observe in working beer or ale putt into it some Yeast but be shure it be not sower and work it as you doe beere and after it hath wrought a bout 8 or 10 hours putt it into the Barrell and hang a little quantity of Ising glass upon a string in the barrell but lett it not touch the bottome of the barrell let it stand a little time unstoped to work over if it will and then bung it down very close and after 12 days draw it off into bottles and putt a small peice of loaf sugar into each bottle.

Notes for interpretation and choices:

- There is a 1:6 ratio of honey to water before the second boiling. However, "so much of the hot water ... as will dissolve it" could imply a higher honey content.
- The amount of spices is not precise.
- Jamaica pepper is allspice.
- There is an option for the use of wood or more neutral containers.
- The recipe uses isinglass, an animal-based clarification agent.
- The use of sugar at bottling could be as a bottling sugar, for back sweetening, or both.

Instructions for Mead MS 1321:

1. Add 1.9 pounds (2 ½ cups) honey to 17 ½ cups water.
2. Bring to a boil and hold for about 30 minutes. Remove scum.
3. Add 5 slices ginger, 1 teaspoon allspice (whole), and 2 cloves. Take off heat.
   [Bring 14 cups water to a boil, add spices. Then add 1.9 pounds (2 ½ cups) honey when slightly cooled.]
4. When cool enough add yeast. Expected OG 1.07.
5. The next day, strain into fermenter with clarification agent (isinglass or preferred).
6. Follow preferred fermentation and aging protocols, ensuring spices are drawn off primary at about 12 days.
7. Back sweeten with sugar {or substitute honey} before bottling.

Methegling MS 3769

Similar to the above recipe, this one written in MS 3769 Parker (1651) on f.41v contains numerous options for variations:

To make methegling

take your hony combes and put them in a sive that the hony may rune from them then put a sufficient quantity of water to the combs and wash them with your hands very well then strayne them very harde and put the licore in a pane and boyle it very fast with continuall stiring of it and let it be as cold as beere or ale befor it is tuned up and as you doe to that so proportionably put brane to it and so let it worke in the vessell all night and the next day tune it up and hange thes spieces in it sinamon cloves nutmugg and mace of each a small quantity after the toning stope it with a corke lightly as it leaveseth working you may know by the hissing so stope it closer.

This recipe provides significant freedom for interpretation. The mead maker with access to drained honeycombs, recalling that modern centrifuges are much more efficient at removing honey than allowing honey to drip from the combs, may choose a literal approach. This honey will contain a higher amount of extra material washed from the comb. Therefore, a longer boiling time of about one and one half hours has been assumed.

Notes for interpretation and choices:

- Decide whether to use honeycombs or substitute honey.
- Decide on amount of honey in must. Assuming a relatively efficient extraction of honey from the combs and using a lot of water, there could be a pound or less of honey per gallon. Combs that were poorly opened before initial extraction and rinsed with a small amount of water, could perhaps give two to three pounds per gallon honey.
- I have interpreted "brane" as barm. It could be argued that bran, i.e. grain husks, is meant and is closer to the written word. However, yeast is often added at this point, and bran would be a unique addition, making barm the likely intention.
- The amount of spices relative and absolute is unclear.

Instructions for Methegling MS 3769 with less honey:

1. Add 1 pound (1 ⅓ cups) honey to 20 cups of water.
2. Boil, skimming, for about 1 ½ hours, returning to 1 gallon.
3. Take off heat and allow to cool. Expected OG 1.035–1.04.
   [Add 1 pound (1 ⅓ cups) honey to water to make 1 gallon.]
4. Add yeast.
5. When fermentation has started add: ½ stick cinnamon, 3 cloves, ¼ nutmeg, and 2 blades mace, crushed and in a bag.
6. Rack off and serve after 3–8 days.

Instructions for Methegling MS 3769 with more honey:

1. Take 2.3 pounds (3 cups) honey, add to 18 cups water.
2. Boil, skimming, for about 1 ½ hours, returning to 1 gallon.
3. Take off heat and allow to cool. Expected OG 1.08–1.085.
   [Add 2.3 pounds (3 cups) honey to water to make 1 gallon.]
4. Add yeast.
5. Once fermentation has started, add: ½ stick cinnamon, 3 cloves, 1/2 nutmeg, and 2 blades mace, crushed and in a bag.
6. Remove spices when mead is moved to secondary.
7. Follow preferred protocols for fermentation, aging, and bottling.

Spices plus One Additional Flavor

Individual herbs (or other non-spice flavorings) are also paired with spices, as seen in the following recipes. The first three feature rosemary, which is the only herb used in historical recipes at the same overall frequency of the top spices: ginger, cinnamon, cloves, and nutmeg.

Ten bee-hives on wooden shelves.
Woodcut by S. Brandt, c. 1580

Mead Like Sherry MS 144

When we see the characterization of this wine as being like "sherry" we should not think of the wine as fortified and sweetened, but rather the geographical origin of a (usually) strong white wine from southern Spain. These wines have been made for well over 2000 years. The importation of these wines to England began as early as the 12th century when the trade was given royal recognition. Consistent fortification of sherry with distilled spirits dates to the later part of the 18th century, after the Wellcome recipes.

MS 144 *Book of receipts* (1650–1739?) on f.87v instructed in a different hand from the initial:

To Make Mead that Drink, like sherry

Boyle a good quantity of spring water an hour, put it in a tub, the next day to Eleven gallons of it put 30 pounds of honey hang it over the fire and when it is near boyling, ad the whites and shells of 18 eggs, stir all well and as it boyles scum it well that being done, put in 6 small sprigs of Rosemary: and cinnamon cut in peices about 2 inches long as much as a spoon will hold; let it boyle in all two hours, then straine it through a fine sive, and when its quite cold tun it into to a vessell that fit it, let it stand 6 months ere you bottle it, then after a month drinke it/

Instructions for Mead Like sherry MS 144:
1. Add 3 pounds (1 quart) honey to 4 ½ quarts of water.
2. Bring to a boil. Add the whites and shells of 2 eggs, mix in well.
3. Boil, skimming for about 45 minutes.
4. Add ½ sprig of rosemary, and a pinch of crushed cinnamon.
5. Boil for another 1 ¼ hours.
6. Take off heat, strain, when cool place in fermenter. Expected OG 1.11.
   [Boil spice and herb in 5 quarts water for 1 ¼ hours, take off heat, strain, add to 3 pounds (1 quart) honey to make 1 gallon.]
7. Follow preferred fermentation, aging, and bottling protocol; recommended bulk aging 6 months.

Mead MS 3082

MS 3082 Johnson (1694–1831) on f.29r gave the following instructions:

> How to make mead.
>
> Put 14 pound of honey to 30 quarts of water boyl them an hour then put in 3 ounces of ginger a little clove, and mace and nutmegs and rosmary then boyle it 2 hours longer then take it off and let it stand all night a cooling then strain it trough a sive and then put it into a barrel and let it stand 3 weeks and then bottle it with a lump of suggar and the next you make tun up to the same lees.

Notes for interpretation and choices:
- The must is cooled overnight and if left open could be infected by wild yeast.
- The instruction to tun the next batch with the same lees leaves an opening to experiment making two serial batches. It could also imply an instruction to continually recycle yeast from batch to batch.
- The recipe does not specifically add yeast to the first batch.
- Sugar added at bottling could carbonate, back sweeten, or both.

Instructions for Mead MS 3082:
1. Add 2.6 pounds (3.5 cups) honey to 22.5 cups water.
2. Boil for 1 hour, skimming.
3. Add ¾ ounce sliced ginger, 2 cloves, 2 blades mace, ½ crushed nutmeg, and ½ sprig of rosemary.
4. Boil 2 additional hours, reducing total volume to 1 gallon.
5. Take off heat and let cool overnight. Expected OG 1.095–1.10. [Boil 18 cups of water for 2 hours with herb and spices. Remove from heat. Mix with 2.6 pounds (3.5 cups) honey to make one gallon.]
6. The next day, strain, and place in fermenter.
7. Follow preferred fermentation, aging and bottling protocols, using priming sugar to carbonate.

Small Mead MS 1795

This small mead has a very short period before drinking. The use of ginger and rosemary is well suited to a summer session drink. MS 1795 *Cookery-book: 17ᵗʰ/18ᵗʰ century* (1685–c. 1725?) on p.210 instructed:

> To Make Small Mead
>
> Take a Gallon of honny and put to it Seaven or Eight Gallons of watter ster it well together and boyle it half an houere or more put in it a race of ~~Nut~~ Ginger or two and a little sprigg of rosemary when it is Boyled and almost cold put it in a Runlett and put in a little yest to make it worke, in a day or two stop it up close let it stand 5 or 6 dayes then bottle it.

Notes for interpretation and choices:
- The recipe has a short fermentation and aging time.
- The recipe does not specify when to take out ginger and rosemary.

Instructions for Small Mead MS 1795:
1. Add 1.6 pounds (2 generous cups) honey to 16 cups water.
2. Boil for ½ hour, skimming.
3. Add 3 slices of ginger and 1 teaspoon rosemary. Boil another ½ hour.
4. Take off heat and let cool.
   Expected OG 1.06.
   [Add 1.6 pounds (2 generous cups) honey to water boiled with herb and spice for ½ hour to make 1 gallon.]
5. Place in fermenter with yeast.
6. Follow preferred fermentation, aging, and bottling protocols, racking off rosemary and ginger after 1 week.

Woodcut of drinking and vomiting

Mead MS 144, Mead w Herbs MS 144

This recipe provides several options for flavoring. The first fits in this category, but the second produces a mead with much more herb presence although it is presented here. The recipe was written on ff.96r–96v of MS 144 *Book of receipts* (1650–1739?):

> A Receipt to Make Mead
>
> Cut your Honey comb into thin peices, then steep it three Dayes and night in water then strain it through a hair sive, and put as much Honey to them as will make the water bare an egg then boyle it with or without these herbs following as you think fitt Rosemary bay leaves balme and sweet Marjorum of each one handfull, tyed together, this quantity of herbs serves half a Hogshead, then boyle it a full hour and keep it with skiming then strain it ofe and when prittie cold, work it up as Beer with Yest tun it before the Yest fall, and when it has done working in the Vessell, hang in a canvis bag, with Mace cloves cinamond ginger and Nuttmigs of each half an ounce sliced or brused then stop the bung close this must stand half a year before its fit to broch and if your Honey be good it may stand a year, befor its bottled one quart of honey to 4 of water will do if you have no comb and put in one ounce of carraway seeds brused with your spice.

Notes for interpretation and choices:
- A hogshead is 63–64 gallons.
- There is a choice of starting with honeycombs or simply using honey.
- The mead maker can choose to add herbs or not.
- The addition of spices after primary fermentation is unusual.

Instructions for Mead MS 144 and variant Mead w Herbs MS 144:
1. Add 2.3 pounds (3 cups) honey to 15 cups water.
2. {For a more complex mead including herbs, add one or more of: ¼ sprig rosemary, 1 bay leaf, 1 teaspoon balm and 1 teaspoon marjoram.}
3. Bring to a boil. Boil, skimming, for about 1 hour.
4. Take off heat. Strain. Let cool
   [Add 2.3 pounds (3 cups) honey, to water in which herbs have been boiled to make 1 gallon.]

5. When lukewarm, add working yeast. Expected OG 1.08–1.085.
6. Follow preferred fermentation protocols.
7. At end of primary fermentation, add bag of spices with: 2 blades mace, 1 clove, and a pinch each of crushed ginger, caraway seeds, and nutmeg.
8. Follow preferred aging and bottling protocols.

Metheglin MS 8097

MS 8097 *English recipe book* (17th–18th c.) on p.77 of the culinary section (from the back) gave the following recipe:

Metheglin.

Take as much honey as will make the water strong enough to bear an egge cold then take a root of angelica, a little gallingale root with a little ginger & cloves, boyle this an hour, when it is cold take out the roots & spice, put to the quantity of 8 gallons a spoonfull of yest if you boyle it in the morning, put the yest to it at night when it is cold, let it work till morning, then tun it up in a barell, when it hath done working stop it up a quarter of a year, if you make it at midsumer let it stand till michelmas so bottle it, & it will be good to drink in winter.

Notes for interpretation and choices:
- Michaelmas is September 29.

Instructions for Metheglin MS 8097:
1. Add 2.3 pounds (3 cups) honey to 16 cups of water.
2. Add 1 tablespoon angelica root, 1 teaspoon galingale, 1 teaspoon dried ginger, and 2 cloves.
3. Boil 1 hour.
4. Remove from heat and let cool.
   [Add 2.3 pounds (3 cups) honey to water boiled with spices to make 1 gallon.]
5. Strain, place in fermenter, add yeast. Expected OG 1.08–1.085.
6. Ferment, age, and bottle using preferred protocols.

Non-Spice (Herb) Focused Meads

Meads focused on non-spice flavors, including herbs plus roots, barks, seeds, and fruits that are not in the abbreviated group of mead spices, are historically somewhat less common than spice-focused meads. About 40% of cataloged recipes contain one or more of these additions, compared to about 50% which include spices. A notable fraction of non-spice focused meads contain long lists of ingredients, many of which are unfamiliar to most modern mead makers. In some recipes, ingredients were selected for perceived medicinal properties rather than for their flavor profiles. That aside, there are a great number of additions which provide diverse and pleasing flavors to mead, ranging from subtle to intense.

The recipes in this chapter represent those where the presence of the non-spice flavors is expected to be dominant in the drink.

Ten bee-hives on wooden shelves.
Woodcut by S. Brandt, c. 1580.

1–3 Herbs or Other Flavors

These meads each contain a few, mostly familiar, flavors and serve as good examples of simpler meads in this group.

Mead MS 7976

This mead recipe was written on p.75 of MS 7976 Palmer (1700–1739):

> To make Mead.
>
> Take 4 Gallons of Water and a pottle of the best Hamshire honey, warm the Water so much as to dissolve the honey, put a good branch of Lemmon thyme in it & boyle it quick, scum it clean, and take it off, let it stand an hour so, & then strayn it into a cooler and the next day tun it, & stop it up close, and let it stand 5 or 6 weeks, and bottle it with a knob of sugar.

Notes for interpretation and choices:
- A pottle is a half-gallon.
- Sugar addition at bottling will provide carbonation, but given the relatively low OG will probably be consumed rather than also providing back sweetening.

Instructions for Mead MS 7976:
1. Add 1.5 pounds (2 cups) honey to 1 gallon of water.
2. Bring to a boil and add a small branch of lemon thyme (2 teaspoons).
3. Boil ½ hour, skimming.
4. Take off heat and let cool. Expected OG 1.055.
   [Add 1.5 pounds (2 cups) honey to water boiled with thyme to make 1 gallon.]
5. Let stand for 1 hour after it is cool, then strain into fermenter.
6. Add yeast.
7. Follow preferred fermentation, aging, and bottling protocol, using priming sugar {or honey}.

Small Meade MS 3582

This mead, written on f.49v of MS 3582 *Miscellany receipts* (1725?) f.49v includes three herbs:

To make small meade

Take 10 Quarts Water, 1 Quart best honey, boyl it ¼ hour scim it very well. Then put in bayes, Rosemary, betony, of each an handfull boyl it ¼ hour, strain it in a sive, and let it stand While it is almost Cold. Then Work it up with Yeast, cover it close a Night and day, then Open it the 4th day you may draw it into bottles putting a Clove in every bottle

---

Notes for interpretation and choices:

- At the end of the word bay is an unclear form that could be "es" (bayes), "&" (bay &), or perhaps the word "or" (bay or). In context "or" seems unlikely, and it does not match ampersands elsewhere in the manuscript, I have chosen "bayes."
- Amounts of herbs added are not specified.
- I have interpreted addition of cloves in bottling as an option. It could be read as required.

Instructions for Small Meade MS 3582 and variant:

1. Add 1.2 pounds (1.5 generous cups) honey to a gallon of water.
2. Boil for 15 minutes, skimming.
3. Add 3 bay leaves, 2 sprigs of rosemary, and 2 tablespoons betony. Boil for 15 minutes more.
4. Take off heat, strain out herbs, let cool.
   [Add water boiled with herbs to 1.2 pounds (1.5 generous cups) honey to make 1 gallon.]
5. Put in fermenter, add yeast. Expected OG 1.045.
6. Follow preferred fermentation, aging, and bottling protocol.
7. {Add 2 cloves during bulk aging if desired.}

4+ Herbs or Other Flavors

Naming conventions for the Wellcome meads are inconsistent, but meads with multiple herbs and non-spice addition are almost always called metheglins. Both of these recipes allow the mead maker to choose the specific additions, which is somewhat common and can be presented in the recipes as an open invitation to choose any desired herbs/non-spice addition, as a choice among a list of options, or as a specific list.

Metheglan MS 184a

This recipe predominately relies on roots for its flavors, which is unusual. The recipe was written on pp.98–99 of MS 184a Catchmay (c. 1625):

The makinge of Metheglan

Take fenill Rootes, parsely Rootes, suckory Rootes, saxifrage rootes, any other rootes as you think good. A handfull of Rosmary to some six gallons of water, make your detoxsion stronge of the Rootes, then lett it settell after you have streined it then put your honey to it, boyle it and ~~straine~~ scume it, then putt it forthe and lett it coole, to a galland of honey you may putt three gallons of water when it is almost colde lesse then bloude warme putt your barme to it, cover it close and lett it stand and worke two dayes, then skime it clene, and stire it togither and ~~lett~~ lett it stand an other day, then take of the barme and tunne it uppe, fill it still as it worketh over when it leveth singinge, stoppe it, it will looke lie colored untill the barne laye barme purged it.

Notes for interpretation and choices:
- Four roots are specified with an option to add other roots. Likely candidates for additional ingredients include angelica, chicory, elecampane, and licorice.
- Boiling times for both the initial extraction of flavor from roots and after honey is added are not defined.

Instructions for Metheglan MS 184a:

1. Take 1 ½ gallon of water.
2. Add, loose, 1 ounce each of fennel root, parsley root, and chicory root. Add also 1 sprig rosemary.
3. Boil for about 1 hour or until the roots are soft and the water has the character of the roots and rosemary.
4. Take off heat, strain, and settle.
5. Take off 13 cups of clear water and add to 3.3 pounds (4 ⅓ cups) of honey.
6. Boil for about ½ hour, skimming.
7. Take off heat, cool, place in fermenter, and add yeast. Expected OG 1.12.
   [Add 3.3 pounds (4 ⅓ cups) honey to enough of the strained and settled water from the initial boil to make 1 gallon.]
8. Follow preferred fermentation, aging, and bottling protocols.

Given the relative complexity of the recipe, I have chosen in my initial recipe to use only the four roots specifically mentioned. Addition of others could follow after the flavor of the simpler recipe was understood.

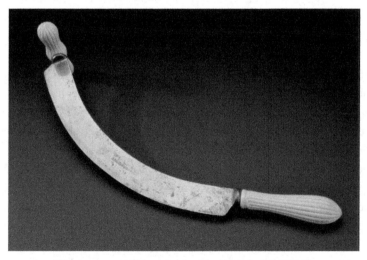

Herb cutter, Worcester, England, 1701-1900

Metheglin for Liver & Spleene MS 7391

This recipe is another example of a metheglin with a long list of additions, in this case with a clear medicinal intent. There are over 30 additions, not including the 7 spices. The instruction to choose which additions to use makes the recipe more accessible, particularly since some ingredients are difficult to find. The recipe written in MS 7391 *English recipe book* (mid-17th–early 19th c.) pp.27–28 is as follows:

Methegline good for the Liver and Spleene.

Take to every gallon of Hony 4 Gallons of faire water, stirr it well together and if it wil beare an Egge it hath hony enough else not. Then take of all such openinge Roots and herbs as be comfortable for the Stomacke, Liver and Spleene or for any other greife that you have, with seede and spice for to breake winde, then first seeth the water and hony as longe as any Scum will rise, and skim it cleane, then put in your Rootes & let them seeth, and then your herbs, and when you feele the tast of your herbs in it then put in your seedes and Spice grosly beaten, and so sethe it uppe, and when tis well boyled, one quarter beinge consumed thereof, straine it through a cleane Cloath into a Stand such as Ale is wont to be put into. And beinge cold put uppon it good Ale yest & cover it and let it stand 4 daies, and then drawe out the cleerest into a firkin, wherein you may keepe it as longe as you list, it wil be better at the yeares end then at the first, let the most your hearbs be pleasant in tast and such as are wholsome. Of such as be bitter and stronge take the lesse quantity. As hysop, Sage, Rosemary, the flowers and the mother of Thyme, Stannary, Horehound, Maiden haire, Scabious, Egrimony Bettony, Hartshorne, Liverwort, Succory Mather, Borage and the flowers of Buglos, & the flowers of Asparagus, fenell and parsley Rootes, Sidrach, Buckhoren, Centry, Polipodinus of the wall, wormwood of Elicampaine Roote, docke rootes, fennell seeds, annis-seede, Coryander seeds Carraway seeds Gallingall spicknell, of these two 1 good handfull, 1 ounce, of Cinamon, Ginger, Nutmegs, Cloves & Mace, Longe pep, of all these 1 ounce and a halfe, bruise them and put them in a little bagge of fine Lawn or Cypres, and a little stone in with them, Put the bagge and hange it halfe way into the vessell by a stringe, fasten it about the Bunge-hole, it being well stopt with Clay. The best makeinge here of it betweene the 2 St. Mary daies, &

not to be drunke before All hallontide. It is very good for any disease in the Liver Spleen or Lungs.

Notes for interpretation and choices:

- St Mary's Day is August 15 (Feast of the Assumption, Mary's death), and St Mary's birthday is September 8 (Nativity of the Blessed Virgin Mary). All hallontide is all Saint's Day–October 31. Total fermentation and aging time is therefore 8–11 weeks.

- Herb identification is challenging. Succory is chicory, herb is assumed because it is listed with other herbs. Saxifrage is burnet. Stannory is scammony. Harts horn is Bucks Horn Plantain – although this means that herb is mentioned twice. Sidrach has not been positively identified as a known herb; a tenuous connection to jujube exists, but is not solid.

- In alphabetical order, herb ingredients by modern name are: agrimony, anise seed, asparagus flowers, betony, borage, bucks horn plantain, bugloss flowers, caraway seed, centaury, chicory, coriander seed, dock root, elcampane root, fennel root, fennel seed, horehound, hyssop, liverwort, maiden hair, parsley root, polypody, rosemary, sage, scabious, scammony root, spicknell, mother of thyme, thyme flowers, and wormwood.

- Spices are: cinnamon, cloves, galangale, ginger, long pepper, mace, and nutmeg. This recipe lists glangale with the herbs; I count galangale as a spice based on overall usage patterns in historical meads.

- The specific choice of herbs (for opening) and spices (to break wind) is left open to the mead maker. Even the mead maker looking for historical accuracy would be advised to use a subset in initial trials.

- In this recipe, I have left placeholders for the reader to choose which additions they want to explore or think will complement each other. The recipe implies one or more choice from each of the categories (herbs, roots, seeds, and spices).

Rosmarinus
(Brunfels, 1532b, p.63)

Instructions for Metheglin for Liver & Spleene MS 7391:

1. Add 3.2 pounds (4 ¼ cups) honey to 17 cups water.
2. Boil for ½ hour, skimming off scum as it rises.
3. Add desired roots and herbs, 1 tablespoon of each.
4. Boil another hour.
5. Add any desired seeds and spices, boil for 15 minutes.
6. Strain and cool. Expected OG 1.115–1.12.
   [Add 3.2 pounds (4 ¼ cups) honey to water boiled with herbs and spices to make 1 gallon.]
7. Add ale yeast.
8. Follow preferred fermentation, aging, and bottling protocols.

Ginger and Other Flavors

Rosemary is the most common herb added to historical meads and was paired with spices in a number of recipes. Similarly, ginger, the most common spice, was often featured with non-spice flavors in recipes. The following are representative.

Another Mead MS 8097, Another Mead w Rosemary MS 8097

The following recipe was written on p.78 of the culinary section of MS 8097 *English recipe book* (17th–18th c.):

Another Mead.

Take to every quart of honey 6 quarts of water, mix the two together till the honey is disolved then let it boyle 2 hours, & as the scum arises take it off, pour in cold water as much as will keep to your first quantity as it wasts in boyleing boyle it a quarter of an hour after the last water is in, & in this quarter of the hour put in some angelica root, sweet bryer, & some races of ginger. 5 quarts of honey make 3 dosen of mead to which put a pint & half of alle yest, let it stand in an earthen stean with a tap, & as the yest rises take it off on the top, for 10 daies constantly as it rises then draw it off & put it into a vessell that will just hold it, & let it stand 6 weeks & then bottle it 3 races of ginger a handfull of sweet bryer 4 sprigs of angelica & a sprig of rosmary is what is usually put in. Lady Nevill.

Notes for interpretation and choices:

- The amounts for the herbs and spices given in the final two lines are in a different hand from the remainder of the recipe. This opens room for the mead maker to vary herb amounts freely.
- This second hand also adds rosemary, which is not specified in the main recipe text. This has been treated as a recipe variant.
- Ale yeast is added as a slightly over two percent of must volume. This will add notable malt flavor, but is not enough to classify this as a braggot.

Instructions for Another Mead MS 8097 and variant Another Mead w Rosemary MS 8097:

1. Add 1.7 pounds (2 ¼ cups) honey to 13.5 cups water.
2. Boil and scum for 1 ½ hours, replacing lost liquid periodically.
3. Add ½ inch sliced ginger root, 1 teaspoon eglantine, and 1 tablespoon of angelica.
   {If desired add also 1 teaspoon rosemary.}
4. Boil another ½ hour.
5. Take off heat, cool, strain into fermenter.
   [Add 1.7 pounds (2 ¼ cups) honey to water boiled with herbs and spices to make 1 gallon.]
6. Add 3 ounces working ale yeast. Expected OG 1.06–1.065.
7. Follow preferred fermentation, aging, and bottling protocols.

Neece Green's Mead MS 3082

This recipe was written in MS 3082 Johnson (1694–1831) on p.68:

> To make Mead Neece Greens Receit
>
> Putt in so mutch honey in to raine watter (it sweet) as will make it bare an egg after well stirring the honey & watter, then sett it on the fire lett it just boyle so as to scum it verey cleane, then put in to 6 galons a handfull of Lemon time a handfull of sweet margarom a little rosemarey & a little sweet bryre a prittey deale of ginger & sum mase Lett all boyle to gether a full howre, then straine it throo a haire sive & when it is Luke warme tunn it up Lay ownley a Cloth over it 4 or 5 howrs & then stopp it up Close doe not sett it in too cool a pleye in winter & if you make it in the somer you may bottle it when 6 months old if made in winter 12 months

Non-Spice (Herb) Focused Meads

Instructions for Neece Green's Mead MS 3082:

1. Add 2.3 pounds (3 cups) honey to 1 gallon water.
2. Bring to a boil. Add 2 teaspoon lemon thyme, 2 teaspoon of marjoram, 1 teaspoon rosemary, ½ inch sliced ginger, and 2 blades of mace.
3. Boil 1 hour. Scum.
4. Take off heat, strain, and when warm place in fermenter. Expected OG 1.08–1.085.
   [Add 2.3 pounds (3 cups) honey to water boiled with herbs and spice to make 1 gallon.]
5. Follow preferred fermentation, aging, and bottling protocols.

Small Meth MS 2323

This recipe was written in MS 2323 Eyton (1691–1738) on f.99r:

To make small meth

Take to 3 pints of hony take 12 quarts of water sciming it all the while then when it is half boyled put in 2 rases of ginger 5 or 6 bay leves & a sprige of rosmary then when it is boyled anoufe take it ofe the fier & let it be as could as you think good then put to it 3 sponfuls of ale yest & cover it close & botell it as soone as it is cleare,

Notes for interpretation and choices:
- The boiling time is not specified.

Instructions for Small Meth MS 2323:

1. Add 1.7 pounds (2 ¼ cups) honey to 18 cups water.
2. Boil for about 45 minutes, skimming.
3. Add about 1 ½ inches of sliced ginger root, 2 bay leaves, and ½ sprig of rosemary.
4. Boil another 45 minutes.
5. Strain, let cool. Expected OG 1.06–1.065.
   [Add 1.7 pounds (2 ¼ cups) honey to water boiled with herbs/spices to make 1 gallon.]
6. Add to fermenter, add ale yeast.
7. Follow preferred fermentation, aging, and bottling protocols.

Meads with Multiple Flavors

The meads in this chapter represent a class of meads with multiple ingredients of sometimes widely varying character.

4–6 Mixed Flavors

The simplest recipes with both herbs and spices include only a few of each. Some meads of this type where either spice or non-spice flavors are expected to dominate have been presented in the previous chapters. The recipes below are expected to present a more balanced flavor.

Strong Mead MS 8002

The collection MS 8002 *Loose receipts* (1663–1740) includes this recipe written on catalog item 108 of the set:

To Make Strong Mead

To every gallon of water putt three pound an half of good honey boyle the water and melt in the honey scuming it as long as any scum will rise, boyle in it a hand full of balm & a handfull of sweet marjerum, some saffron some merigold flowers a litle ginger a litle sinamon in a bag and when it is cold put it into a tub, if there be 16 or 18 gallons or twenty gallons. Put a quart of good Ale yeast then work it up being covered warm for a week or a fortnight beating it in four or five times a day till you finde the honey taste to go of then tunn it up keeping the vent open so long as you heare it hiss in vessell and when it has done hissing stop it up close & keep it for a year in the vessell & when you tap it if it be not fine & have not lost the honey taste then draw oute a quart or 3 pints and then stop it for a month or more then tap it a gain & so continue drawing so till it be very fine, and when it is botle it up for your ease

Notes for interpretation and choices:

- Amounts of herbs and spices are not specific.
- Aeration is instructed four to five times a day for the first two weeks.
- Marigold flowers and saffron may be added for color.

Instructions for Strong Mead MS 8002:

1. Bring 14.5 cups of water to a boil.
2. Add 3.2 pounds (4 ¼ cups) honey. Mix and skim for ½ hour.
3. Add 1 teaspoon balm, 1 teaspoon marjoram, 0.25 gram saffron, 1 teaspoon marigold flowers, 2 slices ginger, and ½ teaspoon crushed cinnamon.
4. Boil another half hour and take off heat.
5. Let cool, strain into fermenter, and add ale yeast. Expected OG 1.115–1.12.
   [Add 3.2 pounds (4 ¼ cups) honey to water boiled with herbs and spices to make 1 gallon.]
6. Use preferred fermentation, aging, and bottling protocols.

Mrs. Wig Mead w Herbs MS 7892

This recipe is a variant for one of five closely related recipes presented with the citrus meads on p.184. It replaces lemons with lemon balm and lemon thyme. While this recipe is the only one of the five recipes in that group which contains this substitution, the use here of lemon flavored herbs in place of lemons is not unique. The recipe is written on ff.56v–57r of MS 7892 *Cookery and medical recipe book* (late 17th–18th c.):

How to make Mead. Mrs Wig:

Take 10 quarts of Water, let it be hot, then take 1 quart of Hony & 1 pound of sugar, let it boil till no scumm arise, then pour it into a pot, or Tub, that hath a Tap, & squeeze in the juice of 4 Lemmons rinds & all in when it is a little cool, put in a sprig of Rosemary, 20 cloves, to 2 Rases of ginger let it stand, till it is just cold, then take 2, or 3 spoonfulls of good yest, spread your Toasts of bread, put them in warm, so let it stand, 4, or 5 days, then bottle it, it is fit to drink in 1 weeks time instead of Lemmons I put in Balm, & Lemmon Time which doth very well.

Notes for interpretation and choices:

- The base recipe for this mead is presented starting on p.182.
- The amount of balm and thyme is unspecified.
- Options for adding herbs include: adding during boil, as is typical for herb additions, during cooling, as a direct substitute for the lemons, or when partly cool with other flavors.

Instructions for Mrs. Wig Mead w Herbs MS 7892:

1. Add 1.1 pounds (1 ½ cups) honey and 6 ounces sugar to 15 cups warm water.
2. Boil for about 15 minutes, take off heat.
3. After a few minutes, add 1 ½ tablespoon each lemon balm and lemon thyme, 7 cloves, 1 sprig rosemary, and about ¾ inch ginger root sliced.
   [Add 1.1 pounds (1 ½ cups) honey to enough water boiled with sugar and to which herbs have been added as above to make 1 gallon.]
4. Place in fermenter and add yeast spread on a slice of toasted bread. Expected OG 1.06.
7. Follow preferred fermentation, aging, and bottling protocols.

**Man working with plants *Kreuterbůch*
(Rosslin, 1550, p.XLIX)**

White Metheglin MS 8687 and Variants

White Metheglin MS 8687, which was written on pp.101–102 of MS 8687, Tully (1732? –), also includes three variant recipes which are colored with clove gilliflowers, using different methods to apply the color. Each method is expected to provide different flavors.

To make white Metheglin or Meath.

Take 4 gallons of Water and one of white virgins hony, boil the Water very well with a little sweet Brier Leaves, and Eringo roots sliced and pour it into a wooden Vessel to cool, and when it's bloud warm put in the hony, and stirr it till it's all dissolv'd, then put in a new laid Egg, and if it's strong enough to bear it up to the top of the Water, it is enough, if not you must put in some more hony till it will, or if it bear it above the Water, more then the breadth of a groat, put in more Water, then put it over the fire in a clean Kettle, with the Whites of 3 or 4 Eggs beat well and stirred in it, and when it boils scum it clean, let it boil about ¾ of an hour, then pour it into wooden Vessels, that it may not stand too thick, for then it will be the longer a cooling, and when its blood warm, put it together in one Vessel, and put some good Yest to it, and let it be covered with a Blanket all Night, and in the Morning tun it into a Vessel that hath had Sack in it, if you have it and hang a Bag of Spice and some Coriander seeds bruis'd a little, or you may steep Gillyflowers in some of it, or in Sack or Spirits of Wine, to tincture it if you pleases, when you boil it put it in, and when it hath done working, stop it up very close, and in a Month you may bottle it, or if you will you may keep it longer. When you tun it take care you leave the settlings in the Bottom of the Tub.

Notes for interpretation and choices:
- Eringo roots were often candied. This recipe does not specify candied or not. Uncandied is more likely; no mead recipe has been cataloged that specifies candied eringo root.
- Removal of herbs is not specified.
- Use of a sack barrel is specified.
- Choice of spices and amounts are left to the mead maker's discretion.
- The section on clove gilliflowers implies they are used for color and can either be placed directly in mead or soaked in sack or

brandy and the tincture used to color the mead. It also appears to direct that the colorant be placed in the boil, removing the alcohol from the brandy or sack if that method is used.

- Amounts and methods for the three coloring options are not detailed.

Instructions for White Metheglin MS 8687 and variants:

1. {If sack (wine) or spirit of wine (brandy) is being used to color, prepare about 1 week in advance ½ cup clove gilliflowers in ½ cup dry white wine OR ¼ cup brandy, straining out flowers before adding to must.
2. Take 1 gallon of water and add to it 2 teaspoons sweet briar and 2 teaspoons cut eringo root.
3. {Add also ½ cup red clove gilliflowers, or add about 3 ounces wine tincture, or add about 3 ounces brandy tincture.}
4. Boil water and herbs for ½ hour.
5. Take off heat and when warm, add 3 pounds (1 quart) honey.
6. Return to heat, add 1 beaten egg white as it begins to boil.
7. Boil ¾ of an hour, skimming.
8. Let cool, rack off clear liquid into fermenter.
   [Add 3 pounds (1 quart) honey to water boiled with herbs and spices to make 1 gallon.]
9. Add yeast. Expected OG 1.11.
10. Add oak cubes soaked in wine to simulate sack barrel (or use other method as desired).
11. Add a bag containing ½ teaspoon coriander, 2 slices ginger root, and ¼ nutmeg crushed.
    {Add other spices in addition to coriander as desired}.
12. Ferment, age, and bottle using preferred protocols.

I have used ginger and nutmeg to provide a noticeable but minor spice presence, intending to focus attention on the herbs in the mead.

Meath for Stomach and Liver MS 2477

This medicinal recipe with an extensive title was written on p.116 of MS 2477 Garside (c. 1655):

An excellent meath to cleanse the stomake, preserve the liver, & very good against the stone

Rx Fayre spring water, and put as much Honey to it, that when it is warm & well stirred together, it will bear an egg the breadth of a groat above the water, lett it stand soe all night close covered, the next day sett it on a clear fire and boyl it, styll scumming it as long as it will rise, then put into it 3 @ of Agrymonie, and 2 @ of Pellitory of the wall, Cynamon 3 oz ginger 2 oz, and 4 or 5 nuttmeggs grosly bruised: put the spice into a litle bagg, of a bullet of lead or a stone to make it slink putt the herbs & spice in a kettle together and let them seeth about halfe an houre: then take out the herbs when you take ~~the~~ off the Meath from the fire, let the bag of spice bee put in the Barrell with it, But it must stand till it bee quite cold before you tun it, this quantity of herbs & spice will serve over 12 Gallons of Meath which is an excellent thing to cleanse the stomache, preserve the Liver, and wonderfull good against the Stones.

The recipe is taken from Alexander Read's, 1651 book *Most excellent and approved medicines & remedies for most diseases and maladies incident to man's body*. The original specifies the herb and spice amounts are for 10–12 gallons, versus 12 gallons in the manuscript version.

Notes for interpretation and choices:
- This bears an egg when warm, not at room temperature.
- The symbol used for amounts for agrimony and pellitory is unusual. With the help of the original recipe, it can be identified as handful.
- A glass weight will help the herb bag sink.

Instructions for Meath for Stomach and Liver MS 2477:
1. Add 3 pounds (1 quart) honey to 1 gallon of water, mix well.
2. Boil, skimming, for 45 minutes ½ hour, then add 1 teaspoon agrimony and 1 teaspoon pellitory.
3. Add also 2 sticks of cinnamon, 3 slices of dried ginger, ½ nutmeg, all bruised in a bag.

4. Boil another 30 minutes.
5. Take off heat, strain out herbs. Expected OG 1.11.
   [Add 3 pounds (1 quart) honey to 3 quarts water boiled with herbs and spices.]
6. Place bag of spices in fermenter.
7. Ferment, age, and bottle using preferred protocols.

White Mead MS 4683, White Mead MS 4759

This recipe using three herbs and three spices appears in almost identical form in two of the Wellcome manuscripts and has also appeared in print.

MS 4683 Springatt (1686–1824) p.55 instructed:

To Make White Mead

Take 6 gallons of water, and put in 6 quarts of Honey, stiring it till the Honey be throughly Melted, then set it over the fier and when it is redy to boyl scum it very clean, then put in a quarter of an ounce of Mace and as much ginger, halfe an ounce of Nutmegs sweet Marjoram, broad thyme and sweet bryar; of all togather a handfull and boyle them there in, then set it by till it be throughly cold, and then Barrel it up, an keep it till it be Ripe

---

MS 4759 Tallamy (1735–1806) f.133r instructed:

To Make White Mead

Take 6 Gallons of watter & put in 6 quarts of Honey stiring it till the Honey be throughly melted then set it over the fire & when it is ready to boyle scum it very clean then put ¼ ounce mace, as much ginger ½ ounce nutmegs, sweet marjoram broad thyme & sweet bryar of all together a handfull & boyle it therein then sett it by till it be throughly cold & then Barrell it up

---

Instructions for White Mead MS 4683 / White Mead MS 4759:

1. Add 2.8 pounds (3 ¾ cups) honey to 15 cups water.
2. Bring to a boil, skim the scum that first rises.
3. Add 4 blades of mace, 1 slice of dried ginger, ⅓ of a nutmeg crushed, and 1 teaspoon each of marjoram, thyme, and sweet briar.
4. Continue boiling for a total boiling time of 1 hour.
5. Take off heat, strain into fermenter. Expected OG 1.10–1.105. [Add 2.8 pounds (3 ¾ cups) honey to water boiled with herbs and spices to make 1 gallon.]
6. Follow preferred fermentation, aging, and bottling protocols.

Spice Focus

This category includes recipes where spice flavors are expected to be stronger than non-spice flavors.

Mead MS 3008; Mead Newer MS 3008

MS 3008 Jackson (1743) p.200 presented this recipe. The postscript is in a different hand:

To make Mead.

Take 5 Gallons of water, take 25 pound of the best honey, put it into a clean brase kettle, & stir it a good while, till the honey is milted, then sett it on the fire, & stir it sometimes, when it boyles, take 4 whites of Eggs well beaten, & put into it, to raise the scum, when it is scum'd, put in a nutmegg cutt in peices some Cinamon, Cloves, & mase, a little sweet marjorum, & a small sprigg of rue, let it boyle about 3 hours, then put it into a tub to work, when it is near cold, spread a white bread tost, with Ale yeast on both sides, & put it in, Lett it stand till nixt day, then take out the toast, & put it in the Vessell, when it hase done working, stop it close down & Let it stand a year in the Vessel.

We now put in but 4 pound of honny to a gallon of water.

Notes for interpretation and choices:

- The mead maker has the choice of the original or modified recipe (original about 5.7 lb/gal after three hours boiling or modified about 4.8 lb/gal after boiling). Both are very high initial gravity, but both are plausible for fermentation (for example see Polish traditional high honey meads). The modified version at an approximate OG of 1.18 is more practical and has been used here.

Instructions for Mead Newer MS 3008:

1. Add 4.9 pounds (6 ½ cups) honey to 20 cups of water.
2. Bring to a boil.
3. Add the white of an egg, beaten.
4. Add ¼ nutmeg, ½ stick cinnamon, 3 cloves, 2 blades mace, and 1 teaspoon each of marjoram and rue.
5. Boil about 3 hours until volume is close to 1 gallon.
6. Strain. When cool add working ale yeast spread on toasted bread. Expected OG about 1.18.

Rue *Medical botany* (Woodville, c.1790, pl. 37

[Add 4.9 pounds (6 ½ cups) honey to water boiled with herbs to make 1 gallon.]

7. After 1 day remove bread.
8. Follow preferred fermentation, aging, and bottling protocols keeping in mind recipe calls for one year bulk aging.

Mead MS 3547

MS 3547 Miller (1660) f.36v instructed:

A very good Receipt to make Mead

Unto the measure of water you intend to make mead of mix so much puer honey as will make it of strength to beare up an egg the breadth of 3 or 4 p & lett it stand all night. The next day seeth the liquor & when it begineth to breake the thirde soun skime it untell it yeeld no more then put two nutmegs & mace ginger & cloves beaten small, liquorish & anniseeds bruised of each as much as you think fitt, boyle all well together a prety while, & then take it off the fire. & put it into a wodden vessell to coole untill ye next day, then take a coorse sheet dobled, lay it over a broad wodden vessell upon stickes under thwart the vessell then strayne it thorough the sheet because at the bottom of the cooling vessel it wil be thicke, take it up softly with a dish, then the clearest may first run thorough the sheet let it passe leasurely thorough all though it be a day or 2 before it be dreigned thorough, this done put it into a new vessell & let it stand unstoped or light tell over for 8 or 9 dayes after stop your vessell as close as you can, & let it be stale before you draw it to A gallon of water ½ an ounce of these spices is enough.

Notes for interpretation and choices:
- The recipe includes an unusual and specific set of instructions for removing settled material
- This recipe starts with as much water as the final volume of mead, giving an evaporation gauge.
- Amounts are not specified for flavors other than nutmeg.
- Recipe phrasing might suggest licorice seeds, but seeds are not commonly used. I have assumed root.
- The boiling must "breaking" refers to the hot break in beer making where after five to thirty minutes of boiling proteins and other components floc and fall out of suspension. Similar clumping of components happens in mead must, but may either take more time or be less notable.

Instructions for Mead MS 3547:

1. Add 3.4 pounds (4.5 cups) honey to 1 gallon of water.
2. Boil and skim for about 45 minutes.
3. Add ½ nutmeg, 2 blades of mace, 4 slices of ginger root, and 3 cloves, bruised. Add also 1 teaspoon licorice root and ½ teaspoon anise seeds.
4. Boil all together another 45 minutes.
5. When returned to close to 1 gallon, take off heat and cool.
6. The next day, strain. Expected OG about 1.125.
   [Add 3.4 pounds (4 ½ cups) honey to water boiled with herbs and spices, making 1 gallon.]
7. Follow preferred fermentation, aging, and bottling protocols.

Methegling MS 4683

MS 4683 Springatt (1686–1824) on f.65 instructed:

Methegling

Take eight Gallons of Fair Water & put to it three gallons & half of Honey; & boil it half an howr, with one handfull of Sweet Majoram & Rose-Mary & a little mother Thyme. Take off which scum shall rise in boyling. And when all shall have boyled together half an hour, run it through a Hair Sieve: & when it shall be cold, tun it up into a vessel that will be full of it; hang down from the Bunghole a Bag of Spices; viz: Cloves, Mace, Nutmegs, & ginger; to the Quantity of two ounces broken alltoger. Then Stop it close; & let it stand one year, or two, before you bottle it after Bottling let it stand till you can forbear it no longer; & then Drink it.

Mrs. Springatts

Notes for interpretation and choices:

- The total amount of spices is specified, but the relative amount of each is not, giving some flexibility. Less cloves and more ginger by weight is a balance typically seen in historical mead recipes.
- The recipe has a high honey content with high alcohol potential and long aging.

Instructions for Methegling MS 4683:

1. Add 3.9 pounds (5 ¼ cups) honey to 12 cups water.
2. Add 1 Tbsp. each of marjoram, rosemary, and mother thyme.
3. Boil for ½ hour, skimming.
4. Remove from heat, strain, let cool. Expected OG 1.14–1.145. [Add 3.9 pounds (5 ¼ cups) honey to water boiled with herbs to make 1 gallon.]
5. Take 4 blades of mace, 4 cloves, ¼ nutmeg and 2 slices dried ginger, bruised and placed in a bag to hang in fermenter.
6. Follow preferred fermentation, aging, and bottling protocols, noting long bulk aging.

Non-Spice Focus

The next pair of recipes increases the involvement of non-spice flavors.

Mrs. Salendines Metheglin MS 3582

This recipe bears a strong resemblance to the previous recipe, and was written in MS 3582, *Miscellany receipts* (1725?) pp.41–42:

Mrs. Salendines Metheglin

Take 8 Gallons of Water, putt to it 8 Gallons of Muscody, as much of time, a handfull of sweet Bryer, & a handfull of sweet Marjoram, Boyl these in the Water One hour Then take it off, and strain it, & sweeten it with honey Untill it will bear an Egg. Then boyl it so long as any scum will Rise, Then take off the scum, & take the Liquor Off the fire and let it stand till the next morning. Then pour it into a Vessel, & take an Ounce of ginger ½ ounce Nutmegs ½ ounce Cloves Bruise these Spices Together, & putt them into a bag, & let it hang in the Drink. And stop up the Vessel close. This is best made att Bartholomew Tyde, and its ready to Drink a Month after

---

Notes for interpretation and choices:

- Bartholomew's tide is August 24.
- The call for "8 Gallons of Muscody" is confusing. It is possible it calls for addition of Muscadine wine, but the next phrase "as much of time" suggests "muscody" is the herb Muscovy and being added with thyme. I believe the most likely explanation is the second "8 Gallons of" is a transcription error and the recipe calls for 8 gallons of water with muscovy and thyme.
- The amount of several of the herbs is uncertain.
- The temperature at which the must should bear an egg is uncertain. I have assumed it is still hot.

Instructions for Mrs. Salendines Metheglin MS 3582:

1. Take 19 cups of water. Add to it 2 tablespoons each of Muscovy and Thyme, and 1 tablespoon each of eglantine and marjoram.
2. Boil one hour.
3. Take it off the heat, strain it, add 2.2 pounds (3 cups) honey.
4. Bring it to a boil. Boil about 1 hour, skimming.
5. Let cool completely, place in fermenter. Add selected yeast. Expected OG about 1.08–1.085. [Add 2.2 pounds (3 cups) honey to water boiled with herbs to make 1 gallon.]

Woodcut of a kettle,
Koch und kellerei
(1549?, title page)

6. Add in a bag, 3 slices dried ginger, ¼ nutmeg, 10 cloves, bruised.
7. Followed preferred fermentation, aging, and bottling protocols, ensuring spices remain in liquid about 1 month.

Mead MS 4047

The following recipe contains a similar ingredients list to the above recipe, but is expected to produce a notably different taste because the spices are boiled in and the herb list differs. It was written in MS 4047 *Receipt Book* (1669) on ff.36v–37r:

To Make Mead

Take good water or raine water and make it so strong with honey that it will raise an egg to be seen above the water when your hony is throwly dissolved then after let it stand one hower then put it over the fire with a good hand full of rosemary lemnon as mush time muscow and sweet margorum and egrimony one ounce of nutmegs one of cloves 2 of ginge brused and put in a bag to hang in the vessell scum it as fast as it rises boile it an hower then let it stand all night in a wooden tub first being cool as thin as you can get vessels so do it and cleend of in the morning poure of ale the cleare and tun it in a barrell fit for it and hang the bag of spice in it it ought not to be drunke till a yeare and botld as you find cauce at halfe a yeare if it be made when hony is new.

Notes for interpretation and choices:
- Volume of batch is not specified.
- Wording "rosemary lemnon as mush time" is unclear as to specific additions. Could be rosemary, lemon, and thyme, or rosemary and lemon thyme. I have chosen the latter explanation.
- One ounce of cloves is over 300. This has been reduced, as that number of cloves would overwhelm the recipe.

Instructions for Mead MS 4047:
1. Add 2.5 pounds (3 ⅓ cups) of honey to 17 ⅔ cups water.
2. Add 1 small sprig of rosemary, and 1 tablespoon each of lemon thyme, muscovy, marjoram, and agrimony.
3. Add also, in a bag, 1 ½ crushed nutmegs, 10 cloves, and ¾ inch sliced ginger root.
4. Boil for one hour, skimming.
5. Let cool then rack clear portion into fermenter (volumes called for should allow for 1 gallon after loss), adding spice bag back in. Expected OG about 1.085.

> [Add 2.5 pounds (3 ⅓ cups) honey to water boiled with herbs to make 1 gallon.]

6. Use preferred fermentation, aging, and bottling protocols.

The amount of herbs and spices in this recipe appears unbalanced, and heavy on the spice. Closely monitoring the flavor during fermentation is recommended to ensure a palatable flavor profile.

8+ Flavors

Herb/spice meads which each include a number of varied flavors make up the final group in this chapter. These meads are challenging and some experimentation will be required to ensure the multiple flavors are all represented and balanced.

Two meads matching this characterization are detailed elsewhere. The version of the Mead II MS 144 recipe including extra herbs is detailed with the core recipe on p.223. Metheglin for Liver & Spleene MS 7391 (p.230) could also be placed in this category.

Mead MS 6812

This recipe was written in MS 6812 *English medical notebook* (1575–1663) on p.146:

To Make Mead

To every quart of honey put four quarts of runing water when it is disolved skim it clean & put in what Cold herbs you please as violet leaves maiden hair & liver wort strawbery leaves & hartstongue leaves before you take it from the fire put in the shells of six eggs being broken in peices let them boyle till they look blackish & the Mead clear then strain it into a clean vessel the next day tun it then take three or four nutmaggs broken in peices, a quarter of an ounce of mace a few cloves bruise all & put them into a bag & put it into the cask then stop it when fine bottle it

---

Notes for interpretation and choices:
- Cold herbs are specified with specific ones named.

Instructions for Mead MS 6812:

1. Add 2.8 pounds (3 ¾ cups) honey to 15 cups water.
2. Bring to a boil and add 1 tablespoon each of one or more of: violet leaves, liverwort, maiden hair, strawberry leaves, or harts tongue. Optionally use other "cold" herbs.
3. Add 2 egg shells, broken up.
4. Boil and skim for about 1 hour.
5. Strain and let cool.
6. Place in fermenter. Expected OG about 1.10–1.105.
   [Add 2.8 pounds (3 ¾ cups) honey to water boiled with herbs to make 1 gallon.]
7. Add 1 nutmeg, 6 blades of mace, and 2 cloves, bruised and in a bag.
8. Follow preferred fermentation, aging, and bottling protocols.

Metheglin MS 3009

MS 3009 Jacob (1654–c. 1685) p.234 of the culinary section (from the rear) detailed:

To Make Metheglin

Take a kettle of water, and hang it on the fire, and put therto of rosemary, brown sage sweet marjoram, broad time, Balme, Egrimony, bettony, saxafrage, of Each halfe a handfull boile these 2 or 3 walmes, then straine the water cleane from the hearbes, and let it stand and settle, then poure it from the bottom, then put therto the honey, and keep it still straining while it is Throughly mix't with the water, then while the liquor is blood warm, try it with an Egge for the strength, and if the Egge Appeare Above the liquor the breadth of a groat it will be strong Enough, if not more honey may be put to it, and when it is made of such a strength, as you would have it, then put it again on the fire, and put therin an Ounce of cloves, halfe a pound of ginger halfe an ounce of cinamehl, a Quarter of an ounce of mace, an Ounce of nutmeggs, and of fennell seeds anyseeds, Caraway seeds, of Each an ounce, all which spices and seeds must be bruised and put into a Linnen bagg, and boile them halfe an houre, keeping of it still scumed as long as any scume will be upon it, then put it Abroad in vessells, and when it is quite Cold, Tun it up, leaveing the

---

bottom or grounds behind; according as you intend to have stat'd: 2 spoonfulls of yeast may be put to a Vessell of 10 or 12 gallons, keeping it open as long as it doth worke. The hearbes, spices, before mentioned are Enough to make 25 or 26 gallons of methegline. A little more then a Quart of honey will serve to 3 quarts of Water, a spoonful of yeast may be put to 5 gallons, not to be stoped almost a month, an ounce of all these spices will serve for 8 or 10 gallons, put most Cloves

Notes for interpretation and choices:

- The egg test is done in blood warm must. A groat is about 24 mm (almost one inch) in diameter.
- The volume for fermentation relative to the amounts of herbs and spices is unclear.
- Liquid loss from boiling is uncertain. The use of the egg test to determine gravity and the temperature at which the test is done give a likely OG range of 1.11 to 1.135.

Instructions for Metheglin MS 3009:

1. Take 5 quarts of water, add to it 1 teaspoon each of rosemary, sage, marjoram, thyme, balm, agrimony, betony, and saxifrage.
2. Boil about ½ hour.
3. Strain and let settle.
4. Add 3.6 pounds (4 ¾ cups) of honey to 14 cups of the clearest of the herb water.
5. Bring to a boil.
6. Add in a bag: 10 cloves, 3 blades of mace, ¼ nutmeg, ½ teaspoon fennel seed, ½ teaspoon caraway seeds, and ½ teaspoon anise seeds. All bruised.
7. Boil ½ hour, skimming.
8. Let cool, decant clear portion and place in fermenter. Expected OG about 1.125.
   [Add 3.6 pounds (4 ¾ cups) honey to the clearest of the liquid from boiling water with the herbs and spices as detailed above to make 1 gallon.]
9. Add yeast.
10. Use preferred fermentation, aging, and bottling protocols.

White Metheglin MS 1511

MS 1511 Carr (1682) recipe number 288 stated:

> To Make white Methegline 288
>
> Take 7 gallons of water put into it as much honey as being dissolved into it will bear an egg when you mingle the honey with the water beat the honey and water with a dish in your hand doe this for the space of a whole hour at the least for this longe beating conduceth much to the whitenesse of it when it is beaten enough set it on the fire in a great kettle when it boyles skim it well when it is skimed clean then take 2 nuttmeggs 3 rase of ginger a few cloavs & a litle Mace cutt the nuttmeggs & ginger & putt all into a litle bagg & soe putt it into the kettle, & a bundle of herbs winter savoury time rosemary sweet margerom tye them together & putt them into the kettle & as the skim rises shall take it off then lett it boyle till a good part be wasted almost halfe then poure it out into some vessell to coole when it is cold tunne it upp into a litle Barrell or some botles it is not good to be drunke of a year at least.

Instructions for White Metheglin MS 1511:
1. Take 3.8 pounds (5 cups) water and add to 6 ½ quarts water, mix thoroughly.
2. Bring to a boil and skim for about ½ hour.
3. Add in a bag, bruised: ½ nutmeg, 1 inch sliced ginger root, 3 cloves, 2 blades of mace.
4. Add also in a bag or tied together a small sprig each of rosemary, savory, thyme, and marjoram.
5. Boil, skimming, until volume is 1 gallon.
6. Let cool. Expected OG about 1.14.
   [Add 3.8 pounds (5 cups) honey to water made from instructions above.]
7. Strain into fermenter.
8. Use preferred fermentation, aging, and bottling protocols.

Complex Meads

The meads in this section are complex due to the number of additions, the types of additions, or the process.

Wheat Flour as Fermentation Aid

Adding flour to mead fermentation, other than in the context of creating a braggot, is a direction in a number of recipes from the Wellcome manuscript era. None of the cataloged recipes provided a specific reason for this addition, but use of flour at the same time as yeast was pitched suggests intent. It seems likely this addition was, similar to the use of toasted bread covered with yeast, an experientially-based effort to improve fermentation through adding nutrients present in the flour and bread.

Meade MS 7721, Meade from Scum MS 7721

MS 7721 *English recipe book* (1675–1800?) instructed on p.45:

To make meade:

Take fare spring water, boyle it halfe an houre sciming it as it boyles, there must be full ten gallons, so let it coole 12 hours, then beat in 2 gallons of Honey to this quantity with a brand stick, it should be so strong of honey as to beare an egge, so let it stand all night then beat it with the stick againe that the hony may be well melted, then boyle it with half a pound of ginger scraped & sliced, 2 handfuls of rosemary, egremony half a handfull, as much sweet bryer, walnut-tree leaves & sweet marierum half a handfull, let it boyle half an howre sciming it well, in the boyling put in 6 egges that is well beaten with there shells & all, which will raise the scim better, and scim it as long as any scum will rise, the next day tun it up when its cold enough, beat a pint of Ale yest with the white of an egge & a little flower and put into it, & when it is worked well, stop it up and let it stand six weekes before you botle it:

You need not loose the scum but put in some water and boyle it & work it for present drinking:

Notes for interpretation and choices:

- Whether the ten gallons is before or after initial boiling of the water makes a small but notable difference in expected OG.
- The last sentence provides an option occasionally seen for the scum from the boiling to be used to make an inferior drink. This is presented as an option below. The amount of drink from this process would be fairly small, even with 10–12 gallons of must. The sugar content of the scum would be very low.
- The recipe calls for eggs "shells & all" to be added. This appears to include the yolk, which would be unusual but not unique. Eggs with yolk are expected to be less effective in clarification.

Instructions for Meade MS 7721:

1. Add 2.3 pounds (3 generous cups) honey to 14 ½ cups water. Mix well.
2. Add 1 ounce sliced ginger, 1 sprig rosemary, and 1 teaspoon each of agrimony, eglantine, walnut tree leaves, and marjoram.
3. Bring to a boil, add ½ of a whole egg, beaten well, with the shell.
4. Boil and skim for ½ hour.
   {Reserve scum for later use.}
5. Take off heat and let cool. Expected OG 1.085.
   [Add 2.3 pounds (3 generous cups) honey to water boiled with herbs and spices, making 1 gallon.]
6. Strain into fermenter. Add 2 ounces working ale yeast, a small amount of beaten egg white (if desired, food safety concern), and 1 tablespoon wheat flour.
7. Follow preferred fermentation, aging, and botting protocols.

Instructions for Meade from Scum MS 7721:

1. Collect all the scum taken from the must while boiling the previous recipe, and place in a pot.
2. Add water, mixing, until foam is absorbed, boil briefly.
3. Cool and ferment.

Best Mead Weak MS 4054, Best Mead Strong MS 4054

The use of anise, fennel, and coriander seeds in this recipe presents a reasonably simple set of additions with many complex flavors. Their addition for only the last few days of fermentation is unusual. The recipe was written in MS 4054 *Receipt-Book* (1690–1710?) on p.190:

> To make the best Mead, another way.
>
> Putt one Gallon of Honey to Six gallons of cold spring water, Lett it boile an houre, taking of the browne skume & stirring the White skum in, Lett it stand till it be as cold as worte, them take a crust of – browne bread & toast it well on both sides, & spread it all over with – new yest, then strew a litle flower upon it & putt it in whole bunge a dish over it, & so lett it worke. When it has worketh bruise of – anyseed, fennell seed, & corianders seed of each a small handfull & putt it into the liquor & lett it infuse so 2 days, then straine it & putt it up into Botles. Some put to 3 gallons of water one of Honney.

Notes for interpretation and choices:

- The recipe offers an alternative for a strong and a weak version with expected OG of 1.075 and 1.13. These will have very different characters.
- Addition of flavors is after fermentation, which is unusual.

Instructions for Best Mead Weak MS 4054 and Best Mead Strong MS 4054:

1. Add 2 pounds (2 ¾ cups) honey to 1 gallon water.
    {Add 3.6 pounds (4 ¾ cups) honey to 14 cups water.}
2. Boil for one hour, removing brown scum and stirring white scum back in.
3. Take off heat and cool to lukewarm. Place in fermenter. Expected OG 1.075 {Expected OG 1.13}.
    [Add 2 pounds (2 ¾ cups) {or 3.6 pounds (4 ¾ cups)} honey to water to make 1 gallon.]
4. Add a toasted piece of wheat bread with active yeast spread on both sides, and spread 1 tablespoon flour over liquid.
5. Follow preferred fermentation protocol. When done working, strain and rack.

6. Follow preferred aging protocol. In last 2 days before bottling, add 2 teaspoons each of anise seeds, fennel seeds, and coriander, bruised.

7. Follow preferred bottling protocol.

The Green Water Meads

The green water meads name themselves by a common instruction to boil water with herbs until it no longer looks green. MS 1026 contains the sole example in the Wellcome manuscripts. These recipes are consistent in the spices used, but vary considerably in the number and specific herbs used. The most basic version uses only rosemary, thyme, and eglantine, while others add up to 20 additional herbs to these. The version here is the only one found to date in a manuscript rather than a printed book. The earliest printed appearances are 4 different variants in Digby's 1669 *Closet*.

MS 1026 Ayscough (1692) p.41 presented the following:

To make White Mead

Take of Rosemary, Time, sweet bryer Pennyriall Baise of each an handfull and what other-herbs you please as Origan Watter Cresses, - Egremony march Mallowes leaves & flowers – Liverwort wood Betony Eye bright scabius of each A like Quantity of the Bark of the Ash tree of Iringo roots green of each A like proportion to the herbs of wild angilico Robwort sanibell – Roman wormwood each such A proportion as is to every handfull of the first herbs, A 16 part of an handfull of these lesser steep them A night & day in A wooden Bowl of water covered then the next day boil them very well in Another water, till the Colour be very high, then take another Quantity of water & boil the same herbs in itt till they look green, soo let itt boil 3 or 4 hour's time or as long as the liquor looks any thing green then let it stand with those herbs in itt A day & A night then put as much fine honey to itt as will make it bear an Egg the Liquor being strain'd from the herbs work & labour the honey & Liquor together A whole day till the honey be consumed then let itt stand A whole night again A clearing, soe set it aboile A ¼ of an hour with the whites & shells of 6 eggs the yolks being taken Out, soe strain itt clean & lett itt stand A day A cooling then put itt into A Barrill if you will have it work soe that it may be riddy to drink presently take the whites of 3 or 4 Eggs A spoonfull of Barme & A spoonfull of wheat flower & beat all these togather & let it work before you stop it, then after wards stop it well with Clay & salt tempered together to keep the longer moist before you stop it up hang in the Barrill A bag of spice beat grossly, as Cloves Mace – Cinnamon & nuttmeggs put them in A linnen cloath & hang them with A third in the Barrell.

Notes for interpretation and choices:

- Some 15 of the 20 herbs named in the recipe are optional. The mead maker must decide the slate of herbs to be used. I chose an abbreviated list of better known and easy to find herbs.
- Washing and boiling the herbs multiple times before the final long boiling will lead to a very different flavor profile than a single boiling period as well as significant overall loss of flavor.
- The volume of water used to boil the herbs is not stated.

Instructions for White Mead MS 1026:

1. Take 1 tablespoon each of rosemary, thyme, sweet briar, pennyroyal, and bay leaf. Take also 1 teaspoon of oregano and agrimony.
2. Leave herbs overnight in enough water to cover them.
3. The next day, boil herbs for about 1 hour in a gallon of fresh water, until it is colored from the herbs.
4. Take off heat, strain, and replace water with 2 gallons of fresh water and boil again for at least 3 hours.
5. Take off heat and let stand for 1 day.
6. Take 2.3 pounds (3 cups) of honey and add to it 14 ½ cups of the water in which the herbs were boiled. Mix well.
7. Bring to a boil and add the beaten white and shell of 1 egg.
8. Let boil about 15 minutes, take off heat, strain and cool. Expected OG about 1.08–1.085.
   [Add 2.3 pounds (3 cups) honey to 13 cups of water at step 5.]
9. Add 1 teaspoon wheat flour and 1 teaspoon yeast, and if desired a small amount of beaten egg white (food safety concern). Add to fermentation, a bag with 3 cloves, 2 blades mace, ½ stick cinnamon, and ½ nutmeg bruised.
10. Follow preferred fermentation, aging, and bottling protocols.

Complex Herbed Meads

The next recipes follow the previous, using a wide variety of herbs.

Metheglin MS 4759

This recipe includes a core version (Metheglin MS 4759) with no spices and alternate versions with spice either in the boil or the ferment (Metheglin w Boiled Spice MS 4759, Metheglin with Spice in Ferment MS 4759). MS 4759 Tallamy (1735–1806) f.174r instructed:

To Make Metheglin

Take all sorts of Herbs that are good as Bame Angilica or wild Lemon time Isop Burnet Egrimony sweett bryer or which herbs you think fitt some field herbs but not to many especily of strong herbs less than ½ a hand full of every sort you must boyle your herbs & strain them & let the Lickor stand till the morning & settle take of the clearest of the Lickor two gallons & a half to one gallon of honey & lett it boyle one hour in the boyling skim it very Cleen then sett it to Cool as you do bear when it is Cold put some Alle Barme in to the bottom of the tub by little & little as thy do beere keeping back the setling that lyeth in the bottem & when it is all together cover it with a cloth & let it work very near 3 days & when you put it up skim off all the Barme Cleane put it into the Vessell but stop it not Close in 3 or 4 days but give it vent for it will work & when tis close stopt Look to it very often & when it makes a noise open the vent or else it will break your vessel, some times I make a bag & put in good store of ginger sliced some Cloves & Cinimun & boyle in it and other-times I put it into the barrell & never boyle it is both good but nutmeg & mace do not well to my tast

Notes for interpretation and choices:
- There is an option to use spices or not, then a choice of using spice in boiling or in fermentation.
- A subset of the called-for herbs can be used. Additional field herbs (herbs which grow in the wild), may be added.
- Proportions of herbs and spices are not detailed.

Instructions for Metheglin MS 4759 and variants:

1. Add to 6 quarts of water, 1 ½ tablespoon each of balm, burnet, angelica, lemon thyme, hyssop, agrimony, and sweet briar. {use a subset of herbs if desired}.
2. Boil together for about 90 minutes.
3. Take off heat, strain, and let settle.
4. Take 15 cups of the clear liquid, add to 4.5 pounds (6 cups) honey and mix.
5. Boil, skimming, for one hour.
   {If desired add bag containing 1 inch sliced ginger root, ½ stick cinnamon, and 3 cloves to boil. But not to fermentation as well.}
6. Let cool, transfer 1 gallon of clearest portion to fermenter, add ale yeast. Expected OG 1.145–1.15.
   [Add 4 pounds (5 ⅓ cups) honey to water that has been boiled with herbs {and spices if desired} as above to make 1 gallon.]
7. {If desired add bag containing 1 inch sliced ginger root, ½ stick cinnamon, and 3 cloves to fermentation, but not to boil as well.}
8. Ferment, age, and bottle using preferred protocols.

Spanish Methegline MS 7892, Spiced Spanish Methegline MS 7892

This recipe is similar to the previous, having versions with herbs only and herbs plus spices, but both the herb and the spice lists differ. MS 7892 *Cookery and Medical Recipe Book* (late 17th–18th c.) f.57v–58r instructed:

> To make Methegline the Spanish way.
>
> Take Rosemary Marjorum Time Balme Angelica, Fennell and Parsloe Roots the pithe taken out Buglos Marygold Flowers Egremony Wild Sage Burnet of each of these what Quantitie you please Boyle the Herbs well in six Gallons of Water then straine them out and let the Water settle till next day then take the cleanest and leave settleing in the Bottle then put to every ten quarts A Gallon of Water A gallon of Honney and mix it very well and if it will bear a new laid Egge it hath Hony sufficient then boyle it an Hour and scum it Continually then set it to Coole and when it is coole put in some good ale Barme in the Tub you mean to worke it in then by degrees put the Cold Liquores into the Barme when all is in cover it up Close with a Cloth, and let it worke almost three days then you may put it into the

vessell having first taken of all the Barm when all is in, cover it up close with A cloth and let it worke almost three days then you may put it into the vessell having first taken of all the Barme and doe not stop it up of 3 or 4 days, and when you stop up the Bung you must have a Hole made on the Top and a Peg to take in and out and When you hear it make a noise give a it vent you may hang in it a little Bag with some whole cloves and a little Nutmeg and Ginger sliced you may Keep it 2 Years, but not use it under 4 Months

Notes for interpretation and choices:

- Angelica, which is used as both an herb or a root, is located between a list of herbs and a list of roots. Based on the position of the comma, I have used it as an herb.
- "put to every ten quarts A gallon of water A gallon of Honney" is ambiguous. I have interpreted it as herb water plus plain water plus honey, giving a gravity of about 1.095–1.10, which will bear an egg with some showing.
- The relative proportions of herbs and spices is not defined.

Instructions for Spanish Methegline MS 7892 and Spiced Spanish Methegline MS 7892:

1. To 1 gallon of water add 1 tablespoon each marjoram, angelica, thyme, balm, rosemary, fennel root, parsley root, bugloss, sage, and agrimony.
2. Boil for about 1 hour until herbs are limp and spent.
3. Take off heat, allow to cool and settle.
4. When cool, take 10 ¾ cups of the clearest herb water and add to 3.2 pounds (4 ¼ scant cups) honey and 4 ¼ cups clean water.
5. Boil 1 hour, down to 1 gallon, skimming.
6. Let cool, add to fermenter with yeast. Expected OG 1.115.
   [Add 3.2 pounds (4 ¼ scant cups honey to 3 ⅓ cups clean water and 8 ⅓ cups of the herb water after step 4.]
7. {Add also to fermenter a bag with 3 cloves, ¼ nutmeg crushed, and 3 slices ginger root.}
8. Follow preferred fermentation, aging, and bottling protocols.

Braggots

A braggot is a mead made with the addition of grain sugars. This is a very old mead type; travelogues by Athenaeus and Strabo in the years BCE speak of drinks made from grains and honey in barbarian lands. While modern braggots are usually made by mixing ale wort with honey or mead must, historical braggots were made with a wider variety of techniques: they could be ale wort mixed with honey or mead must, have honey mixed in after the wort has fermented a few days, mix honey into finished ale or beer restarting fermentation, or even be made by mixing enough ale/beer with associated lees as a yeast source into mead must that the resulting mix has enough grain character to be considered a braggot. Braggots are uncommon across the timeline of historical mead recipes, but are consistently present in all eras.

As with other meads, nomenclature is not always consistently used by period authors. Wellcome manuscript MS 3107 presents a recipe for "Braggot" where sugar is used instead of honey, which would not normally be classified as a braggot.

As discussed on p.34, the distinction between ale and beer is minimal today. In England, in times before the Wellcome manuscripts, ale typically referred to unhopped malt drink and beer referred to hopped malt drink. Through the period represented by the Wellcome mead recipes of the 17th to mid-18th centuries in England it was most typical that both ale and beer contained hops, but ale contained far fewer. The choice of underlying malt drink for these recipes is a potential source of significant variation. Understanding this ambiguity, the malt drink portion for recipes in this chapter is always referred to as ale for simplicity.

Meath with Lemons or Oranges MS 1806

This recipe represents a small group of historical recipes that could be argued are not proper braggots, because the ale is added as a yeast source. I group them as braggots when the amount of ale added relative to the total volume, in this case about 30%, is significant enough that it will be a part of the core flavor. Because the use of only citrus does not align with other braggot recipes, it suggests that this would not have historically been viewed as a braggot.

This recipe was written in MS 1806 *Cookery Books.* (18th c.) on pp.9–10:

To make Mead or Meath &c

To every Quart of honey put five quarts of Water, disolve the honey very well in the water, then put it on the fire, and when its near boiling skim it as the skim rises, let it Boil till it breaks like wort, then take of the Kettle and shire of the Clear, when it is as cold as you wou'd put Guile to barm put 2 quarts of Barm to it and the Juce and rines of sise lemons or oranges, let it stand twenty four hours, then stir it every day for three or four days, but if the barm falls tun it before three days or at three days end put with it the rines of the lemons that was wrought with it – and let it stand Eight or Ten weeks or longer if it be nit fine botle it with lemon peel, this Meath will Drink litle worse than Lemon Wine it ought to be made at Michaelmas it will be fitt to drink at march

---

Notes for interpretation and choices:

- The break in boiling beer wort is the point where proteins and other components clump in the boil. It typically takes place before 30 minutes boiling. Similar clumping of components happens in mead must, but may either take more time or be less notable.
- Michaelmas is September 29, so a total period of five months is called for before drinking.
- The recipe is made with either lemons and lemon peel or oranges and lemon peel at bottling.

Instructions for Meath with Lemons or Oranges MS 1806:

1. Add 12 ½ cups water to a pot. Note liquid depth.
2. Add 1.9 pounds (2 ½ cups) honey.
3. Boil back to about 13 cups (about 1 hour), skimming.
4. Remove from heat and let settle.
5. Remove 11 ½ cups of clear liquid. Expected OG 1.085.
    [Add 1.7 pounds (2 ¼ cups) honey to 9 ¼ cups water.]
6. When cool, place in fermenter and add 4 ½ cups ale barm (including ale). Expected OG varies depending on strength and extent of fermentation of ale, but will be 1.07-1.08 in most cases.
7. Add juice and peel of 4 small lemons.
    {If desired use oranges instead of lemons.}
8. Follow preferred fermentation protocol for 4 days.
9. Rack with lemons {oranges} into new fermenter.
10. After about 2 ½ months bottle with a bit of lemon peel in each bottle.

Interior of a tavern, Marsilius Ficinus (16th c.)

Braggot MS 8097

The next recipe was written in MS 8097 *English recipe book* (17th–18th c.) on p.79 of the culinary section (from the back of the manuscript):

> Bragott.
>
> Take 5 pints of honey & about 5 quarts of old alle, let this boyle & then take it off & scum it, & put it on the fire againe & let it boyle as longe as any scum arises, then take 14 ounces of ginger & bruise it 4 ounces of Jamaco peper, an ounce of bayberrees, Junipe buries, docus seed, caraway seeds, each one ounce, half a pound of aniseeds bruise all these ingredients & boyle them in the alle & honey then take it off the fire & cover it close for 14 hours, then take a vessell that contains about 30 quarts & take a canvas bag, & strain the alle & honey, & add to it as much more alle as will fill the vessell & let it go thro, the Linnen bag which you must tye & hang up in the vessell, this is a welch drink, I made it for mr Wynne.

Notes for interpretation and choices:
- Jamaican Pepper is Allspice
- The recipe is made with "old" ale, presumably referring to aging time, presenting many options for experimentation.
- Boiling the ale after honey addition will cause loss of alcohol.

Instructions for Braggot MS 8097:
1. Add 1 pound (1 ⅓ cup) honey to 2 ¾ cups of finished ale.
2. Bring to a boil, and boil, skimming for about 15 minutes.
3. Add 2 ounces sliced ginger, 1 ounce anise seed, ½ ounce allspice, and 0.1 ounce each of bay berries, juniper berries, docus seed, and caraway seed. All bruised or slightly crushed.
4. Boil about 30 minutes, adding more ale if necessary.
5. Let cool and sit for 14 hours. Honey added will boost OG by about 0.035-0.04.
6. Strain, retaining spices, and mix with finished ale to make 1 gallon. Place bag of spices back into ferment.
   [Add 1 pound (1 ⅓ cup) honey to ale boiled with herbs and spices and finished ale to make 1 gallon.]
7. Ferment, age, and bottle using preferred protocols.

Another Braggot MS 2954

MS 2954 Hudson (1678) p.34, Recipe 113 instructed:

> To Make Braggat Another way
>
> Take 12 Gallons of Ale about a weeke old & draw it of the cropes half an ounce of Cloves an ounce of Nutmegs, & a Ounce & a quarter of Ginger soe much of sinamond and a litle mace, then take two quartes or more of honney and clarrife it in some of the Ale then putt the spices being all beaten small or bruised in a morter together & putt them in a litle bagg being thynn into the honey, & boyle it gentley, then lett the honey Coole & putt it into the Ale, in a fresh vessell, and hange the bagg of spices in it, then take a Gallon of new ale and Barme, & putt to it that it may worke Againe, and after it hath worked stope it for 10 dayes or longer if you please, & then drinke it, and if it be new botle it, and after a weeke in botles it will drinke very quicke and cleare lett your Ale be well brewed, but not to stronge.

Notes for interpretation and choices:

- Choice of underlying malt drink is open.
- The amount of honey added is variable, I have chosen to increase it from the stated minimum.
- I have chosen to simplify addition of new ale to addition of new yeast and have all the liquid be the 1 week old ale.
- This recipe cannot be readily made without boiling the honey.

Instructions for Another Braggot MS 2954:

1. Add to 0.8 pound (1 cup) honey: 10 cloves, ¼ crushed nutmeg, 2 slices dried ginger, ½ stick cinnamon, and 2 blades mace. All the spices beaten and in a bag.
2. Boil honey spice mixture for about 15 minutes.
3. Let cool, then mix honey and spice bag with enough 1 week old ale to make 1 gallon. Effective OG about 1.08.
4. Pitch new yeast.
5. Ferment, age, and bottle using preferred protocols.

Braggat From a Firkin of Ale

Braggat MS 2954, Braggat MS 4054, and Chosin's Malt Drink MS 8903 are three incarnations of this braggot recipe from the Wellcome manuscripts. A similar recipe has been cataloged from a 1684 British Library manuscript. All occurrences to date have been in manuscripts.

MS 2954 Hudson (1678) pp.33–34, recipe 112 stated:

A Recipte how to Make Braggat

Take A ffirkine of good ale, & when it is 3 dayes ould make it in Braggat After this manner: ffolowing, take 3 pintes of very good stow honey and putt it into A conveniant pann; and putt thereto 2 or 3 quartes of worte or new Ale, and stirr them in the pann together, and sett it over the fire to clarrifie, & lett it boyle and ever as it boyleth take of ye scum as cleane as you cain, until it looke as cleare as sirrope then take 3 quarters of a pound of Liquorice, & as much Anna seeds beaten: and putt thereunto like an Ounce of peper and an Ounce of Cloves both beaten with a score of Nuttmegs, all being beaten putt them together into youre clarrified hunney, and set it over the fire to boyle, and if you thinke their be not Liquor Enough to boyle your spices in, putt there unto a quarte or two more of worte, when it is over the fire, and let it boyle A pretty while, and stirr it A boute and then take it of the fire and let it stand and Coole, then uncover youre Ale, and when it is resonable coole poure it in at the at tope of youre ffirkine of ale and worke it very well together, you must lett it stand uncovered, till it hath done workeing, stope it up very closse for 9 or 10 dayes, before you broach it.

MS 4054 *Receipt book* (1690–1710?) p.186 instructs:

To make Braggat

Take a ferkin of good Ale, and when it is 3 days old make it in Braggat after this manner following. Take 3 pintes of Very – good stow Honey, and putt into a conveniant pan, & putt therunto - 2 or 3 quartes of worte or new Ale, and stirr them in the pan together & sett it over the fire to clarifye, and lett it boile, and ever as it boileth take of the scum as cleane as you can, untill it looks as cleare as syrup; then take 3 quarters of a pound of liquorish and as much anyseeds beaten, one ounce of peper and one ounce of cloves both beaten with a score of Nuttmeggs, all being beaten putt them together into your – clarifyed Honey, and sett it over the fire to boile, And if you think there be not liquor enough to boile your spices in; putt therunto – a quarte or two more of worte when it is over the fire; and lett it boile a pretty while and stirr it about, and then take it of the fire and lett it stand and coole. Then uncover your Ale, and when tis reasonable coole poure it in att the top of your firkin of Ale, and worke it very well together, you must lett it stand uncovered, till it has done working, then stopp it very close for 9 ot 10 days before you broach it.

MS 8903, Carteret (1662) instructed on p.86:

To make a kind of Malt Drink Choshins way

Take a firkin of good Ale when it is 3 dayes old & make it after this manner, take 3 pints of good honey & put it into a pan, & put to it 2 or 3 quarts of wort or new Ale & stir the honney well in, & set it on the fire to clarifie & as it boyleth take of the scum, as cleane as you can till it Looke very Cleare then put in halfe of pep, an ounce of Cloves & 20 Nutmegs beat them well & boyle them in your Clarrified Liquor If the Liquor be not Enough to boyle the spices in put in a quart of Ale, more to it, put 2 ounces of Anniseeds & as much Lycurish, when it is boyled let it stand to coole, & then uncover your firkin of Ale & pour it Into your Ale & work it well together, you must Let it stand uncovered

Braggots

The first two versions are identical in every detail, despite significant variations in spelling and punctuation. The third varies in the amounts of spices and when they are added, and also truncates the final instructions.

Notes for interpretation and choices:

- An ale firkin is nine imperial gallons or 10.8 US gallons.

Instructions for Braggat from a Firkin of Ale:

1. Add 0.5 pounds (⅔ cup) honey to 2 cups of ale wort.
2. Boil gently, skimming for 30 minutes.
3. Add 1 ⅓ ounce licorice root, 1 ⅓ ounce anise seeds, 3 grams black pepper, 30 cloves, and 2 nutmegs, bruised and in a bag.
4. Boil about 30 minutes, stirring frequently, adding additional wort if needed.
5. Remove mixture, let cool, add to ale wort that has been fermenting for 3 days to make 1 gallon. Expected OG about 1.07.

    [Add 0.5 pound (⅔ cup) honey to combined wort.]
6. Ferment, age, and bottle using preferred protocols.

Miscellaneous Meads

A miscellaneous category is always useful to capture recipes that do not easily fit elsewhere, such as these four recipes and recipe groups.

Small Mead MS 1796

This recipe for mead including horseradish root has been cataloged in one of the Wellcome manuscripts as well as in several other manuscripts and books. The earliest appearance is 1680 and the latest 1742. The recipes are consistent in ingredients and instructions. Several versions also include variants, although this one does not. It is included in this chapter because the extremely strong and distinct flavor of horseradish makes a unique mead. It was written in MS 1796, *Cookery book: 17th / 18th century* (1685–c. 1725) on p.59:

> A receit for small Mead.
>
> Take 20 quarts of water hang it over the fire, when it is warm put in 2 quarts of honey and 2 pound of sugger then put in a spoonfull of coriander seed brused and put in a bagg a root of horse radish and 6 races of ginger let it boyle well till it be clean without scum, then take it off and tun it warm into an open stone vessel with a top then put in 40 cloves, and 8 Lemmons split and quartered the outward rinde taken off half of them, stop your barrell close about 6 houres after take 2 or 3 toasts of white bread cover them with Yeast put them in warme, stop Vessel close and stand 5 days then bottle it, and in 5 days more you may drink it.

Notes for interpretation and choices:

- The amount of horseradish used is not clear.
- It is possible to replace the sugar with honey.
- This is a small mead with a short time to drinking.

Instructions for Small Mead MS 1796:

1. Take 17 cups of water and warm it.
2. Add to it 1.3 pounds (1 ¾ cups) honey and 0.5 pound (1 cup) raw sugar (equivalent to ¾ cup or 0.55 additional pounds of honey).
3. Add ½ teaspoon coriander seed, ½ ounce sliced horseradish root, and ½ inch of sliced ginger root.
4. Boil for about 1 hour, skimming.
5. Take off of heat, place in vessel, add 8 cloves, and 1 quartered lemon (from which ½ of the peel has been removed).
6. After it has cooled completely, add a slice of toasted bread covered with active yeast. Expected OG 1.07.
   [Add 1.3 pounds (1 ¾ cups) honey to water boiled with herbs, spice and sugar.]
7. Follow preferred fermentation, aging and bottling protocols, keeping in mind specified time to drinking of 10 days.

This mead has a very strong horseradish nose, the flavor is dominated by the cloves. The horseradish flavor is milder than suggested by the nose, present and strong, but not biting, and is an entirely unexpected flavor for mead.

Another White Metheglin MS 3828

This recipe represents one of the few meads that is probably impossible to accurately re-create due to practical reasons. Both musk and ambergris are controlled substances in many jurisdictions, due to being derived from endangered species (musk deer and sperm whales). Legal issues aside, both substances are expensive and are not established as safe for consumption.

Nevertheless, these ingredients are both found in mead recipes, and this recipe provides a representative example.

MS 3828 (1750), Percivall (Mid 18th c.) p.25 instructed:

Another Sort of white Metheglin

Take 8 Gallons of water, and boil in it a bundle of Cithory-Roots sparrow grass roots, Burrage and Bugloss a Bay leafe a sprig of Rosemary, 3 Raices of Ginger 2 Nutmegs slic'd a stick of Cinamon, a few Cloves, 2 blades of Mace let all these boil together till they will bear an Egg & parsly and Fennele Roots, then put into it 2 Gallons of Honey, let it boil, and scum it clean then let it stand a day and a Night, then strain it thr'o a hair sieve let it stand, and settle, then pour it out into another Vessel the clear from the Bottom, so do two or three Times then strain it into the Barrell, put in a Bagg with some spice, & a little Musk, and Ambergrease then stop the Barrell close.

Notes for interpretation and choices:

- Sparrow grass is asparagus.
- Amounts for several additions are not specified.
- The recipe is somewhat complex and could be made either without the final two ingredients, or with an aromatic element to substitute for the musk and ambergris.
- The recipe below omits the musk and ambergris.
- The instruction to boil water and herbs until it will bear an egg is confusing. If this is meant to be bear an egg while boiling after the honey is added, it will be an OG of about 1.11 and about one and one half hours of total boiling for the water portion (final volume eight gallons).
- "Bagg with some spice" could indicate putting previous "bundle" back in or a new set of spices. I have added new spices.

Instructions for Another White Metheglin MS 3828:

1. Take 1 ½ gallon of water and bring it to a boil.
2. Add ½ ounce each of chicory root and asparagus roots, ¼ bay leaf, ½ teaspoon rosemary, ½ inch sliced ginger root, ¼ nutmeg crushed, ¼ stick cinnamon, 1 clove, and 1 blade of mace. Add also ⅓ ounce parsley root and ⅓ ounce fennel root.
3. Boil for 1 hour, skimming.
4. Add 3.8 pounds (5 cups) honey and keep boiling and skimming, for another hour.
5. Take off heat, let cool, and let sit 36 hours before straining into a closed container.
6. After it has settled, rack off clear portion. Repeat. Expected OG about 1.115–1.12.
   [Add 3.2 pounds (4 ¼ cups) honey to clear portion of water boiled with herbs and spices to make 1 gallon.]
7. Put into the fermentation a bag with 1 clove, ¼ crushed nutmeg, and ¼ stick cinnamon.
8. Follow preferred fermentation, aging, and bottling protocols.

Michaelmas to Lent

Over a dozen cataloged mead recipes specify a fermentation and aging period that extends from Michaelmas (September 29th) to Lent. The Lenten season typically starts between the first week in February and the first week in March and ends on Easter Sunday between March 22 and April 25. None of the recipes state whether the aging period ends at the beginning of Lent or at Easter when Lent ends.

Three of these recipes can be found in the Wellcome manuscripts:
- Carr (1682), Metheglin MS 1511
- *Cookery book* (1699), Methegling MS 1792
- *English recipe book* (c. 1700), Metheglin MS 5431

Two of these recipes are almost identical, but the earliest is markedly different in ingredients, proportions and procedure.

Sussex Metheglin MS 1511

This first of the Michaelmas to Lent recipes was written in MS 1511 Carr (1682) as recipe number 295:

To Mak Metheglin the usuall way in sussex 295

After you have drayned the honey of the Combs & laid them in water wash them in 3 or 4 waters untill you have washed out all the sweetnesse strayning the water every time with a course strainer then try the strength of it by putting in a ~~new~~ raw egg to swim therin, & if the egg swim soe high that there appear the breath of 2 pence or 3 pence above the liquor then it is a good ordinary strenght.

But if the egg be all or near it hadd in liquor strengthen the liquor by putting thereto more honey untill it beare the egg as afore said but before you put in the egg after you have put in the honey be sure to stir it well soe that the honey may be all melted or els the mead will be stronger than you expected then when you are satisfied of the strenght thou sett it a boyling over the fire take still the skumm of for 3 quarters of an hour or an hour then put into 6 gallons thereof 2 ounces of Cinamon broken Corriander seeds bruised halfe an ounce of ginger & 2 nuttmeggs sliced & let it boyle 3 quarters of an hour with these spices in it put the spices into a linning bagg then take it off the fire and lett it setle pouring it into an earthen or wooden vessell the bagg continuing in it the next day put up the cleare thereoff into a rundlett or bottles leaveing a smale vent for it to worke out att during the space of a weeke & more as you see it continues working Meed of this strength will keep from Micalmas untill Lent if you have it drunke off sooner you must not make it soe stronge

---

Notes for interpretation and choices:
- The mead maker has a choice of making the recipe from combs as specified or with pure honey.

Instructions for Metheglin MS 1511:

1. Add 3.3 pounds (4 ½ cups) honey to 17 cups water.
2. Boil for 1 hour, skimming off scum.
3. Add 2 sticks cinnamon, 2 teaspoon coriander seed, 2 slices dried ginger root, ½ nutmeg crushed. All the spices in a bag.
4. Boil another ¾ hour with spices.
5. Take off heat and let cool till next day.
   [Add 3.3 pounds (4 ½ cups) honey to 11 ½ cups water boiled 45 minutes with spices.]
6. Strain into fermenter. Expected OG 1.12.
7. Follow preferred fermentation, aging, and bottling protocol.

Methegling MS 1792, Metheglin MS 5431

The other two Michaelmas to Lent recipes below are presented together, as they are almost identical. The first version was written as recipe 231 in MS 1792 *Cookery book* (late 17th c.):

To Make Methegling

Take to Every Gallon of Water one Gallon of honey let your honey be melted Before your Water be to hot and let it be the Best honey you can gitt then put in an Egg and when the Egg Cume up half Way in the Water which you must feel with your Hands then it will be Strong Enough for it will be much Stronger when when cits Boyld and you must boyl these herbes in it 4 or 5 Spriges of Time as many of Sweet marigrom a Sprige of Winter Savory a Good Deale of Sweet Bryer and All most as much Bay Tye all these together with a thread Being a Great handful it will seme to boyl in Ten Gallons then make a quick fire and let it boyl half an hour and no more then Take it of the fire and Set it a Brode in 2 or 3 Wooden Vessells and let it stand 24 hours without stirring then softley Draw it Out leave the Drages Behinde and put the Cleanest into a vessell with a Bag of Spice and if your vessell houlde Ten Gallons put in a Bout 5 Races of Ginger the out sides Paired a Way 2 Nuttmege and a Grote worth of Cinnamon A little mace a few Cloves Brused a little but not to much then put them into a Bag and put it into the vessell cits made in and you must make it at Miclemas And not to be Drunk Tell Lent when cits Drawn put into the vessel an Egg to Trye the Strength it must Bare the Egg no Broder

---

then a Peny and if you Finde it to Strong you may make Some Smaller and mingell them together When thay are Both cold and Be chure you Scum it Cleane as long as aney Scum will Rise

The second version was written on p.60 of MS 5431 *English recipe book* (c. 1700). The "three" in the first line is heavily inked and may be written over the word "one":

To Make Metheglin

To every three gallons of Water one gallon of honey let your honey be Melted before your water be hott and lett it be the best hony you can gett then putt in an Egg and if your Egg come up half way in the water which you must feel with your hands, then it will be strong enough for it will be much stronger when its boyled and you must boyle these Herbs in it 4 or 5 spriggs of time as many of sweett Margoram a sprigg of winter savory, a good deal of sweett bryer and almost as much Bay, Tye ale these Together with a thred being a grate handfull it will serve to boyle in ten gallons. Then make a quick fire and let it boyle an hour and no more then take it of the fire and let it boyle halfe an hour and ~~no more~~ sett it abroade in 2 or 3 wooden vessels and lett it stand 24 hour's without stirring then softly draw it. But leave the dregg's be hind then putt in the clearest into a vessell with a bagg of spice and if your vessell hold ten gallons put in about 5 Races of Ginger the out side paired away 2 Nuttmeggs and a grots worth of Cynamon a litle Mace & a few Cloves bruised a litle but not to much then put them into a bagg and putt it in the vessell's its made in, you must make it at Michalemas and not to be Drunk till lent. When its Drawn put in the vessell an Egg to trye the strenght it must bear the Egg no Broder then a penny and if you find it to strong you must make some smaller and mingle them together when thy are cold and scum it very clean as longe as any scum Rises.

Notes for interpretation and choices:
- A ratio of honey to water of 1:1 in the first recipe is very high. The 1:3 ratio in the second recipe is more typical. Neither instruction leads to a mixture in which an egg is just floating as indicated by the final instruction to bear an egg "no Broder then a penny", which is the metric I have chosen in my interpretation.
- Boiling time for MS 5431 is ambiguous.

Instructions for Methegling MS 1792 / Metheglin MS 5431:

1. Add 2.8 pounds (3 ¾ cups) honey to 20 cups of water.
2. Add ½ sprig of thyme, ½ sprig marjoram, ½ teaspoon winter savory, 2 teaspoons of eglantine, 2 bay leaves, tie up in a bag and set in liquid.
3. Boil 1 hour, remove from heat and let cool uncovered.
4. Let stand 1 day to settle, then draw off 1 gallon of clear must. [Add 2.4 pounds (3 ¼ cups) honey to enough water boiled with herbs to make 1 gallon.]
5. Add in a bag: ¾ inch ginger root sliced, ¼ nutmeg, ½ stick cinnamon, 2 blades mace. Expected OG 1.09.
6. Follow preferred fermentation, aging, and bottling protocols.

Wine Added

Addition of wine to historical meads took place in several ways. Indirect addition via residuals in a wine barrel used for fermentation or storage was common, the flavor addition would have been notable upon the first such use but fade with subsequent uses. Wine was also added directly to mead, usually, but not always, after fermentation. In this latter case, either wine or distilled spirits (brandy) might be used. This wine addition had several purposes stated in the manuscripts, including coloration and preservation; but in other cases, it appears to be for flavor.

The series of recipes using Rhenish wine and syrup of citron detailed on p.194 could also be entered in this category.

As detailed on p.238, MS White Metheglin w Sack MS 8687 and White Metheglin w Spirit of Wine MS 8687 use the added liquor to provide color extracted from clove gilliflowers.

Bibliography

MANUSCRIPTS

Manuscripts from the Wellcome Library. All except the below noted have been retrieved from the Wellcome Library and can be found through the Archives and Manuscripts search tool at https://wellcomelibrary.org/search-the-catalogues/ using the manuscript number (e.g. MS 1026) and looking at the "Item" level result. The manuscripts have been reviewed using the digital scans provided by the Wellcome Library. MS Western 1407 was reviewed at the Wellcome Library.

- MS 144 *Book of receipts* (1650–1739?)
- MS 184a Catchmay (c. 1625)
- MS 1026 Ayscough (1692)
- MS 1127 Bent (1664–1729)
- MS 1321 *Book of receits* (1675–c. 1725?)
- MS 1325 *A booke of usefull receipts for cookery, etc.* (1675–c.1700?)
- MS 1343 Branch (1725)
- MS 1407 Buckworth (1725–c. 1775?)
- MS 1510 Carpenter (1715)
- MS 1511 Carr (1682)
- MS 1711 Coley (mid 18th c.)
- MS 1792 *Cookery book* (late 17th c.)
- MS 1794 *Cookery books: 17th–18th century* (1685–c. 1725)
- MS 1795 *Cookery book: 17th/18th century* (1685–c. 1725?)
- MS 1796 *Cookery book: 17th/18th century* (1685–c. 1725?)
- MS 1799 *Cookery books: 18th cent* (1700–1775?)
- MS 1801 *Cookery books: 18th cent* (c. 1725)
- MS 1803 *Cookery books: 18th cent* (1725?)
- MS 1806 *Cookery books: 18th cent* (c. 1750)
- MS 1808 *Cookery books: 18th cent* (1750?)

Bibliography

- MS 1810 *Cookery books: 18th cent* (1750?)
- MS 1811 *Cookery books: 18th cent* (1750?)
- MS 2323 Eyton (1691–1738)
- MS 2330 *Family receipts* (late 17th c.)
- MS 2477 Garside (c. 1655)
- MS 2535 Godfrey (1686)
- MS 2954 Hudson (1678)
- MS 3008 Jackson (1743)
- MS 3009 Jacob (1654–c. 1685)
- MS 3082 Johnson (1694–1831)
- MS 3087 Johnstone (1725?)
- MS 3098 K. (1735?)
- MS 3107 Kidder, E. and Kidder, K. (1699)
- MS 3498 Matthey (1750–1900?)
- MS 3500 Meade (1688–1727)
- MS 3539 Michel (mid 18th c.)
- MS 3547 Miller (1660)
- MS 3582 *Miscellany receipts* (1725?)
- MS 3768 Parker (1663)
- MS 3769 Parker (1651)
- MS 3828 Percivall (mid 18th c.)
- MS 4047 *Receipt book* (1669)
- MS 4050 *Receipt book* (1675?)
- MS 4054 *Receipt book* (1690–1710?)
- MS 4683 Springatt (1686–1824)
- MS 4759 Tallamy (1735–1806)
- MS 5431 *English recipe book* (c. 1700)
- MS 6812 *English medical notebook* (1575–1663)
- MS 7102 *Recipe book* (18th c.)
- MS 7391 *English recipe book* (mid 17th–early 19th c.)
- MS 7721 *English recipe book* (1675–1800?)
- MS 7787 Peacock (late 17th c.)
- MS 7788 Repp (1703)

- MS 7849 *English recipe book* (late 17th c.)
- MS 7850 Thompson (1749)
- MS 7851 *English recipe book* (late 17th–early 19th c.)
- MS 7892 *Cookery and medical recipe book* (late 17th–18th c.)
- MS 7976 Palmer (1700–1739)
- MS 7979 *Recipe book* (18th c.)
- MS 7997 Heppington. (late 17th–early 19th c.)
- MS 7998 Heppington (17th–18th c.)
- MS 8002 *Loose receipts* (1663–1740)
- MS 8097 *English recipe book* (17th–18th c.)
- MS 8450 *English culinary and medical recipe book* (1680–c. 1740?)
- MS 8687 Tully (1732?–)
- MS 8903 Carteret (1662–mid 18th c.)

Book of cookery recipes. (1640). NYPL Whitney Cookery Collection MS6.

A book of receipts. (1625–1700). Folger Library. Folger MS Add 247. http://hamnet.folger.edu/cgi-bin/Pwebrecon.cgi?BBID=230895

Evelyn Papers. (1651-18th c.) Vol CLXX. *Medical and culinary recipes: 1651–18th c.* British Library Add MS 78337.

Evelyn Papers. (1659-early 18th c.?) Vol CLXXIII. *Collections in two parts, the first of medical and culinary recipes, the second of skills and crafts.* British Library Add MS 78340.

Medical and cookery recipes. (1670–1700). U.S. National Library of Medicine https://collections.nlm.nih.gov/catalog/nlm:nlmuid-2932041R-bk

GENERAL BIBLIOGRAPHY

Acosta, C. (1578). *Tractado de las drogas, y medicinas de las Indias orientales.* Burgos: M. de Victoria. Retrieved from https://archive.org/details/tractadodelasdr00acosgoog

Amman, J., & Sachs, H.. (1884). *Stande und Handwerker mit versen von Hans Sachs.* (Original work published 1568). Retrieved from https://search.wellcomelibrary.org/iii/encore/record/C__Rb2485242

Bibliography

Aouizert, T., et. Al. (2019). Isolation and characterization of live yeast cells from ancient vessel as a tool in bio-archaeology. mBio 10:e00388-19. https://doi.org/10.1128/mBio.00388-19

Augustius, Q. de. (1515). *Dlicht d'apotekers*. Brussels: T. van der Noot. Retrieved from http://search.wellcomelibrary.org/iii/encore/record/C__Rb2138791

Bailey, N. (1742). *Dictionarium domesticum, being a new and compleat houshold dictionary*. London: C. Hitch & C. Davis. Retrieved from https://archive.org/details/b30505513

Barnett, Andrew; Juravle, Georgiana and Spence, Charles. (2017). Assessing the Impact of Finings in the Perception of Beer. *Beverages*, 3, 26. Retrieved from https://doi.org/10.3390/beverages3020026

Bates, F. J. (1942). *Polarimetry, saccharimetry and the sugars*. US Departement of Commerce. Retrieved from Internet Archive Wayback Machine, Jan 3, 2017, http://www.boulder.nist.gov/div838/SelectedPubs/Circular 440 Table 114.pdf

Best, M. R. (1976). The Mystery of Vintners. *Agricultural History* 50:2 (April, 1976) pp.362–376. Retrieved from http://mrec.ifas.ufl.edu/grapes/History/BibliographyChronology/19 76_MysteryOfVintners_Best.pdf

BJCP. (2015). *Beer judge ceritifcation program 2015 style guidelines mead style guidelines*. https://www.bjcp.org/docs/2015_Guidelines_Mead.pdf

Blackwell, E. (1737). *A curious herbal: containing five hundreds cuts. Volume 2*. London: Samuel Harding. Retrieved from http://resource.nlm.nih.gov/2449056R

Brunfels, O. (1532a). *Herbarum vivae eicones ad naturae imitationem*. Retrieved from https://books.google.com/books?id=dfSvObnzPNYC

Brunfels, O. (1532b). *Novi Hernarii Tomus II*. Strasbourg: Ioannem Schottum. Retrieved from https://books.google.com/books?id=iNsHzkWPz-YC

Butler, Charles, (1639). *The feminin' monarchi', or the histori' of bee's*. 3rd edition. Oxford: William Turner. Retrieved from http://search.wellcomelibrary.org/iii/encore/record/C__Rb3033788

Charleton, W. (1669). *Two discourses*. London: R.W. Retrieved from https://books.google.com/books?id=XMc6AQAAMAAJ

Bibliography

Chomal, N., & Bradley, R. (1725). *Dictionaire oeconomique: or, the family dictionary*. London: D. Midwinter. Retrieved from https://babel.hathitrust.org/cgi/pt?id=mdp.39015023902680

Cockayne, T. O. (1864). *Leechdoms, wortcunning, and starcraft of early England. Being a collection of documents, for the most part never before printed, illustrating the history of science in this country before the Norman conquest. Volume II.* London: Longman, Green, Longman, Roberts, and Green. Retrieved from https://archive.org/details/leechdomswortcun02cock

Columbus, C. (1893). *The journal of Christopher Columbus (during his first voyage, 1492–93) and documents relating to the voyages of John Cabot and Gaspar Corte Real.* London: Hakluyt Society. Retrieved from https://archive.org/details/cihm_05312

The complete family-piece: and, country gentleman, and farmer's best guide: in three parts. (1736). London: J. Roberts. Retrieved from https://archive.org/details/101091222.nlm.nih.gov

Cornell, M. (2011). Contending Liquors: how ale and beer remained separate drinks for hundreds of years longer than generally accepted. *Brewery History* vol.144 pp.33–40. Retrieved from http://breweryhistory.com/journal/archive/144/BeerAle.pdf

Culpepper, N. (1651). *A physical directory; or a translation of the dispensatory.* London: Peter Cole. Retrieved from https://archive.org/details/physicaldirector0000culp_s0r9

Culpepper, N. (1665). *Pharmacopeia Londinensis, or, the London dispensatory: further adorned by the studies and collections of the fellows.* London: Peter Cole. Retrieved from https://archive.org/details/b30324464

Culpepper, N. (1725). *The English physician enlarged.* London: Tho. Norris. Retrieved from http://nbn-resolving.de/urn:nbn:de:hbz:061:2-11295

Digby, K. (1669/1967). *The closet of the eminently learned Sir Kenelme Digbie Kt. opened.* St. Louis: Mallinckrodt Chemical Works. Retrieved from https://catalog.hathitrust.org/Record/100618178

Dioscorides. (2000). *De materia medica.* Johannesburg: IBIDIS PRESS. Retrieved from https://archive.org/details/de-materia-medica

Dodoens, R. (1578). *New herball.* London: Gerard Dewes. Retrieved from http://resource.nlm.nih.gov/2232003R

Dublin Society. (1733). *Instructions for managing bees: drawn up and published by order of the Dublin society.* Dublin: A. Rhames. Retrieved from https://books.google.com/books?id=_HdbAAAAQAAJ

Bibliography

Dujon, B. A. and Louis, E. J. (2017). Genome diversity and evolution in the budding yeasts (Saccharomycotina). *Genetics* June 1, 2017 vol.206 no.2 pp.717-750. https://www.genetics.org/content/206/2/717

Elyot, T. (1541). *The castel of helth corrected and in some places augmented.* London: Thomae Bertheleti. Retrieved from http://resource.nlm.nih.gov/2234010R

Estienne, C., & Liebault, J. (1576). *L'agriculture et maision rustique.* Lyon: Jacques du Puys. Retrieved from http://mdz-nbn-resolving.de/urn:nbn:de:bvb:12-bsb10165012-4

Evelyn, J. (1664). *Sylva, or a discourse of forest-trees, and the propagation of timber in His Majesties dominions. To which is annexed pomona or, an appendix concerning fruit-trees, in relation to cider.* London: Martyn & Allestry. Retrieved from https://archive.org/details/sylvaordiscourse00eveluoft

Fitch, J. G. (2013). *The work of farming (opus agricultruae) and poem on grafting.* Prospect Books.

Floyer, J. (1687). *Φαρμακο-Βασανος; or, the touch-stone of medecines.* London: Michael Johnson. Retrieved from https://books.google.com/books?id=t0pfA5O4ZjoC

French, J. (1651). *The art of distillation.* London: E. Cotes. Retrieved from http://lccn.loc.gov/45040251

Fuchs, L. (1542). *De historia stirpium commentarii insignes.* Basel. Retrieved from http://search.wellcomelibrary.org/iii/encore/record/C__Rb1000513

Gallone, B., et. Al. (2018). Origins, evolution, domestication and diversity of Saccharomyces beer yeasts. *Current Opinion in Biotechnology*, Vol. 49, pp.148-155. https://doi.org/10.1016/j.copbio.2017.08.005

Gerard, J., & Johnson, T. (1633). *Herball: or, Generall historie of plantes. Gathered by John Gerarde ... very much enlarged and amended by Thomas Johnson.* London, Adam Islip, Joice Norton and Richard Whitakers, 1633. Retrieved from https://catalog.hathitrust.org/Record/001493539

Gerard, J., & and Johnson, T. (1636). *The herball or, general historie of plantes.* London: A. Islip, J. Norton, and R. Whitakers. Retrieved from http://search.wellcomelibrary.org/iii/encore/record/C__Rb1032686

Glauber, J. R. (1651). *A description of new philosophical furnaces.* London: Richard Coats. Retrieved from https://archive.org/details/descriptionofnew00glau

Bibliography

The grete herball which gyveth parfyt knowledge and understandyg of all maner of herbes and there gryous vertues. (1529?). Treveris. Retrieved from http://search.wellcomelibrary.org/iii/encore/record/C__Rb1148651

Helbach, F. (1604). *Oenographia, weinkeller oder kunstbuch vom wein.* Francfort am Mayn. Retrieved from http://mdz-nbn-resolving.de/urn:nbn:de:bvb:12-bsb11217792-3

Hoff, A. (2017). What is the Density of an Egg? Retrieved November 28, 2017 from http://sciencing.com/density-egg-5127458.html

Hogg, Robert. (1851). *British pomology.* London: William Ford. Retrieved from http://www.gutenberg.org/ebooks/47367

Holland, P. Tr. (1601). *The historie of the world. Commonly called the naturall historie of C. Plinius secundus.* London: Adam Islip. Retrieved from http://penelope.uchicago.edu/holland/index.htm

Jones, O. R. (1986). Cylindrical English Wine and Beer Bottles 1735–1850. *Studies in Archaeology Architecture and History.* National Historic Parks and Site Branch Environment Canada. Retrieved from https://sha.org/bottle/pdffiles/cylindricalenglishwinebook.pdf

Kirkby, J. (1735). *Arithmetical institutions.* London. Retrieved from https://books.google.com/books?id=WyIOAAAAQAAJ

Koch und Kellerei. (1549?). Frankfort: H. Gülfferisch. Retrieved from http://search.wellcomelibrary.org/iii/encore/record/C__Rb1456589

Kuchenmeisterey. (1507). M. Hupfuff. Retrieved from http://search.wellcomelibrary.org/iii/encore/record/C__Rb1220531

Lady. (1737). *The whole duty of a woman.* London: T. Read. Retrieved from https://books.google.com/books?id=SncEAAAAYAAJ

Lawson, W. 1858. *A New Orchard and Garden.* Philadelphia: Robert Pearsall Smith. (Original work published 1623). Retrieved from Internet Archive https://archive.org/details/neworchardgarden00laws

van Leeuwenhoek, A. (1948). *Alle de brieven. Deel 3: 1679–1948.* Amsterdam: N.V. Swets & Zeitlinger. Retrieved from https://www.dbnl.org/tekst/leeu027alle03_01/index.php

Leong, E. (2013). Collecting Knowledge of the Family: Recipes, Gender and Practical Knowledge in the Early Modern English Household. *Centaurus 2013*: Vol 55: pp.81–103. Retrieved from https://archive.org/details/pubmed-PMC3709121

Bibliography

Leong, E. (2018). *Recipes and everyday knowledge.* University of Chicago Press.

Macer, F. (Between 1500 and 1599?). *De viribus herbarum carmen.* Geneva: J. Bellot? Retrieved from https://wellcomecollection.org/works/kh9kcyxg

McGovern, P. E. (2009). *Uncorking the past.* University of California Press.

Markham, G. (1653). *The English hous-wife.* London: W. Wilson. Retrieved from http://search.wellcomelibrary.org/iii/encore/record/C__Rb3034318

Markham, G. (1695). *The husbandman's jewel.* Retrieved from Early English Books Online.

Miller, P. (1740). *The gardeners dictionary.* London. Retrieved from Google Books https://books.google.com/books?id=hkdHTQJ3DwkC

Miller, P. (1807). *The gardener and botanist's dictionary.* Vol. 2 Part 2 Q–Z. London: F.C. and J. Rivington. Retrieved from https://books.google.com/books?id=FfNJAQAAMAAJ

Nasrallah, N. (2007). *Annals of the Caliphs's kitchens.* Brill.

de Orta, G. (1913). *Colloquies on the simples and drugs of India.* London: H. Sotheran and Co. Retrieved from https://catalog.hathitrust.org/Record/01171350946

Paganelli, C., Oloszowka, A. & Ar., A. (1974). The Avian Egg: Surface Area, Volume, and Density. *The Condor.* 76(3), 319–325. https://doi.org/10.2307/1366345

Papazian, C. (1991). *The new complete joy of home brewing.* Avon Books.

Parkinson, J. (1640). *Theatrum botanicum: the theater of plants. Or, an herball of large extent.* London: T. Coates. Retrieved from https://books.google.com/books?id=pFcfNkN8QGYC

Peter, Jackson et al. (2018). Genome evolution across 1.011 Saccharomyces cerevisiae isolates. *Nature.* 556, 339–344. Retrieved from https://www.nature.com/articles/s41586-018-0030-5

Piatz, S. (2014). *The complete guide to making mead.* Voyageur Press.

Portable antiquities scheme www.finds.org.uk

Read, A. (1651). *Most excellent and approved medicines & remedies for most diseases and maladies.* London: Retrieved from Early English Books Online.

Bibliography

Rohde, E. S. (1922). *The old English herbals*. London, New York: Longmans, Green. Retrieved from https://archive.org/details/oldenglishherbal00rohd

Rosslin, E. (1550). *Kreuterbůch, von natürlichem Nutz, und gründtlichem Gebrauch der Kreutter, Bäum, Gesteud, unnd Früchten*. Frankfurt: Christian Egenolffen. Retrieved from http://search.wellcomelibrary.org/iii/encore/record/C__Rb1282297

Rusden, M. (1679). *A further discovery of bees*. London: H. Milton. Retrieved from http://search.wellcomelibrary.org/iii/encore/record/C__Rb1092914

Salmon, W. (1710). *Botanologia, the English herbal*. London: Printed by L. Dawkes. Retrieved from Hathi Trust Digital Library https://catalog.hathitrust.org/Record/101734781

Salmon, W. (1710). *The family dictionary*. The fourth edition. London: Printed for H. Rhodes. Retrieved from https://catalog.hathitrust.org/Record/100158594

Schramm, K. (2003). *The compleat meadmaker: home production of honey wine from your first batch to award-winning fruit and herb variations*. Brewers Publications.

Shakespeare (n.d.). Henry IV Pt 2 4.3. http://shakespeare.mit.edu/2henryiv/full.html

Simpson, J. A., E. S. C. Weiner, and Donna Lee. Berg. (1991). *The Compact Oxford English dictionary: complete text reproduced micrographically*. Oxford: Clarendon.

Spurling, H. (1987). *Elinor Fettiplace's receipt book*. Penguin Books.

A state of the revenue of excise from Michelmas 1662 to Midsummer 1674. (1662-1674). UPenn Ms. Codex 219. Accessed at Penn Libraries http://dla.library.upenn.edu/dla/medren/record.html?q=cider&id=MEDREN_9924864423503681&

Stolarczyk, J. and Janick, J. (2011). Carrot: History and Iconogrpahy. *Chromica Horticulturae* Vol. 51 (2) pp.13–18. Retrieved from https://hort.purdue.edu/newcrop/pdfs/ch5102-carrot.pdf

Bibliography

Svanberg, I., Renata S., Luczaj, L., Kalle, R., Zyryanova, O., Denes, A., Pap, N., et.al. (2012). Uses of tree saps in northern and eastern parts of Europe. *Acta Societatis Botanicorum Poloniae*. 81(4):343–357. Retrieved from https://pbsociety.org.pl/journals/index.php/asbp/article/viewFile/asbp.2012.036/998

de Tournefort, J. P. (1719a). *The compleat herbal. Volume 1*. London: R. Bonwicke. Getty Research Institute. Retrieved from https://archive.org/details/compleatherbalor01tour

de Tournefort, J. P. (1719b). *The compleat herbal. Volume 2*. London: R. Bonwicke. Getty Research Institute. Retrieved from https://archive.org/details/compleatherbalor02tour

University of Michigan. (2013). Middle English Dictionary. Accessed at https://quod.lib.umich.edu/m/med/

USDA. United States Department of Agriculture Agricultural Reserach Service USDA Food Composition Databases. https://ndb.nal.usda.gov/ndb/search/list

Venner, T. (1638). *Via recta ad vitam longam*. London: R. Bishop. Retrieved from https://archive.org/details/TobiasVennerViaRectaAdVitamLongamOrAPlainPhilosophical

Woodville, W. (1790-1793). *Medical Botany containing systematic and general descriptions, with plates, of all the medicinal plants*. London: Jame Phillips. Rerieved from https://doi.org/10.5962/bhl.title.815

Worlidge, J. (1678). *Vinetum britannicum: or a treatise of cider and other wines and drinks*. London: Thomas Dring. Retrieved from https://books.google.com/books?id=ck1XAAAAcAAJ

Index

Index

Index

Index

Index

Index

Index

Made in the USA
Middletown, DE
04 October 2020